Jesus the Mystic

Jesus the Mystic

Pathways to Spiritual Care

Monika Renz

Translated by Mark Kyburz

A Crossroad Book
The Crossroad Publishing Company
New York

The Crossroad Publishing Company
www.CrossroadPublishing.com

© 2020 by Monika Renz
Translation © The Crossroad Publishing Company

Crossroad, Herder & Herder, and the crossed C logo/colophon are registered trademarks of The Crossroad Publishing Company.

All rights reserved. No part of this book may be copied, scanned, reproduced in any way, or stored in a retrieval system, or transmitted, in any form or by any means, electronic, mechanical, photocopying, recording, or otherwise, without the written permission of The Crossroad Publishing Company. For permission please write to rights@crossroadpublishing.com.

Cover design by Monika Renz
Book design by Tim Holtz

Library of Congress Cataloging-in-Publication Data available from the Library of Congress.

ISBN: 9780824596002 (trade paperback)
ISBN: 9780824596019 (EPUB)

Books published by The Crossroad Publishing Company may be purchased at special quantity discount rates for classes and institutional use. For information, please e-mail sales@CrossroadPublishing.com.

Contents

Acknowledgments — vii
Introduction — ix

1. Jesus and God: A Mystical Connection — 1
2. Absent Mysticism and Awakening — 23
3. Jesus the Mystic: A Historical View — 53
4. Jesus' Concept of God: An Answer to Fear — 81
5. Jesus' Concept of the Human Being — 111
6. Jesus' Response to Sin: Mysticism — 133
7. Jesus and Evil — 157
8. Jesus, the Father, and Love — 189
9. Redemption—Newly Spelled Out — 223
10. He Comes toward Me: Jesus the Logos and Christ — 269

Epilogue — 303
Notes — 307
References — 323
About the Author — 339

Acknowledgments

I am deeply grateful to Dr. Mark Kyburz, my translator; to Dr. Gwendolin Herder at the Crossroad Publishing Company for wanting to work with me; to Rudolf Walter, the editor of the original German edition of this book [*Der mystiker aus Nazaret: Jesuanische spiritualität*, 2016], as well as to Prof. Dr. Emeritus Max Küchler, Prof. Dr. Roman Siebenrock, Dr. Miriam Schütt, and my mother, Helen Renz, for their belief in the concerns presented in this book and for many critical discussions. They have all provided valuable suggestions for revising this book, as have Dr. Gotthard Fuchs, Peter Gutknecht, Prof. Dr. Emeritus Heinz Stefan Herzka (of Jewish origin). Between the first and second editions of the German edition lie two journeys to Israel and my encounters with the peoples living there. I served as a spiritual guide on one of the journeys, and I wish to thank the local travel guides and the members of the group. I am grateful to the following medical staff at St. Gallen Cantonal Hospital, where I am based as a psychotherapist providing end-of-life care to terminal cancer patients: Prof. Dr. Christoph Driessen, Prof. Dr. Thomas Cerny, Dr. Daniel Büche, PD.Dr. Florian Strasser. I am indebted to Fällanden Parish for granting me the opportunity to coach its members during the project "Deliverance from Formative Influences." I also wish to thank the many course participants and patients whom I have encountered over the years for their trust and for sharing their experiences with me. Finally, I owe special thanks to my husband, Jürg, whose subtle attention it never escaped—although our attitudes sometimes differed—that engaging with the mystic of Nazareth does me good. As this book grew, his interest in its topic never ceased and he kept inquiring into my progress. He found the title to the German book.

Introduction

Who was Jesus? He has been approached in many different ways. We all know him a little, but nobody really knows him. He is too great to be described in simple terms. Was he the Son of God? Was he a genius? A miracle worker or a prophet? Or rather a fantasist and a failure—a Jew of his time?

I have been deeply moved by discovering Jesus as a mystic. My discovery opened up a new world for me. It was as if I now understood many gospel passages afresh—or even for the first time. Suddenly I "understood" or rather "sensed" Jesus' relationship with God, whom he called "Father." Their relationship is about "being connected." It is similar to how many dying persons or ones who have a near-death experience "sense" another world. This book understands Jesus' relationship with God as *mystical*. By this I mean that the Father corresponds to Jesus' deeper Self[1]—and encompasses even more. Jesus' encounter with the Father represented both: he made contact with God according to tradition, in the outside world, and within his own deeper Self. The Father was thus Jesus' primordial ground. We too can experience God as our personal and primordial ground. Just as our relationship to God can grow ever deeper.

My discovery of Jesus has also helped me to understand what distinguishes us from Jesus: sin. Not only in a moral sense but also in a literal and etymological one: sin as separation and formative influence. Separation—that is, our isolation from God—captures our everyday experience of "disconnection." Sin and separation are inconceivable in purely dogmatic or biological terms. Instead, we need to understand them spiritually, as counterqualities to mysticism.

So what is mysticism? The word comes from ancient Greek [*mustiko,j / mystikos*] and denotes an inner property, a capacity hidden to the outer eye (*mu,ein tou.j ovfqalmou,j* / = to close one's eyes). Thus mysticism means deep spiritual experience—and vice versa (see chapter 2.3).

In calling Jesus a mystic, I mean that the historical Jesus made profound spiritual experiences (e.g., baptism). The gospels agree that Jesus was borne by the Father. He emerged strengthened from the *unio mystica* with the divine. Examples include the transfiguration (Mark 9:2–9) and the experience of the angel in Gethsemane (Luke 22:43). Presumably, Jesus experienced the divine when he actively engaged in the world and when he (occasionally) withdrew from it.

Today, we can also rediscover Jesus' *message*, *healing energy*, and *behavior*. They are all inspired by his mystical source, the "Father." Guided by God, Jesus assumed divine authority. In this book, I seek to understand the *whole*

Jesus—the healer, the one who loves, the "revolutionary"—in terms of his mystical experience. This view—that Jesus was a mystic—casts new light on fundamental biblical statements. For instance, the scene about Jesus' dwelling (John 1:39; see chapter 4), Jesus summoning the people to return to God (Mark 1:15), his understanding of justice (Matthew 5:17–20), his recurring assertion about what "the kingdom of God/heaven is like," his use of the word *reward*, the Beatitudes, or that "one does not live by bread alone" (Matthew 4:4). Jesus experienced *himself* as nurtured by the Father and wanted us to participate in this secret. He experienced the heavenly kingdom as a place of fullness. Being so close "to the source of sources," his person and message could become the content, path, and goal of introspection and contemplation ("I am the way, and the truth, and the life," John 14:6). His immeasurable love and devotion are unimaginable without the "Father" (see chapters 1, 8, and 9).

Yet Jesus never lost himself in mystical conjunction—that is, he was never narcissistic nor disconnected. His experiences of God and transcendence corresponded to his *strong personality*. Even amid his intense experience of God, Jesus, the mystic of Nazareth, remained down to earth. He "held" his experience of God, and it could thus take effect.

One aspect of Jesus' strong personality was his high level of consciousness. His behavior suggests that the historical

Jesus lived an *inherently conscious* life. He saw through obsession and could deal with demons. He saw the truth behind appearances and phenomena. He recognized many human symptoms of fear. He "understood" diseases and healed them.

This book seeks to understand Jesus' inner source. What, though, do we know about Jesus and his times? (For a historical-critical perspective, see chapter 3.) The New Testament illumines the customs and thinking at the time. It also teaches us a mystical, "connected" way of life. As I will show, especially the Gospel of John helps to better understand Jesus as a mystic (see chapters 4, 5, 8, and 10).

In this book, I also attempt to understand the profound mystery of salvation in terms of its psychological components—as far as this is possible. Redemption is mystery *and* "working" (see chapters 1, 5.3, 7.3, and 9). It follows psychological patterns. It is about love and being conscious. Above all, though, it is about a new spiritual initiation. But why? And how? Jesus' capacity for love was both extraordinary and very powerful. His awareness and his highly conscious behavior helped others to achieve consciousness. He brought light into the darkness of archaic human imprinting (John 1:1–10).

Importantly, this book develops guiding ideas for a spirituality based entirely on Jesus. Each chapter concludes with the following question: What are the consequences of a mystical interpretation of Jesus for our everyday spiritual practice; for meditation, contemplation, and spiritual care? What must spirituality be like if—contrary to today's tendency toward randomness—it looks to *Jesus* for guidance? Central to such spirituality is establishing a deep connection with God and trusting him as a Father. Jesus' love and mysticism were not detached from the world but oriented toward it. They provide an answer amid our present lack of spiritual orientation. This book analyzes this crisis, in which religion risks being forgotten, even before its rites and pronouncements, and their deeper meaning, have been understood (see chapters 2, 8, 9, and 10). When religion degenerates, we lose an important cultural asset. In the West, we have become alienated from our spiritual roots. As a result, we are no longer able to put our spiritual experiences—and thus ourselves—into perspective. Our cultural development toward reason would also be a resource. Many of us would like to "understand." This makes us search for the convincing aspects of Christian religion, which I believe would stand the test of such inquiry. Not only does Christian religion have great potential but its image of God and human beings is most impressive (chapters 4 and 5). The future of the churches lies not only in the Far East or in Latin America but also in a new spirituality and in a new understanding of Jesus—both of his person and his message.

This book is about *experience*. Understanding is one matter, *being touched* another. What really matters occurs when we summon the courage to move from observing God to encountering him. Without encounter—that is, experience—neither religion nor Jesus will touch us. Jesus will remain external to us. Time and again, my work with hundreds of cancer patients and dying persons, as well as with individuals from different denominations and religions, has inspired my mystical and contemplative view of Jesus. My work has taught me that what we need most in life and suffering is spiritual experience (see my *Hope and Grace*, 2016). Spiritual experiences can also be crucial to rediscovering Jesus. Touched by Jesus, we will find our own answers and will discover the next steps on our spiritual path. Being touched comes first, interpretation afterward. But what about our personal freedom? Jesus may serve as our model. He lived freedom paired with connection. He respected human freedom and regarded the human being as a subject—as a friend. He seldom gave spiritual instructions. We do not need them if we are connected.

But how can Jesus touch us? This happens time and again when we envision his words, his person, and his particular way of life and love. This book wants to make contact with or to connect with Jesus, whatever our denomination or religion. I believe that understanding Jesus as a mystic may serve as a bridge between the separated Christian denominations. The focus *on Jesus* and *on religious experience* helps us engage in interreligious dialogue. (Every) Religion first needs to find itself. If it does, religious diversity will become a gift for those seeking a mutually respectful and mature dialogue with one other (Renz 2017, 301). We need not anxiously restrain Jesus and his message. Nor do we need to dress him up in doctrine. It is enough if we liberate both. If we manage to do this, Jesus and his message can take place—as deep *experience*—within individuals and communities.

I have accompanied over one thousand dying patients. They are my teachers. My daily work as an end-of-life carer is not limited to the spoken word. It also involves dreams, trauma therapy, music-assisted relaxation,[2] and imagination. Sometimes, these resources are inspired by metaphors and biblical images and often require depth-psychological interpretation. Thus my approach to Jesus has grown from my encounters with the dying, with workshop participants, and with those severely ill persons who bear their suffering and become mature. They are silent mystics. Many know the secret of coming very close to God—or whatever they call this Supreme Being. They are "exegetes of the message." This (mystical) experience (see Renz 2016) makes us "see"— now and at the time of Jesus. Richard Rohr (2010) calls this "learning to see like the mystics."

I have divided this book into ten chapters:

Chapter 1 presents my basic hypothesis: Jesus was a mystic and defined by his close connection with God. My approach sheds new light on Jesus' message, love, and redemption. Jesus' strong personality makes his mysticism seem natural. In other words, he was not divorced from reality. For spiritual practice, this means that "discovering" Jesus as a mystic provides us with deep inner experience.

Chapter 2 analyzes the current crisis of Western Christianity. The better we understand this crisis, the better we will heal and become conscious. I think that religiosity will find a "landing strip" in our life and soul if we long for connection. For spiritual practice, this means that reconnection happens briefly, when we make contact with our deep longing and by *interpreting the great experiences of life* (e.g., discovering our vocation, finding our life partner, enduring suffering, etc.).

Chapter 3 explores the *historical* Jesus. What do we know about him and his words? I see the historical Jesus as a mystic. This view bridges the historical distance between Jesus and us. For spiritual practice, this means that if—or rather, because—the historical Jesus was a mystic, his power is timeless. *He* can thus become the content of our meditation, contemplation, and prayer—Christ (see introduction, note 3).

Chapter 4 considers Jesus' *relationship* with the Father. This is not opposed to a motherly understanding of God, but provides an answer to human fear. Why fear? What is fear? Where does it begin? Ontologically, fear only occurs in an ego-bound world. The heavenly kingdom and salvation, two key concepts for Jesus, describe qualities beyond ego-bound categories. The spiritual idea guiding practice is that we too can live beyond fear, even if we experience this mode of existence only in very brief moments. We too can enter into a relationship with the Father. If we embrace this "offer," we too will feel accepted, nurtured, and loved from the primal ground. We can accept ourselves. And we are related. This mystical relationship to God is the Alpha and the Omega of a spirituality based entirely on Jesus.

Chapter 5 explores *Jesus' concept of humankind*. He assigns us dignity. Nevertheless, he senses that we need healing, not least because of our remoteness from God and because of our fear. Behind all his acts of healing emerges one primordial healing, which means returning home to the Father. Jesus healed *"as a person"*—that is, through engagement, compassion, and relationship. His profound connection with the Father meant that Jesus personified "primordial trust." The key spiritual terms guiding practice are that Jesus is an inner therapist. Faith is about daring to trust. Praying is about coming before God. This also involves motherly therapeutic aspects.

Chapter 6 discusses "sin," separation, and formative influences in terms of developmental psychology. Since time immemorial, the dominant response pattern in the human soul has been separation. This contrasts with Jesus' unbroken relationship with the Father. For a spirituality oriented entirely toward Jesus, this means both *reversal* (coming home) and *exodus* (leaving home). To overcome "sin," we need to follow long paths of maturation. Thereby we make closer and closer contact with ourselves. C. G. Jung speaks of individuation (i.e., self-becoming). Can we accept the inner call to exodus and individuation?

Chapter 7 shows that Jesus was influenced by the prevailing view of the demonic at his time. But this alone does not explain the impressive way in which he dealt with *evil* and obsession. I understand evil as what has been split off, as what has closed itself off from the totality or wholeness of God. Separation involves an ongoing process and leads to a dynamic of splitting, rupture, imitation, and projection (e.g., mimesis; Girard [1972] 2005). The spiritual idea guiding practice is that we must take evil seriously, beyond naivety and diabolization. Like Jesus, we need a strong personality. We also need to renounce destructiveness. And we need to engage in shadow work—that is, to confront our dark sides and failures. Thereby we might overcome evil. This is most likely to happen when we are fully present in the here and now *and* related to God/the Supreme Being.

Chapter 8 asks about Jesus' *love and devotion*. Both occur when we are free. They establish identity and initiate a dynamic of love, which slowly changes the world. Yet what does love mean? The hypothesis of the mystical Jesus also lends a new nuance to the commandment to love one another: love does not (neurotically) overwhelm us but is itself nurtured. Here, I distinguish *philia* (*fili,a*; brotherly love, affection, friendship) from *agape* (the highest form of love, charity; God's love for us and ours for God). Jesus asks his disciples for agape. The Last Supper and Jesus washing his disciples' feet exemplify his love. For spiritual practice, this means that we should grow ever deeper into the love lived by Jesus.

Chapter 9 discusses *redemption*. Which ideas and customs at the time shaped the centuries-long interpretation of Jesus' death as atoning sacrifice? Can these notions and practices be reconciled with his behavior and conception of God? Jesus' Passion and crucifixion arose from a hostile collective dynamic. Further, his particular capacity for love (devotion, loyalty, and consequence) opens up a redemptive, spiritual path for all of us. Jesus never acted or reacted in terms of power and violence, not even in the Passion and crucifixion. Instead, he remained connected with the Father. His life shows us that connectedness can overcome separation. We have the chance to follow him. Redemption, then, leads to a second identity. It enables peace, and even a capacity for forgiveness. It marks the beginning of a new pattern of behavior, a new human constitution. Here, the spiritual idea guiding practice is that Jesus offers us a new beginning. He initiated a new spiritual path. The path was and is about "experience": many encounter Jesus as Christ,[3] while others experience themselves as guided, liberated, rescued, or inspired.

Chapter 10 offers a teleological view of the dynamic between God and human beings. This dynamic can be summarized as "God also comes toward us/me." In particular, the Prologue of the Gospel of John envisions this dynamic. Its language is metaphorical, similar to near-death experiences, spiritual dreams, and many visions of the dying. This teleological view already inspired the early Christians when they developed the faith and rituals of Christmas, Easter, and Pentecost. For spiritual practice, this means that "faith is an option" (Joas 2014). We are not only going toward God. We also can accept that "He comes toward us/me." Jesus' life and behavior manifest God's coming. Yet we too can experience instances of grace through our spiritual experiences. We are not simply determined by our origins. Nor are we simply "caused" (i.e., the result of causation). We are instead also directed toward a goal (i.e., finality and meaningfulness).

My Approach to the Bible

The Bible is a complex text that has come down to us partly by word of mouth. My understanding of theology is Johannine. It is based on the experiences of many dying, and on personal spiritual experiences during severe illness and while experiencing a skiing accident followed by months of rehabilitation. Extreme life events and experiences can help us to perceive in other ways what the gospels mean by the kingdom of God/heaven or the Beatitudes (Matthew, Luke). I do not interpret the kingdom of God/heaven primarily in sociopolitical terms (i.e., as a new political option) but in mystical ones. Deep connectedness and maturation are the emotional foundations capable of changing early imprinting and patterns of behavior. In this book, I link the Gospel of John with various synoptic themes (e.g., the Beatitudes, the healing of obsessions, the "lost" prodigal son). I also establish connections with the covenant theology of the Old Testament. Like the synoptics, I believe that a *development* occurred within Jesus and that he took his decisions in real freedom. In general, I consider three modes of Bible interpretation:

1. Revelation: a collection of sacred texts containing revelation. The authors of the Bible produced many important

contents based on their deep connection with God (Old and New Testament) and their experiences of Christ (New Testament). They were spiritually inspired.

2. Historical-critical interpretation: the Bible as a book written by human beings *after* the death of Jesus. Consequently, we need historical-critical exegesis for the purposes of analysis. This inquires into the origin of the biblical texts and occasionally relativizes their absoluteness. Underlying any image of God is a conception of humankind and an expression of a particular time.

3. A book whose metaphorical language is closer to our modern dream consciousness than our reasoning and waking consciousness (see figure 1, chapter 4.3). As far as we know, such language was customary at Jesus' time. A depth-psychological interpretation often approaches the language and thinking of those times more closely than pure reasoning. The symbolic language of many biblical passages is comparable to that of other sacred cultural treasures (e.g., religious murals, myths).

These three ways of interpreting the Bible also help to illuminate the sacred scriptures of other religions. Revelatory moments enable us to recognize God himself and provide a bridge to the absolute. Historical-critical interpretation lays bare the human and all too human (e.g., an era's patriarchal or law-based thinking). It may also reveal an author's or gospel's individual bias and "marketing strategies." The revelatory is absolute, while the human is conditional. Unlike other approaches to the Bible (and other sacred texts), this book includes the *experiential* dimension, insights from depth psychology, and an affinity with symbolism (see also Renz 2017). My approach is similar yet different to the early writings of the German theologian Eugen Drewermann. I am a practicing psychotherapist and end-of-life carer. I like to rationally understand what I believe, and yet I regard God as our ultimate and innermost point of reference.

CHAPTER 1
Jesus and God
A MYSTICAL CONNECTION

1.1. Jesus' Secret

Jesus' life and words attest to his incomparable autonomy. He healed. He withdrew. He observed commandments, though not for their own sake. He empathized and forgave. All these actions and the way Jesus performed them bear testimony to his deeply rooted freedom and authority. His behavior was fundamentally new and original in many respects. It has historical value, like some of Jesus' words, which we know he spoke himself.

Where did Jesus' autonomy come from? His incredible charisma and authority required no earthly confirmation. He was a charismatic personality. He was neither a guru nor a conceited maverick, but deeply human and loving. His entire life was devoted to his message, to others, to God. Theology speaks of *pro-existence*, that is, existence for the sake of others. But what empowered Jesus to give himself to others without becoming neurotic? How did he know inherently about right and wrong? What allowed him to see through people so profoundly that he knew what they needed to heal? While his message was ingenious, how did he come by it? What was his secret?

I presume that Jesus would not have succeeded on his own. Instead, his life rested on a secret: his absolute closeness to God: "The Father and I are one" (John 10:30). What exactly do these words tell us? They determine the atmosphere of the entire Gospel of John. Unless we develop a deeper understanding of these particular words, I believe that the essence of Jesus' life will evade us. All four gospels and Christian tradition speak about the close relationship between Jesus and God.

In this book, I approach this closeness from the perspective of mystical experience. Jesus was a mystic. His *message*, *healing energy*, and *behavior* were all inspired by his mystical source, which he called "Father." Jesus was guided by God and thus assumed divine authority. He was intimately "connected" with God. "Being connected" is not just the opposite of "being disconnected" (unrelated, divorced). Being connected also contrasts with the experience of "existential loneliness" (McGrath 2002, 644; Sand, Strang, and Milberg 2008). Thus connectedness is more than mere connection; it means *being* versus *having*, which are two categorically different modes of existence (Fromm [1976] 2014).

It implies relationship and relatedness in contrast to more or less autarkic egotism, in which the ego is thrown back upon itself.

Being connected or disconnected: this is the alternative and the ultimate question in life and death, for Jesus and for us. Connectedness is based on primordial trust (see Renz 2018), being, and love—in contrast to primordial fear.[1] Whereas primordial trust allows us to feel loved and to love, primordial fear is the basis for patterns of compensation such as avarice, craving for power, or thirsting for glory. We are mostly unaware of this connective mode of existence in daily life. Connectedness is about absolute relationship and relatedness, which grow from deep acceptance. It is the opposite of an all-embracing mistrust, which results in a more or less autarkic ego. Connectedness enables us to even endure our fundamental dependence (which is experienced by many severely ill and dying persons).

> *"I'm happy to be," a young dying man who did not believe in God told me. His wife caressed him. Her tenderness, which was like music to him, was deeply sensual. "I'm whole, although I'm totally powerless and dependent," he said.*
>
> *A confused old man was nervous and had back pain. He tossed back and forth. "Cable, cable . . . cut," he cried. I told him, and I'm sure he couldn't understand this with his*

mind, that we could rediscover our reconnection. I touched the bottom of his spine. He calmed down. This happened several times. That night he dreamed of a bridge that was like a rainbow. The next day he died.

"I dreamed about a great sheepskin. God himself was this sheepskin and comforted me. I can't do anything anymore: I can't walk, eat, or read, but I can feel. God is near me, sometimes almost too close. Then he overwhelms me." These words were spoken by a religious, seventy-year-old woman.

Our connection with (or disconnection from) God, whom I also understand as the greater whole, is, in fact, a matter of *perception*. Our sense of connectedness depends on how ego-bound we feel or indeed are. Beyond our everyday, ego-bound perception lies a completely different sensibility (see, for instance, near-death experiences, chapter 2). Connected, we see and hear "more" than our eyes and ears. Connected, our perception does not depend on everyday consciousness, selection, and divisions. Nor is it automatically guided by self-interest and personal motivation. Instead, it is unfiltered. Connected, we are bound neither to our ego, nor only to our instincts and affects. Instead, we are radically open—to the world and even to transcendence. Connected: this electrical metaphor gets to the heart of matters: the "grid" or the "network"—what is offered by the other side (i.e., grace, the presence of God)—always exists. Often, however, we are not "plugged in," not connected. Our formative influences, ego, needs, wounds, and prejudices stand in our way.

me days later, the elderly woman mentioned above was angry and hungry. She felt abandoned, motherless. She had another dream: "There was a bridge to heaven, but it was broken. There was no crossing." We talked about Mother Teresa's spiritual darkness. This helped the woman to accept her situation. A few days later, the feeling of the great sheepskin recurred. This woman immediately understood the metaphor of Jesus as a good shepherd.

Let us return to Jesus. He was completely open to the greater whole. He was rooted in the (heavenly) Father. He even let himself depend entirely on the Father. Nowadays, we would say he was "with himself." But being with ourselves is not about ego-boundness but *relationship*: Jesus was so entirely related to God that he was not cut off from divine energy by any blockages, fears, and narcissisms. The Father was his source of trust and strength. Jesus' connectedness allowed him to regenerate, for instance, by withdrawing into, and finding strength, in prayer. He seldom needed to retreat from the world. Behind this fact, and behind his behavior in general (his divine authority, his radical love, his healing), we can sense Jesus' connectedness. All the time, God was "there," ever present in what Jesus did and said. Jesus speaks of oneness. This, however, was a mystical union, which should not be misinterpreted as symbiosis nor as narcissistic appropriation. It was a *dialogical* mystical reality.

Already the covenant of the Old Testament expresses an intimate relationship between God and humankind. Given to Abraham (Genesis 15:1–21), the covenant repeatedly served Moses as a bridge between Yahweh and his people or, psychologically speaking, between God and the person coming to consciousness. Both the Old and New Testament covenants frame the evolving relationship between God and humans: God's unconditional loyalty, God's summons to see eye to eye with humans, the growing human response to his call, the binding of the people to the law (Torah). We can recognize a development: the relationship shifts from a one-sided covenant (Genesis 15:1–21) to a reciprocal one; from an outer covenant to an inner one, as was first prophesied as a new covenant by Jeremiah (Jeremiah 31:31–34). If I call Jesus a mystic, I mean that his mysticism includes all these relational qualities and further deepens them. (On the relationship between Judaism and Christianity, see chapter 3.)

1.2. A Strong Personality

Neither his intense encounter with God nor his intimate closeness to the Father meant that Jesus dissolved into mystical conjunction. He did not live a life apart. On the contrary, he combined a relationship to reality with mystical presence. His personality seemed to be exceptionally strong, his mysticism down to earth. He was never suffused by the spiritual (see his reaction after the transfiguration—namely, his decision not to build any dwellings; Mark 9:2–10). Obviously Jesus knew how to deal with his closeness to God and to the numinous (from Latin *numen*, the overwhelmingly large). We "ordinary" mortals only ever achieve this more or less approximately.

Biblically, Jesus was strong enough to withstand the temptation lurking behind all temptations. He never let himself be dissuaded from God as the Lord and as the basis of primordial trust. Jesus never abused either his closeness to the divine (sonship) or his power—that is, to serve his own ends. His way of dealing with divine power was special: he remained a servant. All the time, he was conscious of being part of God as the whole. Power, for Jesus, always remained identical with the "Father." In the story of the temptation, he saw through false worship. He rejected avarice, the greed for power, the thirst for glory, and the determination by fear.[2] His life bears witness to exceptional clear-sightedness. Examples include his warning against greed (Luke 12:13–15) or his unmasking of the hypocrites (Matthew 23:13). He trusted the Father, and when he fell out of this trust he immediately retrieved it (e.g., in Gethsemane: "Yet, not what I want, but what you want," Mark 14:33–36; and on the cross, Luke 23:43–46).

Like other great mystics, Jesus suffered godforsakenness, but even more strongly. He endured this plight and remained connected with God. Both are signs of his strong personality. Which is how I interpret his words on the cross: "My God, my God, why have you forsaken me" (Psalm 22:1). They are the beginning of a prayer. Quite probably, Jesus did not say this prayer by accident. No, it articulates *an ultimate spiritual challenge*: the need to traverse God's remoteness; not becoming an atheist but standing firm in faith. The experience of God's absence is part of the relationship with God (chapter 9). Nurtured by the Jewish treasure of prayers, Jesus entrusts himself to God as the Lord. When the dying make similar experiences in approaching death, and thus traverse their spiritual darkness to some extent, this expresses utmost dignity (Renz 2015, 34–35). As for Jesus, his dignity was most apparent during the Passion.

1.3. The Basis of Message and Mission

Jesus' mystical connection with God is also the basis of his message about the loving Father, the kingdom of God/

heaven, the Beatitudes, his call for reversal, and his healing. Jesus recognized what humankind lacked. He suffered deeply from the discrepancy between his oneness with God and his fellows' disconnectedness. He saw their fickleness, their barren and brittle spiritual foundation. He endeavored to explain, but his disciples had already misunderstood his words often enough. He realized how much humanity needed redemption (chapters 5, 6, and 7). And he knew intuitively how healing and even salvation may occur (chapters 5, 8, and 9).

In this book, I outline Jesus' idea of human nature, even if the available sources permit no more than a partial answer. His idea of human life was shaped by Jewish tradition, by Hellenistic influences, and by apocalyptic fears.[3] Beyond, however, lay something that originated solely in Jesus. I believe this had to do with *Jesus as a mystic*. His mysticism explains why Jesus remained misunderstood, as well as remote, alien, and envied. His presence and ministry were fascinating and yet unbearable. His mysticism also explains his deep understanding of humankind, which came from his connection with God. He saw through the human soul and its spiritual abysses. He understood the tragic alienation of humanity from its primordial ground (*conditio humana*). This separation meant that, beyond Eden, human beings lived in fear and compensation. Jesus invites us—we who are caught up in this mode of existence—to "trust the primordial ground as the 'good Father,' and thus to live with *more* kindness ourselves" (Kessler 2006, 35).

In this sense, reversal (Mark 1:15) and reconnection are linked to mysticism and trust. Reversal means returning into a relationship with the Father. It also means coming home, because God is the primordial ground. From old Greek *metanoia*, reversal denotes a "turning inward," a change of mind. For the ancient Greeks, this happens in the heart. Thinking was not a cerebral activity but a matter of the heart.

Reversal and healing are not unique events. They are spiritual processes, comparable to a journey. While gaining knowledge is important on this journey, it does not constitute the entire path. We may reap the fruits on our path, but we cannot be spared suffering, as the word itself suggests. *Suffering* describes a highly creative process of arriving at another place.[4] Behind numerous biblical healings lies more than a straightforward narrative, as we see in the gospels. The brevity of the stories told by the evangelists detracts nothing from their processual nature. When Jesus discharges the healed with momentous words (e.g., "Your faith has healed you"), he is recapitulating an entire process. These concise stories make sense if we assume that *Jesus united important salutary capacities in himself.*

1.4. The Capacity for Love

Jesus' extraordinary capacity for love and devotion stems from his connection with the Father, paired with his strong personality. Two thousand years of Christianity tell us that love springs not merely from a moral commandment. We cannot understand the command to love only ethically. We would miss our aim to love, and we would end up neurotically altruistic. Instead, love is rooted in being loved, being nurtured, and living in another state of being. Being connected to God and his abounding plenty (Psalm 65:9) is crucial. Once we have experienced this mode of wholly (holy) being, we endeavor to do good ourselves, out of inner motives. We then also feel an existential sufficiency: we are happy and feel no gaping hole that needs to be compensated.

Biblically, Jesus lived in unity with God. He accepted being totally connected and related. He was never cut off from God. His deep bond[5] connected him with God's fullness. It also made him open to the world and to human beings and their afflictions. Jesus did not understand solidarity and love as a duty (unlike the Pharisees) but as a state of being and longing. He felt urged to give nothing less (to others) than himself (chapter 8). Benedetti (1993) has described this utmost human sympathy with the therapeutic notion of "existential being-with." Jesus' being-with was intense and went even further.

The most impressive testimony to the power of love occurs amid suffering. We often find the quality of being-with in hospitals. Many relatives are so moved by the suffering of their loved ones that they want to help or at least be present.

> *So did the mother of a very young, severely ill man. Whenever he wanted her to, she watched football on TV with him. Whenever he was tired or upset, she left him alone, without any bad feelings. It was obvious that she was not protecting but loving him. She told me, "I am just trying to show him that he is important to the world." When I asked how she looked after herself, she replied, "This [her son's situation] is immensely important right now. I go walking every day. Having my dog helps."*

Our wish to give love can be so strong that we "take" the other person's suffering upon ourselves: relatives or caregivers may relieve the dying person of their suffering; sometimes, the dying may take a family's suffering upon themselves.

Some relatives have told me that they have dreamed of being "infected" by the sufferings of their loved ones. These dreams were so powerful that they changed their dreamers.

> *The husband of an elderly dying woman did something magnificent: he brought her flowers every day, as if to tell his wife,*

*"I love you so much." Later, when his wife was readmitted
and once again feared the symptoms and her powerlessness,
she dreamed of all her husband's flowers. They formed a large
carpet of love. She was moved and realized her husband's
great love as never before. She died peacefully two days later.*

Let us return to Jesus: his mystical connection allowed him to love to the utmost. He also understood the commandment to love one another in this way. This is more than sheer ethical admonition. Even if values such as justice, responsibility, and education are important cornerstones of our society and culture, they do not in themselves enable us to give openheartedly. Jesus' commandment to love stems from his closeness to God (chapter 8). Like Mark the Evangelist (12:29–31), I would say: Love will emanate from us whenever we come to trust /God "with all our heart, soul, mind, and strength." Love will emanate from us whenever we feel so connected as if *we* too were the beloved son or daughter of God. Consequently, we will love ourselves as who we are, as we will love our neighbors, brothers, and sisters as who they are. We will even be able to forgive ourselves and others. And, as an extreme consequence, we will be able to imagine loving our enemies. Being grounded in greater love is the source of our capacity for love. It is also the essence of a spirituality entirely based on Jesus.

In Jesus' case, the Passion and his suffering on the cross bear witness to his love. He remained faithful to himself, to his message, to his way of love, and to the Father (chapter 9).

1.5. The Secret of God's Son

Was Jesus a human being or God's Son? This question, crucial in ecclesiastical history, remains unsolved. We will never prove either answer. From the perspective of mystical experience, I understand Jesus' relationship with the Father neither dogmatically nor biologically. It is instead a deep spiritual reality (Steindl-Rast 2010). In his *Confessions* (3.6.11), Augustine speaks of an outermost and innermost reality, of God's presence as "more inward than my innermost and higher than my uppermost" (McMahon 2006, 11). By analogy, Jesus was related to the Father as the innermost and the outermost. His connection could not have been greater. His loneliness also meant togetherness.

In 451, the Council of Chalcedon hypothesized that two natures resided in Christ: that of a true human and that of a true God. Some deemed this view ingenious, others unfortunate. We will better understand this hidden conception if we understand it as a *deeply mystical*, inner reality. Jesus *was* entirely human, but also "at one" with God, in an almost unbearable intensity. From *behind* the dogma and its instructional function ought to emerge a final secret. This, however, remains inaccessible.

A final mystery implies taboo and functions similarly: though completely hidden, it nevertheless urges toward disclosure. *Taboo* (from Polynesian *tapu*) denotes what is forbidden under the most severe threat if violated. In earlier cultures, taboo-breaking entailed psychogenic death: people died of horror and fear, even without any external threat (Riedel 1994). A taboo, although shrouded in silence, nevertheless urges toward conscious realization when the time is ripe. Interestingly, some folktales tell us that, at times, the tabooed must be uttered, at others kept silent, just as its breach must be denied.

Let us transpose these reflections onto the secret of Jesus' intimate relationship with God. Their connection reveals something truly magnificent. Like the sun, which warms and scorches us, we experience an absolutely challenging, at times even overwhelming spiritual reality. For the human being, God is taboo: if experienced close up, its existence is almost unbearable. We therefore need and seek a "mediator" (the New Testament bears witness to Jesus Christ as the mediator between God and creation). Yet his closeness to the absolute still makes us avoid him. Thus the oddly ambivalent approach to Jesus throughout history makes sense: he was—and still is—fascinating *and* frightening.

Yet what can open the door to the secret of an intimate closeness to God? It is the phenomenon of spiritual experiences. At the time, this happened during Jesus' healings. For "outsiders," these events were magnificent and awe-inspiring. For "insiders," the healed ones, the healings were like a key. Similar to Jesus the mystic, they had personally experienced divine power. Among other precepts, they were instructed to remain silent. Jesus' healings revealed deeply hidden inner realities, for which neither language nor self-awareness (yet) existed. The healed were partly initiated into God's secret while, as with breaking a taboo, they were themselves tabooed.

Jesus was strange and dangerous. Not just because he healed, radicalized, and polarized. His mystical connectedness, and hence his person, exerted fascination as well as incomprehension, fear, and resistance (Luke 8:26–39). Even his disciples barely understood his explanations of himself, his nature, and his Father. A few decades later, Paul and the evangelists struggled to capture this secret in words.

Unlike a dogma, a (tabooed) secret urges toward disclosure. It seeks to raise consciousness. When Jesus said, "The time is fulfilled" (Mark 1:15), he might have intuitively felt what was at stake (*kairos*, a unique fortunate turning moment in history had arrived). Jesus often calls us to follow him. If we understand his secret, his *mystical* union with the Father, his call makes sense: like Jesus, we can also allow an ever-greater mystical connectedness with the Father to occur. Once we see the closeness to God as an extreme secret and taboo, we will understand redemption as the overcoming of human separation (i.e., sin). This process, in turn, is like overcoming a taboo. Through it, we find our way back to our primordial trust and closeness to God.

"The Father and I are almost one," a young, nearly quadriplegic woman told me after an experience she had made while praying. Amid suffering and illness, she was deeply happy.

1.6. Deliverance from Formative Influences

Redemption, on the one hand, involves freeing ourselves from bondage and formative influences. On the other, it is about becoming able to be reconnected with God. We can become more and more able to endure that closeness. We can imagine a final state as mystical. It means "remaining near God." In reality, this state occurs time and again because it is interrupted by the dynamics of sin. Thus redemption occurs through various processes: suffering, enduring, becoming more and more conscious, and loving.

Jesus was a role model; he led the way. Redemption happens when we follow the way, but also by grace. In modern terms, Jesus initiated a new neurophysiological program. This consists of new patterns of behavior—for example, unconditional love based on being loved by the Father. Jesus' groundedness in the Father represented a redeemed existence. He was free. His message, healings, and love were redemptive. His exceptional behavior is evident, both in life and above all in the Passion up to his crucifixion (chapter 9).

Jesus initiated a new spiritual path. He was a pioneer. He involved and still involves those who follow his path toward a new connectedness. He unburdened and unburdens us. He led the way and thus opened up a new way of life and a new way of loving. He gave us a new, God-related identity. He allowed new patterns of behavior (e.g., trust instead of fear, being instead of having, devotion instead of the thirst for power and glory). They replace the prevailing formative influences and determination (sin, separation). These new patterns of behavior, based on a new connectedness to God, bring forth new individuals and new patterns of collective behavior and reorganization. A positive formative influence counters the once-prevailing negative imprinting (Renz 2017).

We need to see redemption as a long process. Jesus underwent it as a pioneer. At its end stands no more than a "formula of redemption."[6] Those who follow the pioneer's footsteps have a smoother path ahead of themselves because *someone*—in our case, Jesus—has undergone the process (of achieving consciousness) before us. In terms of depth psychology, Jesus became an archetype in our soul. This involves more than being a role model.

Let me illustrate the secret of redemption.

A middle-aged Catholic woman dreamed about a deeply impressive person like the pope or a similar great authority. Time and again, this figure had to forge a path through the wilderness. Yet he was handicapped and physically unable to perform this task. He had to apply mental strength instead, resisting one temptation after another. Looking back, he saw a new path and many people following it. The dreamer was told to take this path and to widen it. In the dream, there was no doubt that its message concerned the inner secret of Jesus.

Several people who have attended one of my workshops, as well as severely ill patients, have dreamed of "Christ's trail through the desert," of "religion as an underground system," of "Jesus who points the way," or of corresponding words and music—beyond analytical reasoning (see chapter 9).

1.7. Human Answers: Faith in Freedom and Responsibility

The new beginnings, the Jesuanic response pattern, have often been blurred or buried. This is the fate of many paths, trails, or initiations. But deep down, they have existed in our unconscious—for two thousand years. The salutary potential of this pattern urges toward conscious realization, in the individual and in human history. Once it exists, the path is waiting to be revealed and to be taken. This is the deeper meaning of Christian faith, and of Jesus' words, "Follow me." We can live our faith ethically, with utmost responsibility, as well as mystically. For instance, we can attribute dignity to a suffering person because we want to or because we feel with him or her.

One final, still unresolved question remains: What came first—the path or our imitation of Jesus' behavior? In the first case, the path is initiated by Jesus. We become conscious of it through following and internalizing it (mystical and depth-psychological viewpoint). In the second case, our following Jesus' example becomes our new formative influence (behavioral and ethical viewpoint). This brings the path into existence. Like all questions of faith, this one also demands that we make a personal decision (chapter 2). It is also a question about grace versus good works.

My approach is mystical and depth-psychological. It is about achieving consciousness rather than about implementation. If we seek and allow ourselves to become conscious, then faith will acquire a new, mature, and inner dimension.[7] In this case, we must search for what governs our inner life and find our way back to God as the Lord of our life (a major issue throughout the Old Testament). This spiritual journey corresponds to the biblical development from an outer to an inner covenant. It also corresponds with a new—and yet very old and mystical—interpretation of Jesus' person and message, as well as with a new understanding of fellowship as internalization. The beginning of such a mystical reinterpretation already exists: it is a new desire for Christian spirituality. Spiritual traditions speak of an entirely different reality (Dietrich Bonhoeffer, Dorothee Sölle, Thomas Merton, Anselm Grün, David Steindl-Rast, Richard Rohr, Franz Jalics). So do other disciplines (medicine, psychiatry, psychotherapy, body therapy, the study of near-death experiences, and quantum physics).

I close with Jeremiah's words about the new covenant: "I will put my law within them, and I will write it on their hearts; and I will be their God, and they shall be my people. No longer shall they teach one another, or say to each other, 'Know the Lord,' for they shall all know, from the least of them to the greatest, says the Lord; for I will forgive their iniquity, and remember their sin no more" (Jeremiah 31:33–34; see also Hebrews 8:8–12).

CHAPTER 2

Absent Mysticism and Awakening

2.1. Christianity in Crisis

The name Jesus has become lifeless in the Western world. It is now barely able to serve as a basis of Christian culture and religion. Western Christianity has been in crisis for decades. This began as a crisis of the Church and has since evolved through a crisis of faith to a spiritual crisis. Many lament the empty churches, the lack of credibility among ecclesiastical dignitaries, and the unwillingness to engage in dialogue within church hierarchies. Also criticized is the declining profession of faith: How do priests see themselves today? Are they merely social workers? Can theology, and can individuals, still self-confidently embrace the essence of Christ and his message—without being branded fundamentalist? The power of a Christian life based on faith is often no longer even considered. Many of us no longer bother with Jesus. Churches lacking credibility and the misdemeanors of pastors have long become an excuse for, and an argument against, Christian religion.

Another aspect of this crisis is Christianity's lack of *inner* orientation. For centuries, the churches mainly considered themselves exoteric (Greek: *evxw, teroj*, "external," "outside"). They oriented themselves toward the outside world, focused on doctrine and proclamation, and forbid themselves and their members any personal experience of God.

The historical background of the Church's shunning of experience—its fight against Gnosticism[1]—is understandable. And yet it is problematic: the center of Christian existence—Jesus Christ—was only taught by hearsay. (See Job 42:5: "I had heard of you by the hearing of my ear, but now my eye sees you.") Crucially, however, it was no longer felt or experienced. In contrast, esotericism has become a hodgepodge of spiritual, indeed spiritistic doctrines, and thus also a term of abuse.[2] Esoteric teachings, which partly invoke early Christian Gnosticism, encourage human fantasies of self-redemption and the hubris inherent in such ideas. Although esotericism may be about experience, it is no longer about Jesus Christ. Christ is no longer considered "necessary." Nor is he experienced. His absence has long made Christ an argument against Christ.

I believe that Western Christianity's most severe crisis is *spiritual.* This is evident in a sprawling spiritual randomness, a quasi-McDonaldization of religion. As Fulbert Steffensky (2012) has aptly pointed out, "Everything tastes the same."

This explains why *mindfulness*, a term borrowed from the East, is greeted so enthusiastically—as if it were a religion itself. Even if mindfulness is important, and even if it promotes tolerance, body perception, and self-awareness, it is *not* the content of religion. Religious arbitrariness spells emotional, spiritual, and even cultural degeneration. It dissolves the core of all religions. For Christians, this means we need neither Jesus, the redeemer, nor his message of the kingdom of God/heaven. As a result, we are increasingly unaware of our Judeo-Christian roots. Our Western culture, its history of ideas, and its knowledge are wasting away. Worryingly, we barely ever discuss this decline.

New generations are growing up not only without sacraments and ecclesiastical symbols but also without the Bible, Jesus, the Jewish-Christian worldview, "the God of our fathers," and awe-inspiring religious experiences. Judaism and Christianity, wherever they are still practiced, are becoming ghetto religions. Around them, spiritual-religious awareness, differentiation, and binding commitment are considered less and less desirable. Ever more people have ceased asking about the ultimate meaning, about immanence and transcendence.

For decades, people raised as Christians have been reaching out *to other religions*. This is not unproblematic either. Studying other cultures teaches us how different we are as human beings. It makes us necessarily respectful of others. Ultimately, however, nothing from the outside can replace our lost original roots. The development of culture and religion is a reciprocal process. Religion is a response to deep human desires and to culture-specific influences— for instance, our unconscious primordial fear or alienation from God. In other cultural contexts, religion might also be a reaction to their early imprinting (e.g., lethargy, want, illusion, or whatever they are). I was not born in Tibet, nor on a Native American reservation. However, I am convinced that we cannot fully compensate for our own deficiencies by resorting to the answers from another religion. At times, the other religion remains alien and eludes judgments from a (securalized) Christian perspective. For instance, a week ago I provided therapeutic support to a dying Tibetan Buddhist and the family gathered at his bedside. The atmosphere was utterly different (e.g., calm, collected, indifferent). In contrast, the family of a just-deceased African Muslim was crying and lamenting in the next room. Even if I was touched, I was merely a witness in both cases—as I am with dying Sufis, Jews, and Hindus. We can only understand another religion *from within itself*. Thus we first need to establish which formative influences a particular religion responds to. Second, we need to explore its salubrity, its health-promoting capacity. It seems to me that only then will any interreligious dialogue bear fruit (Renz 2017, 277–95; see also Renz 2013). In sum, anthropological precepts and religion must go hand in hand.

Today, many diverse attempts exist *to combine religions*, schools of meditation, and spiritual paths (e.g., the Prayer of the Heart with the Zen approach). Some approaches are fruitful—for instance, ones that initiate a mature dialogue between an "I" and a "Thou." Others are marred by irrational (allergic) reactions to the Church, to God, to their own father, and to responsibility. In my experience, self-made spirituality tends to conceal personal deficiencies. Spiritual alignment glosses over the differences between various worldviews. Thus attempts to interconnect religions often risk dilution. They fall prey to hubris, despite the best intentions. We do well to remember that neither a cultural heritage nor answers to the final questions (which have developed over millennia) can be cobbled together at will within the space of *one* generation. *Mature interreligious dialogue* is characterized by the capacity to endure tension.

The spiritual crisis of Western European Christianity is also evident in its shallow cults and rites. Today, we barely ever address our deepest human desires. Barely any culture-establishing precepts remain, except perhaps for the Eucharist or Holy Communion. Whereas other cultures have traditional rites and meditation practices, ours largely lacks the guide rails of a spiritual path. Awe, stillness, and celebration—all appropriate to the mystery—have yielded to activism, eventism, and a freedom from obligation. Are we risking profanation, indeed the desecration of the sacred?

And yet there are movements in our culture that give us reason for hope: the Spiritual Exercises of St. Ignatius of Loyola (Jalics 2011), contemplation (Rutishauser 2011), the Prayer of the Heart, the Camino de Santiago, the songs of the Taizé community, the gospel songs, and the like. They do not, however, disguise the waning of Christianity. Even the inherent transformative potential of central liturgic rites such as the Eucharist and the Holy Communion is not duly recognized. These rites (could) resonate in our soul without many words or much "action." And they (could) initiate processes of reconnection.

So why are attempts to *invent* cults and rituals doomed to fail? Because cults and rites grow very slowly from the depths of collective development. And because they are central to what a culture considers sacred. Cults take hold when they spring from such depths. They are then intuitively understood by the human unconscious (Jung 1969) (see chapter 4.2). But who still has access to these roots? No one understands—even if Jesus' legacy still resonates in the sacred texts, and even if the rites still encircle it.

Religio/religare means "to reconnect" and "to recollect." The liturgy executes recollection. Of what? We are about to lose Jesus' path (see also the metaphor of the "trail," chapters 1 and 9) even before it has appeared in our soul. It seems to be buried. Those of us who had an *inner* relationship with Jesus as children are often still fascinated—even if we fail to understand. Many others are unmoved. Ever more Christians are alienated from Jesus. Thus we are witnessing a widespread search for spiritual well-being on the one hand, and a spiritual vacuum on the other. Many of us speak of spirituality, but we are actually self-centered. Sometimes, even extreme experiences (dying, deep crises, religious peak experiences) are deprived of their existential depth and are reduced to purely natural phenomena. We no longer ask what transcends our existence—in life and in death. We no longer question or reproach the God of our fathers for the justice and benevolence now absent, but which he promised us. Today, the problem is no longer the "poisoning by God" (Moser 1976). Nor is it whether God makes us sick. No, God seems nonexistent. The divine now merely seems to be a cosmic dimension. Johann Baptist Metz spoke of a "God-crisis" already in 1994 (cited in Peter and Urban 2004, 34). What Metz prophesied has since crept into reality: for many, God is beyond experience and has become an argument against God. Today, life and death can occur without him. We have bid farewell to our deep longing.

2.2. A Turning Point

A crisis can *turn* for the better if we perceive what is missing and are frightened by our own shadows. The current spiritual crisis demands our inner and outer attention. *Within our soul*, we who have bid farewell to all longing can search for our lost sacredness and rediscover our spiritual thirst. Thereby, "landing strips" for the sacred may slowly emerge in our soul. They will once again provide *religio*, connection.

> *A nonreligious man had lost four people close to him. He had a spiritual experience with each of the deceased, either during the day or during a dream at night. In these dreams, the deceased were "alive." Yet the man did not understand. Every day he craved hot chocolate. His wife, an open-minded, searching Christian, intuitively understood her husband's spiritual thirst. She made sure that he had enough chocolate, but also took him to empty old chapels with an inviting spiritual atmosphere. Then he dreamed about being close to his wife.*

Here is another example:

> *An elderly lady dreamed about giving birth to a child. Its head, however, looked upward. As a former midwife, she*

knew that no child would be born like this. It had to be a divine child. The newborn looked at its mother insistently, indeed so powerfully that the woman did not forget the dream for years and gradually embarked on a religious path.

Yet how does the crisis of Christianity demand outer attention? Christian institutions, spirituality, and biblical proclamation need *purifying* and *centering*. They need to be focused on the essence of religion. It is not enough to revive traditions long abandoned unquestioningly and to reintroduce even stricter variants. Beyond a well-founded theology, Christian religion needs a knowledge capable of providing a deeper yet more human understanding of both the sacred texts and of Jesus and his message. This knowledge can extend from Christianity to Judaism and also to other religions. In addition to theology, I believe we also need the insights of depth psychology and psychotherapy. Both approaches help to interpret metaphorical passages in the Old and New Testaments. The metaphorical language of the Bible, like fairy tales and dreams, goes back to older evolutionary stages of human consciousness (see "My Approach to the Bible" in the introduction). A new understanding of religious language and forms helps us to rediscover Jesus' path or trace.

I see spirituality as gift and grace. We do not have to acquire it because it is given to us. Thus we "have" it. Deep in our soul, we are connected with the divine. All we can do is accept that connection and allow ourselves to feel it. We *are* relational beings, and we discover our personal center through a "Thou." In this book, I accept God as the principal and most extreme Thou. I also accept him as our innermost center. And yet he is almost unbearable to experience because God is the Whole. He is tremendous and our greatest taboo (see the introduction). Yet instead of being mystics, we are afraid, due to and as part of our imprinting (chapters 4–7). Today, we do not have a Thou as our center, but rather a "gap" lurks deep within us (Siebenrock, personal communication). Thus I am convinced that our deepest longing is spiritual.

> *A young boy who occasionally came for therapy pointed to his chest and told me, "There's a hole there." His mother's death, two years before, had left more than a hole. He was so thirsty, he said most accurately, but didn't know what for. Knowing that a gaping hole loomed inside him, we could begin our search. What filled/fulfilled him? Initially, Coca-Cola. Though not really. Then chocolate. Though not really either. Most of all, and quite simply, it was closeness. Though not really. He was moved by the picture of a great, yellow angel in my therapy room. When the angel put his hand on the boy's heart, it would get warm. The music of angels, flutes, and praying to his mother and God helped the boy.*

He prayed, "Mister God, why are you so far away?" One night he dreamed about a yellow angel coming down from heaven. This made him happy.

2.3. Spirituality as Experienced Religion

Spirituality comes from religious experience. *Spirituality*: whether the word fascinates or frightens us, we barely know its meaning. Positively, spirituality is now reemerging and being discussed.[3]

Spirituality triggers less aversion than *religion*. Nor is it bound to any particular worldview or denomination. But it may tend to become meaningless, arbitrary, and exchangeable. Still, it extends beyond mere well-being. Etymologically, spirituality is close to mysticism: the Greek *mustiko,j / mystikos* denotes the impenetrable, the mysterious, what is hidden deep inside from the outer eye (*mu,ein tou.j ovfqa-lmou,j*, to close one's eyes). Derived from Latin, *spirituality* implies breath, spirit, pneuma. While *mind* refers to cognitive abilities and states (e.g., intentionality, reason, intellect, cognition, memory), *spirituality* describes inner, highly mystical, or religious experience. Around 200 CE, the adjective *spiritualis* translated Greek *pneumatiko,j / pneumatikos*: "spiritual." Used in connection with baptism, the word meant a deep inner event, akin to breathing, that the person to be baptized (an adult in those days) experienced—or did not. The verb *pne,w / pneo* meant to blow, breathe, or smell.

In this original sense, our ego can neither produce nor grasp spirituality at will. Nor can we "have" or own it. Rather, it guides us toward an inner home and source. It is about individuals and their transcendental experiences. We open ourselves toward the infinite and experience "something." Thereby, relationship occurs, even if we only know one part of this relationship—ourselves. Unlike today's randomness, spirituality connects and enables us to enter into binding commitment. It involves and binds us much more than a journey into another state of consciousness. To make my point: spirituality means to *experience* the divine/God. God is not an otherworldly, remote being. He is instead our term for the Whole and its inherent dynamics. He is substance *and* energy and encompasses "being" (the Supreme Being) *and* "relationship" (connection).

The well-known Catholic theologian Karl Rahner (1971, 15; Klinger 1994, 47) famously remarked, "The devout Christian of the future will either be a 'mystic,' one who has experienced 'something,' or he will cease to be anything at all." It is no coincidence that Rahner's view is one of the most-cited theological statements of the late twentieth century. While mysticism fascinates us, it also makes us shy away and become awestruck. It points to that sacred place where we experience God not just indirectly but directly: as a presence, as a voice in a dream, as light, as part of an encounter with another person. Without this connection with God or the sacred, our soul starves and is left wanting. Rahner knew what he was saying: he had experienced both the dark nights of feeling alienated from God and the luminous moments of feeling close to God. He spoke of God as being existentially *here* for us, as *experiencable*. Either by addressing us or by remaining silent.

To summarize: Our thirst for spirituality is more than a trend. Worldly existence involves us in an ego-bound, survival-driven perception of reality. Normally, we see, hear, and feel as egos. We consider "development" as the abilities and skills acquired. But this idea of perception is limited. Neurophysiologically, it stems from a mechanism of selection—that is, the selective reception (and emission) of stimuli and vibrations. Because we are ego-bound, we automatically screen out what would otherwise overwhelm, flood, or threaten us. Or, of course, what is simply less important. The Swiss palliative care physician Daniel Büche puts it this way:

> The human being has a filter that varies from one individual to another. It slackens in dying and other crises and may sometimes overwhelm us. Certain medication (neuroleptics, Ritalin) seeks to reinforce this filtering

function, to ensure that perception is more selective and more focused (personal communication).

Our longing for spirituality involves our desire to return and to move forward to our own unfiltered wholeness and connectedness. It expresses our longing for another world.

2.4. Between Two Worlds: Four Near-Death Experiences

Near-death experiences capture the unspeakable in highly condensed words and images. Mystical closeness to God—or however else we interpret changes in our consciousness and the unspeakable—is often described in visual metaphors. It involves images, astonishment, and awe. As Saint-Exupéry's little prince says, we understand best with children's eyes and with a heart still able to marvel. We feel as if we have experienced something sacred. Yet all language languishes behind such experience. We stammer or fall silent. We find ourselves at the limits of time and space, in a sphere removed from our ego.

The cardiologist Pim van Lommel (2010, 301–25) has examined the patterns of near-death experiences (NDE) in an attempt to understand such experiences against the background of quantum physics. He speaks of out-of-body experiences, of immersion in an all-embracing, timeless, non-local consciousness. This is also known as a higher, cosmic, divine, transpersonal, or unitary consciousness. So-called deathbed visions, which are socially even more taboo, are just as far-reaching. Van Lommel (2010, 325) concludes "that the essence of our endless consciousness predates our birth and our body and will survive death independently of our body in a nonlocal space where time and distance play no role." He claims that actual near-death experiences usually seriously affect brain functions. Hence ego-bound fear is no longer an issue in such experiences (Van Lommel 2010, 144–45).

In contrast, van Lommel (2010, 310–311; Fenwick, Lovelace, and Brayne 2009) assumes that *persons who have deathbed visions* are time and again present in their (ego-related) waking consciousness. Thus they can experience fear, as my observations of several hundred dying persons confirm (Renz et al. 2013; Renz 2015; Renz 2017). Many experience fear from time to time. Even if they are unable to escape their inner scenario, they can still communicate with their surroundings in that state or between such states. When we cross a threshold of consciousness and draw ever closer to death, our fear loses itself completely time and again (out-of-fear experiences).

In *Dying: A Transition* (Renz 2015), I distinguish three stages of the dying process: *pre-transition* (before the threshold in consciousness), *transition* (across the threshold), and *post-transition* (after the threshold). Post-transition is comparable to near-death experience. In this stage, patients are free of fear. They seem to be "on the other side," though still in the here and now (see also the concept of "terminal lucidity"; Nahm et al. 2012).

The contents and quality of images during deathbed visions and near-death experiences are similar. Characteristic of exceptional states of consciousness in the liminal sphere of death are their intensity and lucidity: light, colors, beautiful landscapes, happiness, and an atmosphere of love. What is experienced in that state is felt to be real, not imagined, as one patient told me: "It was reality, not fantasy." The so-called panoramic view belongs rather to near-death experience. According to van Lommel, such deep experience includes illumination experiences or ones of unity during medication or during total relaxation in regression therapies involving LSD.

Our attempt to understand experiences and their various categories points us toward the books of the dead from various traditions, experiences during spiritual crises (see Grof and Grof 1989), and C. G. Jung's insights into the collective unconscious and its archetypal world of images. The symbols seen during such experiences are not accidental. They seem patterned and convey energy. Many dying seek to express themselves through word fragments, sounds, mimicry, and gestures. Medical and psychiatric experts often speak of "delirium." But this is normal in dying processes (in 65–80 percent of all cases according to the palliative care physician Daniel Büche). I prefer a metaphorical approach: judging by their symbolic language, such patients are in a world of images, even of vibrations (music) and energy. Some even try to articulate their closeness to the sacred.

> *The meadow:* A cancer-stricken Muslim woman facing difficult family circumstances drew strength and confidence from a near-death experience that she had many years ago (when she was pronounced clinically dead). At the time, she saw "a gate and behind it a beautiful green meadow—simply and purely green." Gripped by sadness ever since, the word meadow was enough to make her smile and to feel reminded of that former peacefulness. She lived with her cancer for years, never completely forgetting the meadow. At the same time, she couldn't constantly think of the meadow because otherwise she would have forgotten the demands of daily life. Once, she decided to consider the experience her secret. "It overcame me," she said about this decision. No one understands the value of this inner meadow. For her it was paradise, where she would return one day. Years later,

she was dying. She was restless, only for the unspeakable to recur. She now saw that "everything is green." She became peaceful and died.

The need to love: *A cancer patient who had suffered from depression for years, and who had almost died after an operation a year earlier, told me, "I've returned and would like to spend the time that remains loving." Trying to explain, he added, "No words exist for what I've seen . . . a radiant whiteness, a globe that was looking at me (!) . . . At some point appeared a throne, surrounded by incense and beautiful music." He paused and continued, "It's impossible to describe! But I clearly heard the words, 'You must love more.'" Even though the man's life had grown lonelier and more tense, it was also more beautiful and intense. The depression had gone. He felt compelled to give his wife and son presents or to smile at a child in the street.*

ONE light, the one: *On his readmission to hospital, a patient suffering from diffuse chronic pain in one of his legs and in his back and who had resigned himself to his condition once again approached a magnificent near-death experience he had made many years previously. Music-assisted active imagination, especially the sounds of a monochord, transported him into a spheric mood. He cried and* *told me, "It happened while I was diving in the Red Sea. I couldn't reach the surface. At first I became desperate, but soon a strange calmness overcame me. I knew that I was going to die. I saw light. Everything became increasingly suffused with this light. I don't believe in God, you see. But this light was . . . 'God.'" He paused, before continuing, "You know, there is only one light. EVERYTHING is light. Behind everything is light—THE light. And I saw this light. I seemed to be in this light. I realized that I had been rescued and became angry." He cried. Interestingly, he had no pain, neither during music-assisted relaxation and active imagination nor while telling me about his near-death experience. Hours later the pain returned. We repeated our sound-related relaxation during the next few days. The man saw this light again and again, sometimes similar to a presence. Music therapy became a source of hope. Two weeks later he was ready to think about life and death once more and to reconsider his resignation. He still didn't believe in God, but he did believe in the light—no, he KNEW of the light. The pain kept subsiding considerably.*

White in white, the circle squared: *After a serious operation and a subsequent pneumothorax in the intensive care unit, an elderly woman cried out for help, exclaiming that* *she "felt as if she were trapped in a near-death experience," which she later described as "being forlorn in a barren landscape of death." She was caught between powerlessness and beholding the indescribable. She uttered various words: "timelessly long," "doors and corridors," "deserted." When I approached her bed, she recognized my voice. When she heard the sounds of my harp, a smile flashed over her face. She fell silent, awestruck, and stammered, "God is . . . , God is . . . , there is." I asked her whether it was so sacred that it made her fall silent? "Yes," she smiled and then drifted away again. A few days later, this educated religious woman told me more about her experience: "There were huge vaults, then fewer and fewer contours, only some few lines. In the end, everything was white in white. There was no fear there. A luminous white circle, before it a rectangle. I stood in the rectangle—a tiny figure—and 'knew' immediately: this is the circle squared; I stood before the question about God and yet can't find my way into the circle." For several days the woman oscillated between two states: unfathomable, unseeable being, with the almost tangible presence of God, on the one hand; a fearful in-between state on the other. Gradually this led her through more and more seemingly worldly vaults toward life. "And there wasn't anything else?" I asked. "Yes, there was: eyes, nothing but eyes, human eyes, the eyes of particular animals." In these she saw archaic symbols of the divine—a profound sense of being looked at. A few weeks later, I asked her whether her fear of the in-between state and the landscape of death had fallen into perspective? "No!" Her voice thickened, she struggled to smile, and then she resumed, "I must probably go back to the core of my experience, to understand things better, to be able to live without this fear." It took another few weeks, during which she worked through what she had seen with the help of painting and imagination, until she regained a foothold in the real world.*

"Far away and yet so close": this is how these four patients described their experience of the divine. They felt as if they were in another state, as if they were touched by the sacred, as if they were connected. They felt this way even if their transcendental experience was surrounded by a fearful in-between state or by a spiritual experience of darkness. Both states can characterize the liminal sphere of the sacred (see Renz 2016). The mysterious light; the wonderfully peaceful atmosphere; the radiant, luminous whiteness at the heart of such experience—these are all merely images of the unviewable. This is also true of abstract forms, of roundness, of shapeless colors, of the timeless green (meadow), of wonderful music and incense. Other images—namely, awe-inspiring rooms, an indescribable throne, a tower—are slightly more tangible. Expressive eyes or a voice ("You must ...," "You may ...," "I am!") indicate the experience of being looked at, called, and somehow chosen to live. Sent. These symbols become an answer amid forlornness, lethargy, and a crisis of meaning or identity. Those who have such experiences are moved. They know intuitively that their experience is magnificent and unconditional. What they have seen and heard signifies the greatest possible experience of relationship and connectedness. Such experience often leads to deeper love and to a more conscious life.

Their visions sustained these four patients for months. They needed to remain connected with their experience and the sacred in order to go forward and to once again live freely. If these feelings of connectedness and peace failed to recur, these patients barely managed to live without pain, fear, or unbearable longing. But when they felt close to their experience, they longed or felt urged to give love and grant forgiveness. Spiritual experience—that is, mysticism—turns distress into something positive. But we can neither appropriate spirituality, nor greedily or narcissistically make it ours (Rutishauser 2011, 64). All four patients mentioned above experienced the sacred. Nevertheless, they still had to ask themselves: "What do I believe?" "Does God exist or doesn't he?" This question—faith versus atheism—remains a decision. Herein lies *the* agnostic question.

2.5. God as a Point of Reference: A Decision

Is anything in our life sacred or awe-inspiring? In the epilogue to *Life of the Beloved*, his account of modern spiritual life, the Dutch Catholic theologian Henri Nouwen (2002, 95) sums up the basic question of religion:

> Is there, among the things we do, the people we know, the events we read about in the newspapers or watch on TV, someone or something that transcends it all and has the inner quality of sacredness, of being holy, worthy of adoration and worship?

With the benefit of hindsight, Nouwen has since stated that he ought to have begun his book with this question. This would have allowed him to reach his agnostic friend,[4] at whose request he had written the book and whom he had shown the manuscript. But his friend was disappointed, remarking that *Life of the Beloved* was written out of a foreign tradition and only for initiates—that is, faithful Christians. Already Nouwen's underlying claim—that we are loved by God—had eluded his friend. The latter would have asked other questions: Who is God? Who am I? Why do I exist? How can I make my life meaningful? How can I come to believe? For Nouwen's friend, *Life of the Beloved* did not really empathize with the secular mind-set. Nouwen's (2002, 101) account, which was published despite his friend's reservations, culminates in the question: "Where and how can we rediscover the sacred and give it the central place in our lives?" The differences in religious outlook between Nouwen and his friend persisted. But so did their friendship.

The question about the sacred in our life is personal. It goes to the heart of who we are. There is no scientific answer, only a personal one. Our answer involves a *decision*: How do I intend to interpret the great experiences of my life? The moments of love, happiness, and well-being? Those of protectedness and reconciliation? However impressive, we can interpret all experiences either as coincidental or as encounters with God. There is neither right nor wrong. Instead, it all adds up to "I believe, I want to believe" or "I do not believe." We can neither prove nor refute God. He/It will always elude human thought. We are mistaken to search for evidence of God's existence, even if theologians and philosophers have done so for centuries. I can only *decide* for (or against) "God" as a horizon of interpretation. It is still a matter of whether I accept what I am given from the outset. If I do, it becomes my inner truth. Biblically speaking, I must accept that I am God's beloved son or daughter. But who or what helps me take this decision? Those of us who experienced this astonishment as children, and who found the divine behind providence and positive experiences, can later rely on this basic trust. We might once again be overcome by astonishment. Moreover, we will let ourselves be guided by our own feelings and longing.

Matters are more complicated if we are wholly secularized, if we are cut off from our inner, wide-eyed child. I realized this when I met a nurse at the hospital where I work.

She had been born and raised in the former German Democratic Republic. For her, the letters G-O-D were interchangeable with a car make. And yet she felt a gap within herself. She envied those dying patients who were religious for their capacity to trust. A few months later, she had an accident: her car overturned and crashed down the side of a hill. I shuddered at the thought and was startled that she did not. She placed the accident in the context of her past, as if it were irrelevant. Was this a sign of toughness or indifference? A colleague standing next to us grabbed the woman's shoulder and exclaimed, "You could have died. But you're alive, almost unscathed! That's a miracle!" Over lunch we discussed encountering God. The nurse now faced the question of how to interpret her experience. She had no idea but had the courage to wait. A few months later, she fell in love. This feeling was so strong that she began reading the Bible and attending faith classes because she wanted to find out who her partner's God was.

This story shows that *feeling* precedes decision-making. Being moved is conditional. Divine experience—that is, encountering God—is about attainability, astonishment, awe, indeed fear. It is, in sum, about our capacity to feel. Highs and lows, pain and bliss, desire and abundance are able to touch us. Yet most of us are overwhelmed by really experiencing feelings. We rationalize instead, denigrate whatever eludes rational understanding—or we quickly explain before we can feel astonished (by a great experience of love, joy, or protectedness). We deny great experiences the chance to make themselves felt as what they are—namely, great and life-changing.

Religious astonishment is also obstructed by bitterness. If we never really endure, grieve over, or overcome suffering (a stroke of fate, an unfulfilled lifetime wish, longing to have children, excessive ill fortune), our resentment will increase. More and more Western people take a negative decision about the question of God. Instead of arguing and fighting with the absent God, they lament and raise another, theodicean question: "How can I decide for God if there is so much suffering and injustice in the world?" I keep feeling appalled by how often theologians and laypersons argue along these lines. Their negativity conceals the need to make a *personal* decision. They carry neither a yes nor a no toward God within themselves. Instead, they have allowed thought systems and a sense of doom to take hold and to intervene between their experience and reason. What remains is an inability to "experience" (the sacred). The result is spiritual emptiness.

Suffering is reality. What, then, emboldens us to embrace God as a horizon of interpretation, despite disappointment and despair? Speaking on Swiss television (*Sternstunde Religion*, May 1, 2011), the German theologian Norbert Reck discussed his many conversations with Holocaust survivors. When asked about his engagement with these people's distress, Reck replied that he had abandoned the theology of quick assurances and had no answers to such terrible experiences. Did he still believe in God? "Yes, I do," he replied. He added that *during* such conversations he experienced the Absolute, for instance, when a survivor's gaze touched him (which he allowed to happen). He had felt how something absolute had demanded him to listen to these people. Radically, unconditionally. It wasn't Reck's ethical and charitable determination that enabled him to listen and to decide to believe in "God" but rather his *experience* and perception of an absoluteness. It was not about him listening and empathizing but rather *allowing* something greater to happen through him. Crucially, *he* perceived and approved of this greater force.

We can *want* (to make) such an existential decision. And yet it is a matter of grace. Like the greater yes that occurs over the course of life. The decision *overcomes* us. It enables approval and interpretation from within. Nevertheless, amid despair, amid coping with everyday life, we often find it impossible to approve. However, if I "wait," if I am open, if I expect (that "God/the divine may occur"), I have already been "taken into" the decision. If I allow this to happen, then something inside me resists agnostic inquiry. It resists turning away from God and instead relies on hope. According to Hans Kessler (2006), rabbis distinguish two kinds of divine immanence in this world: God lives in everything and lives where he is allowed to enter (Buber [1947] 1991, 277). A theology of redemption would miss its inherent goal without a corresponding anthropology of reception (see Wöller 1989, 17).

2.6. Spiritual Practice: An Anthropology of Reception

What are the consequences for everyday spiritual practice, meditation, contemplation, and spiritual care?

We cannot instigate or "prescribe" mysticism like medication. On our spiritual path, we depend on gifts and grace. We are challenged to grow open to what we are given. Caught up in immanence, we can strike out once more in search of our primordial desire and longings. We may need to let go of "our" spirituality, which we have come to possess, and to open ourselves up toward God as the eternal "Other." If we do, we will be transformed.

Great experiences occur either quietly or more obviously in every life. If I interpret such experiences openly yet "religiously" (i.e., through my reconnection with God), I will become transformed. As a result, my concepts of God will become increasingly mature.

CHAPTER 3
Jesus the Mystic
A HISTORICAL VIEW

3.1. The Life of Jesus

Who was the mystic of Nazareth? May we consider the historical Jesus a mystic? With regard to interreligious dialogue, as Christians we need to distinguish between the *knowledge* about Jesus that has been handed down to us and *faith*—what we believe and why. The historical details mentioned below are based on my own reading, further training, two journeys to Israel, and several conversations with Professor Max Küchler, chair of New Testament Studies at the University of Fribourg (Switzerland).

Origin, Name, Family Background

Jesus is said to have been either a Jew from Israel, a Judean, or a "Palestinian" Jew.[1] Galilee and Judea belonged to a province on the periphery of the Roman Empire. Jesus is Latin for Greek *Vihsou/j / Iesous*, Hebrew *Jeschua* or *Jehoschua* (God/Yahweh helps, saves, heals). The name is formed from

Hebrew *yascha* (to save or help, to lead out into the open). *Yascha* is one of eight Hebrew words forming the basis of the later term *redemption*, which has no direct cognate in Hebrew (Renz 2017, 166). As Christians, we are familiar with *yascha* as *hoschi'a-na* (Help!), *hosanna*. *Jeschua* was a common name at the time.

Jesus had no proper last name. He was probably called Jeshua Ben Yossef, in keeping with naming practices common at the time. These stipulated that a first name meant providing details of the child's father, family home, or place of origin. Jesus came from a modest background in Nazareth. Archaeological findings (including buildings and tableware) suggest that his native village had about four hundred inhabitants. Jesus appears to have led a simple life within a traditional Jewish community (family, school, and synagogue). While his mother's name is mentioned (Mary), his father's (Joseph) is not. The latter is referred to as Mary's future husband. Jesus was born as the first child of Mary and is said to have had several brothers and sisters. According to Flavius Josephus, the Jewish historiographer and opponent of Christ, Jacob, who was sentenced and stoned to death in 62 CE for transgressing the law, was "the brother of Jesus, who was called Christ."

Date of Birth

It is impossible to determine Jesus' exact date of birth. He is said to have been born circa 7–4 BCE; in any event, before the death of Herod the Great in 4 BCE.

Language, Education, Occupation

In daily life, Jesus spoke Aramaic. It is assumed that he knew biblical Hebrew as the language of the liturgy and spoke this language in his readings at the synagogue. His frequent question "Have you not read . . . ?" (Mark 2:25, 12:10, 26) suggests that, like all Jewish boys at the time, he could read and write, even if no writings have been traced to him. He was probably a *te,ktwn / tekton*, a "carpenter" or "mason." His knowledge of building is evident in various parables (Luke 6:47–48; Mark 12:10). But he may have been a shepherd, farmer, or fisherman (Luke 5:1–7; John 21:4–6). Visual representations of Jesus (beard, long hair), which should not be considered historically accurate, go back to the Veil of Veronica, which has legendary value.

Career, Way of Life

Jesus led an unremarkable life near Nazareth before moving to Capernaum.[2] His work spanned at most three years (according to the Gospel of John), though perhaps even only a year. John the Baptist appeared in 28 CE, in the fifteenth year of the reign of Emperor Tiberius (Luke 3:1). So when Jesus began his proclamation, he was thirty-two to thirty-five years old. This corresponds to Luke's account that "Jesus was about thirty years old" (Luke 3:23).

Spiritually, Jesus was close to John the Baptist, at least in the beginning. The latter preached repentance and the end of time. He also initiated a messianic awakening, which clashed with priestly and scholarly circles (Pharisees, Sadducees). A personal mystical experience, after baptism (as described by Mark, Matthew, and Luke), must be considered historical fact. This deep experience must have "made Jesus recognize the religious dimension of the 'beloved son' of the God of Israel and catapulted him into his own vocation" (Küchler, personal communication). His message, spiritual attitude, and way of life changed thereafter.

Historical evidence suggests that Jesus was a brilliant orator and narrator. That he preached and healed. That he was proexistent—that is, he devoted his life wholly to the cause and to God and gave himself to others. While his teachings first addressed his Jewish contemporaries, Jesus subsequently transcended the confines of religious law (pure versus impure; sacred versus profane) and developed "glad tidings" (the gospel) for everyone. He spent his life as a wandering preacher (unmarried and without a family, possessions, or a home). He performed his work very intensely because he believed that God's rule was so close that he (Jesus) would not even reach "all the towns of Israel."

To spread his message, Jesus gathered twelve men (analogously to the twelve tribes of Israel) from different backgrounds. The Jesus movement included not only many other followers (men and women) but also many sympathizers and financial backers. The disciples called him *Rabbi* or *Rabbuni* (my master), a term consonant with Greek *dida,skaloj / didaskalos* (teacher; didactics). Quite probably Jesus saw himself not as the founder of a new religion but as the renewer of Judaism.[3] The Jesus movement struck the outside world as unconventional—indeed, as provocative.

Jesus disregarded the acute threat posed by Jerusalem, the religious center at the time (and also the political one during festivals). He journeyed there on Passover (Hebrew, *Pesach*; Greek, *Pascha*) in the year 30 CE (possibly 33 CE). According to Luke (13:33), Jesus knew that a prophet would "not be killed away from Jerusalem."

Death, Crucifixion, and Background

It is undisputed that Jesus was flogged in public and crucified. He did not shirk this awful death. He died quite quickly, scorned and derided by those present. He died uttering a final prayer (Psalm 22: "My God, my God, why have you forsaken me?") and a loud exclamation (Mark

15:34–37). At the time, crucifixion was the most gruesome method of execution and ordinarily led to death by suffocation. Although Jesus was crucified by the Romans, for Jews crucifixion meant being cursed by God.[4] Formal grounds for this punishment included inciting an uprising against Rome or causing public unrest. The fact that Jesus was hailed by a large crowd as the future Messiah (Mark 11:1–10) barely left the Temple priests and the high council unconcerned—out of fear and because they were keen to maintain their power. This fear was justified: the day after arriving in Jerusalem, and without explanation, Jesus drove the merchants and buyers out of the Temple and began overturning the tables of the money-changers (Mark 11:15). The Temple cult was profitable, so that Jesus' actions would have alienated religious Jews. Needing to act, the high council thus looked for ways to arrest and eliminate Jesus (Mark 14:1–2).

Today, we can no longer establish whether Jesus "was handed over to Pilate after a lawful trial before the high council or merely after being interrogated by the high priests and by some members of the council" (Limbeck 2009, 373). He was accused of blasphemy, for his criticism of the Temple and for his alleged messianism. But politics (i.e., the fact that the "king of the Jews" was a source of potential unrest among the people) also proved decisive. As for the date of

Jesus' death, current research relies more on the Gospel of John than on the other gospels. It is unlikely that Jesus was crucified on the highest Jewish holiday. He would have died on the Friday *before*, during preparations for Passover (John 19:14).[5] He was thirty-four or thirty-five years old, an average age of death at the time.

Pontius Pilate, the Roman governor of Judea who ordered the crucifixion, had little tolerance for Jewish traditions. He is at times described as cruel, at others as arrogant and conceited. He is characterized as humane in the gospels, probably as much more humane than he actually was.

According to the gospels, Jesus was spared the shame of burial at the place of execution (Golgotha was a quarry). His corpse is said to have been buried by Joseph of Arimathea in a tomb hewn out of rock (Mark 15:42–46; see also Acts 13:27–29; Küchler 2014, 427). This was dangerous in the Roman system, as was sympathizing with a crucified person (in this respect, we might better understand the flight of the disciples when Jesus was captured or the women who watched the crucifixion from a distance or indeed the role of women in general). Joseph wrapped the corpse in pure linen; Nicodemus performed the customary anointment of the body before burial (John 19:39), before Joseph rolled the stone before the tomb. Why the tomb was supposedly empty a few days later defies historical explanation.

3.2. After Death, Mystery

Jesus' death was followed by *mystery*. Historical knowledge of Jesus ceases with his death. But does this exhaust the subject of Jesus? Not in the least! "Neither the life of Jesus, nor his teachings, nor his personal faith ... led to the birth of a new religion" (Jörg Lauster, cited in Schromm 2015, 135). Central to the Christian movement are the events *after* Jesus died: he appeared, resurrected, to many people, including disciples, Romans, and Jews. (According to the gospels and the Letters of Paul, these people included Mary Magdalene, several women, the apostles, the disciples of Emmaus, Thomas, the "many," and Paul.) Even his adversaries declared that rather than his power waning after his death, it increased.[6] The witnesses reported Christ's presence. In their experience, Jesus was awakened—or rather, resurrected—by God. This was the perspective from which Paul (50–ca. 53 CE) and shortly afterward the evangelists wrote about Jesus. His historical influence was immeasurable. Not even the persecution of the Christians, which began soon after his death, changed this. On the contrary. Thus the early Christians were profoundly spiritual and mystical.

3.3. The Words of Jesus

Which words did Jesus speak? What did he or did he not say? We can trace some of his words (*ipsissima vox*)—or even their intention—to Jesus himself, even if the relevant theological debate is not uncontroversial.[7] Below, I repeat some of Jesus' words—to let his voice resonate, and because they encapsulate some key aspects of his message. My focus is mystical. Can we can understand Jesus' words in terms of his mystical horizon of experience, his deep relationship with God?

Father

The most important word is *Father*, Jesus' word for God. This had already appeared in the Old Testament, and in early and classical Jewish literature, in association with the creator, the redeemer, the merciful one, and the Father of Israel.[8] Jesus speaks about the Father several times. And intensely. He uses the Aramaic word *abba* three times (Mark 14:36; Romans 8:15; Galatians 4:6). His relationship with the Father is central to Jesus' proclamation and spirituality (chapter 4).

The Kingdom of God/Heaven

Jesus' second concern is the (dawning) kingdom of God (Mark, Luke), the kingdom of heaven (Matthew), or the rule of God: "The time is fulfilled (Greek: *o` kairo,j / o kairos*, "the fullness of time"), the kingdom of God has come (near)" (Mark 1:15). Thus only the good God ("our Father") should ultimately determine human life.

Reversal and Conversion (Metanoia)

Immediately after the good tidings about the kingdom, Jesus issues a summons to "return" (Mark 1:15). The three aspects of the proclamation (Father, kingdom of God/heaven, reversal) would be inconceivable if they were not rooted in Jesus' mystical background. We need to understand Jesus addressing God as "Father" in both fatherly and motherly terms. The word corresponds to Jesus' experience as a "beloved Son." It also stands for utmost love. After Jesus was baptized, a heavenly voice could be heard (literally "emerged"; Greek: *evge,neto / egeneto*): "You are my Son, the Beloved; with you I am well pleased."[9]

Most scholars consider Jesus' baptism a well-established fact (e.g., Gnilka 2010, 51–52). Nevertheless, we need to interpret the heavenly voice as a—mystical!—initiation. It tells the story of Jesus' calling. It also recalls other encounters with God, other callings, in the Old Testament (Moses, Samuel, Isaiah, Jeremiah, Jonas, etc.). The word *Father* is actually less "originally Jesuanic" than the assertion about the beloved Son (Schelbert 2011). Here, the much-described dove appears as a symbol of love. The relationship between

Father and Son could not be more intense at this point. On the one hand, the assertion of love is directed at Jesus and constitutes his extraordinary capacity for devotion. On the other, nowadays people also have exactly the same experience, most of all in extreme situations: they dream of being God's beloved son or daughter. This points to a corresponding structure in the depth of the human soul: we humans are also *relational* creatures.

I suppose that Jesus had other mystical experiences with God as the loving Father (e.g., his occasional retreats into prayer), even if historical understanding eludes us today (another example is the transfiguration of Jesus). Jesus' mystical experiences were—and still are—constitutive. I believe this is true because his mysticism shifted his proclamation: away from the baptist's concept of God, away from repentance, and an eschatological tribunal, and also away from the scribal and Pharisean cult of purity, and toward the "Father." Essentially, the Pharisees and the scribes pursued a perfectly honorable objective by asking, "How can one lead a good Jewish life in our present time—that is, be sacred before God whilst doing justice to the Torah?" In the New Testament, the Pharisees and the scribes are ciphers of the traditional Jewish interpretation of the law, which also determined the concept of God. Today, we would speak of jurists, theologians, ethicists, politicians, and public administrators. Jesus rejected these institutions and chose a direct relationship with God. He realized that a juridical interpretation of the sacred texts had become central in religion and that, by distinguishing purity from impurity, it humiliated rather than liberated the human being into a freedom toward and from God. In contrast, Jesus chose neither fear nor the safeguarding of power, but emphasized the personal relationship with the Father and his kingdom of God/heaven. Jesus' mystical experiences tell us that God is the loving Father. That God is benign and demanding, merciful and consequential (another term for God as judge, who invites rather than excludes). If this is true, then *everything* changes: the concept of God, of humankind, of the world.

His mysticism and his relationship with the Father were crucial for Jesus. They are also his most important message, concern, and program *for us*. Mysticism and its subsequent relation to God must affect our behavior and politics. It is also crucial to the interpretation of the kingdom of God and to conversion/reversal (chapters 1, 4, 6, and 8). Jesus believed in the power of mysticism. He also believed in its explosive force, also within us.

Jesus' Understanding of the Torah

Jesus' approach to the Torah and to Jewish scripture and legislation was prophetic and mystical. He rejected the primarily juridical interpretation of the scriptures by the eldest, the scribes, and the Pharisees. But he did not reject the Torah. On the contrary. He immersed himself in it (Matthew 5:17–20). Accordingly, Jesus lived the Torah—that is, engaged in a particular "experiment": "What is he who embodies the Torah permitted? What corresponds to him? What does not?" (Siebenrock, personal communication). Jesus did not consider abiding by the scripture and the commandments juridically or morally—that is, in terms of purity or observing the Sabbath. We may trace the tone and concerns of the Sermon on the Mount—"You have heard.... But I say to you . . ."—(Matthew 5:21–48) to Jesus himself. He had a very powerful and different sense of justice, one that did not follow the law alone but constituted a heavenly and also an inner justice. For Jesus, fulfillment (and justification)— and this is my basic assumption in this book—occurs mystically. As a spiritual process. Through connectedness with the Father. Partly on earth, though beyond all ego-bound categories and reckonings. Thus fulfillment makes us free and blessed.

Beatitudes

The Beatitudes, particularly the first three in the version recorded in Luke (see Luz 2007, 185), articulate a genuine Jesuanic concern:

Beatitudes—Matthew 5:3–6	**Beatitudes—Luke 6:20b–21**
Blessed the poor in spirit, for theirs is the kingdom of heaven.	Blessed, you who are poor, for yours is the kingdom of God.
Blessed those who mourn, for they will be comforted.	
Blessed the meek, for they will inherit the earth.	
Blessed those who hunger and thirst for righteousness, for they will be filled.	Blessed, you who are hungry now, for you will be filled.
	Blessed, you who weep now, for you will laugh.[10]

It was unusual to utter such words at the time. Their reversal of values is typically Jesuanic. We need a psychological interpretation to understand the Beatitudes. For they are spoken by someone who experienced, almost better than anyone else, *fundamental* connectedness with the divine, with God. We cannot purchase nor can we work for that connectedness. It already exists in our primordial existence. This is the deeper meaning of poverty as proclaimed by Jesus (see chapter 4.3. for a model of psychic layers; see also chapter 4.6). Bliss and connectedness lie within our reach whenever we long (i.e., the hungry). It also lives in our capacity to feel and let go (i.e., the weeping, the mourning). We are blessed whenever we are not determined by otherwise powerful formative influences: possessiveness, power-craving, envy, and a hardening of the soul. Thus it is fitting that Jesus knew another kind of nourishment (e.g., the feeding of the four thousand; chapter 4). Even the gospel "nurtures": "In the same way, the Lord commanded that those who proclaim the gospel should get their living by the gospel" (1 Corinthians 9:14; Greek: *zh/n / zen*, "living, to be alive, to come back to life"; in Luther's translation, "to be nurtured by the gospel").

Most beatitudes are future-oriented: you *will* be blessed, you *will* be filled, you *will* laugh. The heavenly kingdom is not static, but dynamic. Nor is it past. It cannot be brought back solely by returning to a primordial time. It is final. Jesus' mystical connectedness enabled him to actually "realize" (i.e., see) the kingdom of God/heaven. We should not, however, understand this in magical or purely ethical terms. Jesus was neither a magician, politician, or zealot. Instead, the Beatitudes announce a mode of existence beyond the categories of time and space. Jesus knew of this kingdom. He knew that what has existed "there," since time immemorial, from God and in God's presence, is not ephemeral. Nor is it confined or locatable (i.e., occupying a specific locale).

Jesus "lives" in this kingdom, in this (primordial) state of being.

Is blissfulness, and the inner freedom it expresses, exclusively Jesuanic? Not necessarily, I suggest. Other spiritual traditions (e.g., the Essenes, the Desert Fathers, monastic traditions, Eastern traditions, Sufism) also emphasize the liberating aspect—for instance, of an ascetic life, of letting go, of solitude. Interestingly, eighth-century Sufi ascetics saw Jesus as a model of renunciation. Jesus, though, did not speak of renouncing the world. He spoke of turning toward it.

Fasting

Unlike John the Baptist, Jesus preached neither austerity nor deprivation. On the contrary. His enemies branded him "a glutton and a drunkard, a friend of tax collectors and sinners" (Matthew 11:19). Jesus *lived* a radical life. He abstained, in certain respects and at certain times (e.g., celibacy, fasting for forty days in the desert; Matthew 4:1; Luke 4:1). Still, his concern was not ascetic. No surviving accounts indicate that he fasted. As a religious Jew, he obviously adhered to the law of fasting (Leviticus 16:29). Even if the evangelists did not consider this worth mentioning. His persistent concern (in fasting, prayer, suppers and feasts) was to be *connected* with the Father, to be joyful and free (heavenly kingdom).

And whenever you fast, do not look dismal, like the hypocrites, for they disfigure their faces so as to show others that they are fasting. Truly I tell you, they have received their reward. But when you fast, put oil on your head and wash your face, so that your fasting may be seen not by others but by your Father who is in secret; and your Father who sees in secret will reward you." (Matthew 6:16–18)

Thus fasting is not a commandment. Nor does it pertain to the Sabbath (Matthew 12:1; Luke 6:1–5). Its power lies in its inherent nature (of being rewarded, also in secret). It should occur at the right time and in fitting circumstances: "Can the children of the bridechamber [not the wedding guests in general] fast, while the bridegroom is with them?" (Mark 2:19).

Prayer

Prayer has a similar effect (reward). Jesus' instructions for prayer are also Jesuanic. They point to a deep inner event, in contrast to the purely outer observance of commandments:

And whenever you pray, do not be like the hypocrites; for they love to stand and pray in the synagogues and at the street corners [Greek: *plateiw/n / plateion*, "places"], so that they may be seen by others. Truly I tell you, they have received their reward. But whenever you pray, go into your room and shut the door and pray to your Father who is in secret; and your Father who sees in secret will reward you. (Matthew 6:5–6)

In Greek, the *tamei/o,n / tameion* was a storeroom or pantry. No one suspected that those entering this quiet chamber did so to pray. According to common belief, they went there to eat (or to snack on the sly). Küchler (personal communication) has suggested that a completely hidden activity—praying—took place there. I would add that this is not the selfless action of a strict superego. This would contradict the association of prayer with reward. Prayer is worthwhile. It is allowed to be nurturing. And it takes place where we may feed ourselves good things.

The Lord's Prayer ("Our Father") also comes from Jesus (Luz 2007, 311–13). Three versions are known to exist (Luke 11:2–4, Matthew 6:9–13; and Didache 8.2–3).[11] They raise two controversial questions: First, which version is more original? Second, was the Lord's Prayer, an integral part of the liturgy at the time, redacted? (Luz 2007, 309–10).

Matthew 6:9–13	Luke 11:2–4
Our Father, he in the heavens,[12]	Father,
hallowed be thy name!	hallowed be thy name.
Thy kingdom cometh!	Thy kingdom cometh!
Thy will be done,	
as in heaven, so also on earth!	
Our daily bread [Greek: *to.n evpiou,sion / ton epiousion*], give us this day![13]	Our daily bread [Greek: *to.n evpiou,sion / ton epiousion*], give us day after day!
[12] And forgive us our debts,	And forgive us our sins,
as we forgive our debtors!	for we forgive everyone indebted to us. And do not bring us into temptation!
[13] And do not bring us into temptation, but rescue us from evil![14]	

Exegesis distinguishes *thou* petitions from *we* petitions. There are no *I* petitions. The petition *behind* the petition is: may God alone determine what happens on earth. Aramaic is assumed to be the original language of the "Our Father," whose first part rests on the *Kadosh*, a Jewish prayer. As the prayer of the new covenant, the "Our Father" was long considered un-Jewish. Only later was it found to be *primordially* Jewish. Thus Jesus' prayers were based on Jewish prayers (e.g., the prayer on the cross; see Mark 15:34 and Psalm 22). We need to take seriously both Jesus' alignment with Judaism and his departure from it: although he lived with the God of the Old Testament, Jesus brought to bear his altered concept of God and humankind.

Jesus is said to have prayed intensely—on his retreats (to the wilderness) and in his work (among the people). His authentic speech, love, and rebellion—and his wholesale rejection of hypocrisy—suggest that he could only pray authentically. This means entrusting ourselves to God, as who we are and as how we feel, in worship and in lamentation. And in the question that we are (see Karl Rahner's theology of prayer; Rahner 1997, 12–13; 2005, 32). Jesus was true to himself; he prayed radically and honestly. Two relevant instances include "Do not bring us into temptation" (does God bring us into temptation?) and "Your will be done." Later, in Gethsemane (Matthew 26:42), he struggles with temptation. Through prayer, he finds a way out: "not as I want it, but as you want it." At the time, "Your will be done" meant that one prayed for the strength to actively associate oneself with God's will (Luz 2007, 316–17). Prayer, then, resembles two other processes: conversion/reversal and suffering/healing.

Discipleship

Jesus' call to discipleship is also typically Jesuanic. His call meant more than if a rabbi called for the people to observe God's instructions. Among others, Jesus demanded that his followers sever ties with their family, occupation, and home. Psychologically, it was about following him. Discipleship began and still begins with us taking our abode (entirely) in God. We must be rooted in God. Jesus' radicalness suggests that he was convinced that these roots and this spiritual foundation were salubrious and necessary. He must have been absolutely sure that his message and concept of God were true.

Jesus and the Question of Evil

Jesus' worldview extended beyond goodness to the notion of demons prevalent in early Judaism. At the time, evil spirits were caused by fallen angels: "Wherever Jesus drove out evil spirits, he created an open space for the rule of *God*" (Küchler, personal communication; see also Luke 10:18). Jesus was neither exorcist nor shaman. His mission was to serve the Father. Connected with the Father, Jesus even saw through evil—a task that overwhelms us.

"I watched Satan fall from heaven like a flash of lightning" (Luke 10:18). These words rest on a vision. Jesus does not see Satan as the accuser who comes before God (unlike in the Book of Job). Jesus' concern is not the impending trial or Last Judgment, but the coming kingdom. The above-cited words describe the mystery surrounding Jesus: he defeats Satan and sees him fall. His total connectedness with the Father makes Jesus part of the Father's "victory over evil"—whatever such a victory means (see chapters 5, 7, and 9). I suggest that this is how we ought to understand his words: "But if it is by the finger of God that I cast out the demons, then the kingdom of God has come to you" (Luke 11:20).

Honorific Titles

Opinions differ about how Jesus referred to himself. He is unlikely he have called himself the "Son of God." Although familiar across Greek, Hellenistic, and Roman regions, this designation was only partly known in Jewish areas.[15] It is also quite inconceivable that Jesus spoke reverently *of himself*—that is, that he used honorific titles such as Kyrios (Lord) or Messiah (Christos).[16] He is said to have used a broader term: *Son of Man*. This *may*, yet *need not*, refer to the Son of Man promised in the Old Testament (Book of Daniel). Other terms (*doctor* and *bridegroom*) are also likely to go back to him. Whatever the terminology, Jesus appeared and acted so authoritatively that he was assigned such honorific titles. His sovereign behavior and speech coincided with his assertion: "I am a king" (John 18:37). This captures his *behavior* and reflects that Jesus intuitively grasped his own significance. Jesuanic utterances sound something like this: "Who is close to me, is close to the fire. And who is far from me, is far from the kingdom."[17]

Devotion and Supper

Jesus' sovereignty is most evident in his unconditional yet unneurotic devotion. While he intuitively grasped his own significance, this knowledge always came with utmost devotion: he sensed that his life was a path of suffering, one of giving himself to others. We find an important utterance to this effect in 1 Corinthians (11:23–25): "The Lord Jesus on the night when he was betrayed took a loaf of bread, and when he had given thanks, he broke it and said, 'This is my body that is for you. Do this in remembrance of me.' In the same way he took the cup also, after supper, saying, 'This cup is the new covenant in my blood. Do this, as often as you drink it, in remembrance of me.'" Celebrating supper mattered deeply to Jesus as it represents sympathy, connectedness, and devotion (chapter 8).

3.4. The Work of Jesus

Jesus was not only a man of words. He was in manifold ways also a man of action and presence.

Healing Energy

Jesus acted and healed. How exactly? What does a miracle or a sign (Gospel of John: *shmei/on / semeion*) mean in the Jesuanic context? According to Söding (2011, 393), the signs of wonder reveal Jesus' magnificence (John 2:11; 6:16–21) or God's (John 11:4, 40; John 20:30). Even if we call an event a sign or a miracle, it will still elude us today, however enlightened or inquiring we are. So how might we approach Jesus' miracle-working?

We can interpret many of Jesus' healings and motives psychologically, similarly and yet differently to the German Eugen Drewermann (chapter 5). Nevertheless, a purely psychological interpretation of Jesus' work would seem to fall short. What Jesus did partly eludes our thinking, as this has been shaped by the natural sciences. Thus we need "another" dimension of understanding and faith. This was not so foreign to people at the time (in ancient literature, miracles were also attributed to other persons).[18] Mark the Evangelist, however, changed the genre of the classical miracle narrative by not applauding Jesus the miracle worker (Theissen 1983, 212–21). This view concurs with my own assumption that although Jesus acted in a most sovereign and healing manner, he never gave the impression that his work was about him. He never acted out of self-interest. When I was preparing to write this book, I read entire gospels several times in one sitting. I was moved on every occasion. The person of Jesus, his authority, and his sheer incredible power made a lasting impact on me. I asked myself: Why have we forgotten to believe these stories? Is it simply because they sound so unbelievable at times? It is equally impossible to *refute* or to prove Jesus' miracle-working. Like his contemporaries, we are left with unsolved questions: What exactly did Jesus do? Who was he?

Committed to the Poor, the Destitute, and Women

Jesus and his work had great impact. Especially on the poor, the sick, the ostracized, and those in need. This is a social statement. But not only: Jesus affected those who had nothing to lose and those who were open to help. These were (and are) rarely the powerful. His behavior toward women was almost revolutionary. Not even the fact that none of the twelve disciples was a woman detracts anything from Jesus' openness toward women but corresponded to expectations at the time (the model of the twelve patriarchs). According to the evangelists, women played a central role among Jesus' followers. This is remarkable, as they were not admitted as witnesses to court and were only allowed into the outer forecourt of the Temple (the women's courtyard). Jesus' treatment of women is remarkable because of its autonomy.

What does our fragmentary knowledge of Jesus add up to? I believe that his relationship with God is decisive. The wandering preacher, who occasionally did not know where he would bed down, rested in something greater: the Father (John 1:18).

3.5. Spiritual Practice: The Work of Christ Extends Beyond Time and Space

What are the consequences for everyday spiritual practice, meditation, contemplation, and spiritual care? What does spirituality mean in terms of Jesus if we consider the historical dimension?

What may we Christians hope for? What remains in the face of such relativity and uncertainty about religion? In the fact of the fragmentary records from those times? I have two answers. First, we know a fair amount about Jesus, his words, and his exceptional behavior. These are good reasons to believe in him. Second, like people at the time, we need to take a decision about faith after we have been touched by Jesus (see chapter 2.5). First and foremost, religion is tradition, which begins with recorded *experience*. Today, as in the past, we can only access religion through religious *experience*. Thus we are never "right" about religion in terms of extant—historical—knowledge. Instead, our encounters with God and our spiritual experiences tell us something about the mystery. Yet we must accept that all experience falls far short of the essential truth. Nor should we be discouraged by the fact that the writers of the gospels and epistles wrote from their own perspective. We do not need less divine experience or fewer "encounters with God." We need to be touched deeper by this dimension of God. Thus we need churches and a theology that permit "the transcendental experience of God/the divine" (an experiential theology/Christology; see Renz 2016).

My *guiding* spiritual idea is that the historical Jesus was a mystic. Thus he was not bound to his historical context. He transcended and acted beyond his times and hence bridges the historical gap to us. Consequently, as Christians we do not need spirituality methods or programs (e.g., fasting, stillness, yoga, spiritual instructors), even if they may be helpful at times. Rather, Jesus himself is the heart and center. *He* can become the content of meditation. Of prayer. Of our spiritual quest.

Whether we believe or have doubts, whether we are healthy or sick, we can make contact with Jesus. We can experience him as present and at work within us. This is the mystery of Christ.

CHAPTER 4

Jesus' Concept of God
AN ANSWER TO FEAR

4.1. The Gospel of John: The Mysticism of Abiding

What did Jesus say about God? How did he see God? What was his concept of God? May we ask these questions?

We have no direct access to Jesus' concept of God. He did not enter history as a philosopher but as a wandering preacher, healer, and doctor. Yet his words and actions bear (indirect) witness to his concept of God. For Jesus, this highest authority did not ask questions about a person's name or station. Nor did he focus on the meticulous observance of the commandments. And God was more than a judge: he was a wise, merciful, and loving Father. The word *Father* is not opposed to the feminine nor to utmost dignity. For Jesus, God was the Alpha and the Omega. He lost none of his respectability by turning fully toward the human being—that is, by exposing himself to the world. God epitomized the highest power and sanctity and was at the same time a Father. We need to bear this important point in mind with regard to interreligious dialogue. Jesus could love *and* at the same time revere the Father. But why? Perhaps by virtue of his healthy spiritual nature: Jesus seemed to have no problem with God's omnipotence. Nor with his own power or with power per se. He did not harbor any sense of rivalry. He was not conceited. Nor did he have an no issue with his self-esteem.

For Jesus, the Father was his point of reference, also personally. For his thinking and his judgment. The Father was where Jesus brought his fear, grief, and wrath.[1] *This* relationship enabled Jesus to forgive others and to overcome his suffering ("Father, forgive them, for they do not know what they are doing," Luke 23:34). As I mentioned at the beginning of this book, Jesus' life rested on a particular secret: his absolute closeness to God ("The Father and I are one," John 10:30).

We do well not to explain the unity of Jesus and the Father only in dogmatic terms (as regards the Holy Family: Mary living without sin, Joseph as a mentor, the virgin birth of Jesus, the immaculate conception). Instead, this Father-Son connection was a *mystical* reality. Jesus was completely *relational*. He lived an unbroken relationship with God, with his fellows, and with himself. No ego, nor any ego-bound perception, stood crosswise to this relatedness.

The mystery between Jesus and God is described in the Gospel of John (90–110 CE). Its mystical character distinguishes it from the other gospels. Although it contains complex theological material, its language and style are straightforward. It is composed like a fugue and only includes some very few insertions. Like the First Epistle of John, the Gospel of John also grew out of a specific community's spirituality.[2] Evidence suggests that it was written by several authors (Childs 1993, 282). The evangelist and final redactor never saw Jesus himself and hence could not have been the apostle John but perhaps one of his students.[3] The Gospel of John is essentially spiritual: it is written from the perspective of transfiguration, by persons who were moved by their inner experience of Jesus.

The Gospel of John raises various key questions: Where does Jesus live? What is he rooted in? Thus the first disciples asked him, "Rabbi (i.e., Teacher), where are you staying?" (John 1:38). Their question implies which village (Capernaum). And yet, importantly, it also means which *inner* abode? What were his roots? What was his secret?[4] Jesus' disciples were so attracted to Jesus that they followed him. Just like that. In this light, his answer, "Come and see" (John 1:39), makes sense. We cannot explain the secret of inner settlement. We must *experience* it, physically and spiritually. We must follow Jesus to understand his relationship with God, his dwelling place: "They came and saw where he dwelt (Greek: *me,nei / menei*, "forever present"), and abode (Greek:

e;meinan / emeinan) with him that day: for it was about the tenth hour" (John 1:39).[5]

Living/abiding (Greek: *me,nw / meno*): This term is central in the Gospel of John and often occurs in connection with rootedness. For instance, in John 15:1–5, Jesus is the vine. This vine has very strong roots. In this image, Jesus offers himself to us as a mediator, so that we, too, can be connected with what nurtures: "Abide in me as I abide in you" (John 15:4). In the terms of this book, this means, "stay connected." Thus, according to John, Jesus captures in words a "mysticism of abiding." He articulates the need for roots:

> I am the true vine, and my Father is the vine-grower. He removes every branch in me that bears no fruit. Every branch that bears fruit he prunes to make it bear more fruit. You have already been cleansed by the word (*lo,gon*, meaning, connection, Logos) that I have spoken to you. Abide (*mei,nate / meinate*) in me as I abide in you. Just as the branch cannot bear fruit by itself unless it abides in the vine, neither can you unless you abide in me. I am the vine, you are the branches. Those who abide in me and I in them bear much fruit, because apart from me you can do nothing...." (John 15:1–5)

Images and symbols reach deeper than words. They were understood intuitively at the time, when people thought and lived more intensely in images. If we only observe religion from the outside, as many Christians do today, we will struggle with the Bible's symbolic language. And yet we can still understand these images today. Intuitively, beyond analytical reasoning, in those deeper layers of our psyche where something inside us yearns for fulfillment. Thus the biblical image of the vineyard occasionally appears in dreams today.

One night, a dying woman, plagued by unquenchable thirst, had a dream. "Vines, colors," she stammered. I asked if she had dreamed about a vineyard. She nodded. She no longer felt thirsty afterward.

A younger woman, a theologian who lived in a city, dreamed about an old convent that was set in a Tuscan vineyard. In the dream, she had to take up residence there, to restore the derelict building, and to become abbess and govern the convent. Now that she was more consciously rooted in her faith, the vineyard became a place where she could become fruitful in a new way.

The primal ground—that is, the ground of being, which Jesus calls the Father—always exists, even if many of us discover it only after long inner journeys. Kessler (2010, 53) speaks of God as the creative primal ground. The Gospel of John (10:30–38) describes being connected, being one with the Father, as the basis of fertility ("apart from me you can do nothing," 15:5b), as reciprocal flowing, as mysticism ("Abide in me as I abide in you," 15:4).

4.2. A Category Shift: Human Fear— a Model of Conscious Development

For Jesus, "God was the loving Father." This conviction is not directed against God as mother but against human *fear*. But why?

First of all, Jesus was responding to his times and their historical precepts. But he was also reacting to a particular human constitution and imprinting, to individual developments and collective patterns of behavior. We need to see what the Bible describes as the *alienation from God* in the myth of Adam and Eve as an inner reality (see chapter 6 for a discussion of sin).

Let me provide some psychological background to help us better understand Jesus. Early human development is comparable to a *category shift*—from the mode of being to that of having (Fromm [1976] 2014), from unconscious primordial connectedness to our everyday, ego-centered disconnectedness. This shift springs from an even older, deeply unconscious fear. As I explain below, my sense of the development of human consciousness grew over a period of ten years, through studying the depth psychology of C. G. Jung and his student Erich Neumann, through practicing music therapy with patients, yet above all through conversations with Heinz Stefan Herzka[6] and through personal spiritual experiences. In my therapeutic practice, I first worked with patients suffering from early formative experiences. Contrary to every theory about early imprinting, they could unexpectedly make salubrious experiences through music-assisted relaxation: for brief moments, they experienced themselves as intact, as whole. Whether they were religious or not, many felt "touched" by a higher, divine entity. Little did I know at the time that this idea of humankind would one day provide me with a key to understanding what happens in dying. And to reinterpret Jesus' Sonship and message mystically.

My approach involves an early and final transitional process, a transformation of perception, a category shift from being part of a whole to being ego-bound.

Let me explain my model of transition:

As far as the spiritual and mental origins of human life are concerned, the concept of humankind is based neither on a *tabula rasa*, nor on sheer coincidence or ultimate nothingness. Instead, it rests on being in God/in the divine as the Whole. The Whole is both the outermost and the innermost reality: God as ultimate substance, as Being. This is what we as human beings originally participated in. We can imagine this Whole in religious terms but also just as a mental state of Oneness. Human beings emerge from the Whole, from this state of Oneness. In its greatest closeness to this One, humankind began to become itself. This means the "development of the subject," which subsequently no longer participates in the Whole.

In death, by losing not only our ego but also our ego-based perception and our subjecthood (the fundamental laws that makes us feel as a subject), we return to the Whole. Some dying people experience this crossing of an inner threshold as moving backward, others as going forward (in religious terms, God comes toward them).

Thus we need to understand the early stages of ego-development as a *crystallization* process. The individual crystallizes out of his or her context and emerges from the original Whole. Not once but repeatedly. And ever more clearly. This involves a transformation of perception: the rudiments of the future ego and of ego-consciousness begin to perceive *more and more selectively*—that is, become confined to their own vantage point. Their sensibility is ego-related—that is, oriented toward the ego as the center of perception and steering. Now, the focus is on the ego, on the individual and the particular, and no longer on the Whole. What we take for granted—that sensibility and perception are subjective, differentiating, and focused on their own survival—is essentially both an achievement and a tragedy of early human development: we feel, act, and think as an ego. In this way, we become more and more conscious of our individuality. But at the same time, we lose our connectedness to the Whole. Thus power is no longer epitomized by God/the Whole. No, it becomes increasingly ego-driven. The pursuit of power in egomaniacal terms progressively comes to determine the course of history (Weber 1978).

This category shift—from being part of a whole to becoming an ego—is *ancient*. It is plainly evident throughout human history and evolution: in plants stretching up toward light; in animals obeying their own needs and instincts; in prehistoric humans "recognizing" themselves as themselves, and thus reacting out of self-interest and self-preservation; and in humans considering and judging matters in their own way (i.e., based on their ego-related perception). Ontogenetically, this shift is apparent in the fetus hearing independently of the mother, as well as in the infant eating and oscillating between waking states and dozing.

Ego-consciousness awakens repeatedly in early development. Examples include prehistoric humans engaging in battle. Infants protesting, making the world their own, and gradually understanding words such as "mother" or "car." And realizing that fairy tales are just fairy tales. We need to see an *entire* period of evolution (phylogenetically) and of childhood (ontogenetically) as a *transition* from participation to subjectivity, from dozing to wakefulness. This transition involves a shift to selective, subjective sensibility.

During transition, the moments in which we experience initial wakefulness are crucial. For on the threshold to recognition and knowledge the ego is fragile and vulnerable. Here begins early imprinting. We may experience these moments as salubrious, extreme, or fraught with tension. Our experience becomes fateful for future individual or cultural development. Thus fear is aroused either strongly, abruptly, overwhelmingly, or moderately. Accordingly, self-esteem and power are more or less of problematic.

Fear is central to the emergence of culture and personality. It determines human development. We can detect primordial fear (or the preliminary stages of fear) already on a microbiological scale: in human history, in the fearful reactions of animals and prehistoric humans; in the individual; in the mother's womb—for example, in response to vibrations (intrauterine hearing).[7] We enter the world of categories in our transition from participation in wholeness to becoming (and being) an ego. Here we become subjects and gain consciousness. Fear, in essence, is an expression of subjecthood: in an ontological view, we are afraid because we are interested in and also afraid of *ourselves*. Anxiety depends on our ego-bound perception and corresponding state of being. We know from people who have had near-death or other deep spiritual experiences that *some states of mind exist beyond fear*. The dying also experience this time and again. Our original participation in God/the Whole was "fearless." Our final states will be too. Fear is absent from deep spiritual connectedness.

What does this original fear consist of? In terms of developmental psychology, fear occurs as the nascent ego emerges. The rudimentary ego perceives from its own perspective, and thus the world becomes its environment. This happens instantly, as our "gaze" changes, individually *and* at the beginning of the culture. On the threshold to recognition, prehistoric humans *suddenly* experienced themselves: first, as outside the Whole; second, in opposition to the Whole.[8] They felt threatened and alone.

There are two aspects of primordial fear (see Renz 2015 and 2018):

1. Forlornness: this sense of lost unity arises from feeling outside and suddenly separated from the Whole.

2. Being delivered and "threatened" due to sudden exposure to the outside world. This fear also becomes a fear of the numinous because we feel helplessly small when facing the numinous Whole.

The first aspect concerns the shift from the Whole to the ego. As perception begins to focus increasingly on the ego, the nascent ego cannot feel oneness with the Whole anymore. It "falls out" of the Whole (see the terms *Fall of Man*, *Fall from Paradise*). It no longer participates in the Whole or its power. As a result, it also loses its basis for natural self-esteem. The nascent ego—even before developing—is thrown back upon itself, leaving a gap (chapter 2) and creating a breeding ground for diffuse sadness and greed.

The second aspect concerns the early forms of "existential" fear. The nascent ego cannot endure the sight of the tremendous Whole because it feels its own existence. Facing the numinous, it feels its own miniscule existence (and its miniscule intrinsic value), just as it fears extinction, as if it were exposed to an anonymous, numinous Other. It feels delivered and "threatened." The nascent ego experiences the Whole as devouring and overwhelming and is unable to differentiate its surroundings (the sum of all vibrations, influences, etc.) into individual factors (mother, teddy bear, storm). The fetus experiences the surrounding vibrations as the entirety of sounds (i.e., noise is an *acoustic* experience). The infant perceives the tense family atmosphere as threatening. Prehistoric humans were threatened by the constant struggle for survival (climate conditions, the fight against animals and hunger).

This experience of an overpowering Whole finds expression in various mythological themes: in the dragon, in the devouring primordial waters, and in ancient images of the fearsome or angry God. These symbols and images are all distorted by projection (e.g., the image of God in the Fall; see chapter 6).

These experiences at the beginning of human development imprint themselves very deeply and become part of the human unconscious.

4.3. Topography of the Unconscious, Part I: Psychic Layers and Primordial Imprinting

Depth psychology (e.g., Sigmund Freud, C. G. Jung, Stanislav Grof) has defined the topography of the human unconscious in different ways. I would describe it in terms of various *psychic layers.* All our experiences, including our original participation and our subsequent crystallization, are stored somewhere.

Here is a model of psychic layers:

As the lowest and innermost psychic layer, we are *a priori* part of the Whole and its powerfulness, regardless of whether we understand this state of being religiously or non-religiously. We may only speak of wholeness if no one "falls out of" this ultimate reality of being. Our *connection* with God/the Whole is (or would be) our source of sources. Our primordial trust comes from this primal ground. Here, we find "memories" of our belonging to everything and together. Such traces of memory flare up in deep longings and extreme situations: approaching death, spiritual experiences, deep symbolic or mystical dreams. Thus, from time to time, we experience ourselves as connected, as safe, as healed, as both whole and holy. We discover a piece of our original spiritual home. Or of our native, motherly soil, as my patients often do through music-assisted relaxation. Many severely disturbed patients whom I worked with in my previous job, and many dying patients whom I look after in my current job, have taught me that we can all have these experiences, regardless of background, attitude, and biography. Yet the same patients have shown me that the painful traces of separation and lost unity, as well as our earliest irritations and sensations of being threatened, are also deposited in the depths of our soul (see figure 1). Pain and threat have superimposed themselves on our original trust, happiness, and bliss.

So what about primordial trust and fear? Looking back, and seen from the diverse psychic layers, primordial trust and primordial fear are neither equally original nor contrasting alternatives. We should not, as Erik Erikson ([1959] 1980) claimed, consider them opposing poles—that is, primordial trust *versus* primordial distrust. While both exist and are stored in our soul, primordial trust lies *deeper* than all fear (Renz 2018; Renz 2015). It exists indestructibly, despite often being overshadowed by fear, disconnection, and so many formative influences. The shift from connection to disconnection described above (see chapter 4.2.) can characterize both individual and cultural development. Overshadowing has detached the ego—and in a cultural perspective, ego-centered consciousness—from the primal ground, which is perceived as darkened (see figure 1) or cut off. In religious terminology and history, God was projected into a remote distance, which enabled the vulnerable ego to keep its primordial fear at arm's length.

To return to Jesus, this extraordinary and highly sensitive man intuitively realized just how much human beings are separated from God as the Whole. Yet Jesus himself also felt connected, deeply rooted in God. Therefore he knew that—deeper down—we, too, are part of God as the Whole. Jesus' message is an ingenious answer to our disconnection and to our primordial fear in both its aspects (forlornness and

96 JESUS THE MYSTIC

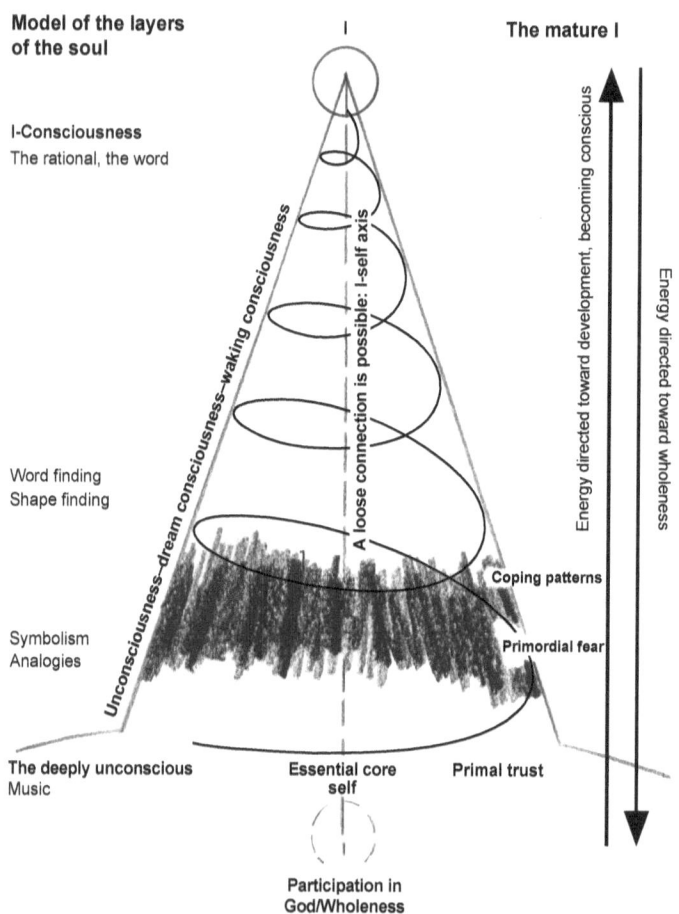

deliverance—that is, feeling "threatened"). So, too, is Jesus' fatherly and motherly concept of God.

4.4. God as Father: An Answer to Fear

Jesus' message of the loving Father can heal us deep inside. Jesus must have felt urged to put things right, even if he merely intuited the fears and traumatic background of the people and cultures around him. And even if he only saw partially through their images of God. These were obscured by projection: God as the merciless judge or as the wrathful avenger. Jesus told the fearful, and thus also us: "Imagine that God as your primal ground is a loving father or mother. If you do, you will neither fall out of God's love nor must you fear him." He was able to relativize this fear based on his own fundamentally different experiences with God.

How does Jesus speak about the Father? The word *abba* (Mark 14:36; Romans 8:15; Galathians 4:6) used to be interpreted as an affectionate term of address, just as children speak endearingly to their father (Schwager 1999, 29–30). Jeremias (1966) understood *abba* as an Aramaic vocative. For him, this word of Jesus had to be heard as "new and incredible" (Jeremias 1966, 63). He argued that Jews could hardly have used this unceremonious address in their prayers to God without seeming disrespectful of Jewish sensibility.

Current research holds a slightly different view and emphasizes Jesus' experience of *being a beloved Son* (Schelbert 2011; chapter 3.3). On all accounts, a highly intense—mystical—relationship occurs between Father and Son.

This notion is explosive, both in psychological terms and with respect to interreligious dialogue: for Jesus, the mystic, God did not abandon the human being to forlornness (the first aspect of primordial fear described above). He did not consider God to be appallingly numinous (the second aspect). Nor did he see him as a distant, omnipotent ruler or as an abstract—that is, present yet absent—divinity. Psychologically, all these notions express the human coping with primordial fear. Instead, Jesus saw God as a loving, reliable, and motherly Father. This assertion opposes the prevailing notion of God at the time, and of God as a superego. For Jesus, neither the strict observance of laws demanded by the Pharisees nor any internalized, enslaving fears and commandments decide how and who God is. Instead, God is essentially good, intangible, and powerful. This utmost authority need not be prayed to at any special place (the Temple), nor at traditional sites. It has its place within our innermost: mystically, in the spirit (*pneuma*) and in truth, in the heart, and thus in the act of loving our neighbor. As Jesus tells the woman at the fountain of Jacob: "The hour is coming when you will worship the Father neither on this mountain nor in Jerusalem. . . . But the hour is coming, and is now here, when the true worshippers will worship the Father in spirit and truth" (John 4:21–23). Thus, psychologically, Jesus epitomized God as an inner source even if he neither rejected the Temple nor Jewish law. On the contrary. Jesus loved and honored the Temple as the sacred abode of the Father. He threw out the traders and merchants. And he observed the Torah, the Jewish set of instructions (Matthew 5:17–20).

4.5. Heavenly Kingdom: Justice, Reward, Fullness

The Father also opened up that particular fullness, wisdom, and justice that Jesus associated with a key *metaphor*: the kingdom of God/heaven. The relationship with the Father is the pivotal point from which what is pending reaches fulfillment. It is also the point from which that reward, which is neither earned nor calculable, is given. Jesus talked about the kingdom of God/heaven on countless occasions. Rarely was he understood. He said that in the end justice and righteousness will also reach fulfillment. Yet this will come from the heavenly kingdom and from the Father, not from the law. Now, this does not automatically mean that Jesus rejected the law and worldly arrangements. The emperor should be given what is his (Mark 12:17). We should not, however, attempt to grasp in earthly categories what can only occur in divine ones. A key passage in the Sermon of the Mount accurately expresses this idea and illustrates Jesus' relationship with the law (Torah):

> Do not think that I have come to abolish (*katalu/sai / katalysai*) the law or the prophets; I have come not to abolish but to fulfill (*plhrw/sai / plärosai*, i.e., "to bring to fullness"). For truly I tell you, until heaven and earth pass away, not one letter, not one stroke of a letter, will pass from the law until all is accomplished. Therefore, whoever breaks one of the least of these commandments, and teaches others to do the same, will be called least in the kingdom of heaven; but whoever does them and teaches them will be called great in the kingdom of heaven. For I tell you, unless your righteousness (*dikaiosu,nh / dikaiosünhe*) exceeds (*perisseu,sh| / periseushä*, "flowing in excess" due to its connection with fullness) that of the scribes and Pharisees, you will never the kingdom of heaven." (Matthew 5:17–20)

Thus Jesus did not intend to alter one single letter of the law—the Greek text says neither a jota (*ivw/ta*, the smallest letter of the Greek alphabet) nor a dot (*kerai,a / keraja*, the smallest letter of the Hebrew alphabet). The law may provide guidance on worldly affairs, but it does not *overcome* injustice in the world. Nor does it lead to nurturing or sufficiency. Nor does it provide that fatherly fullness, freedom, and love that alone make us humans capable of love. Jesus saw through human hypocrisy and coldheartedness—for instance, when the scribes or Pharisees preached brotherly love according to the law but did not follow that commandment themselves (see the parable of the Good Samaritan, Luke 10:25–36); or when they heaped unbearable burdens upon others without moving a finger themselves (Luke 11:45–46). Jesus did not regard the coming fulfillment as a juridical or moral issue. No, as this book claims, he saw this as the outcome of mystical reality. Heavenly righteousness is more than worldly justice. It grows from within, from the experienced fullness of the heavenly kingdom. To an excessive, heavenly extent. Compared to those who narrow-mindedly insist on their rights, those connected with the Father and his heavenly kingdom are capable of another, generous righteousness from within themselves. The same psychological consistency informs the talk of *reward* in the heavenly kingdom. Jesus often thought in terms of the ultimately connected person. He thus stood in the tradition of the forefathers and the prophets.

"The kingdom of God/heaven" points to Jesus' concept of God. Where God is, there is a heavenly kingdom. This provides sustenance of a different kind, as Jesus tells the disciples: "I have food to eat that you do not know about.... My food is to do the will of him who sent me and to complete his work" (John 4:32, 34). For Jesus, the relationship with the Father leads to the experience of fullness, even to overabundance: note the theme of living water (John 4:10) and the feeding of the four thousand / five thousand (John 6:1–15). God provides food and is himself like food.

> You are looking for me, not because you saw signs, but because you ate your fill of the loaves. Do not work for the food that perishes, but for the food that endures for eternal life, which the Son of Man will give you." (John 6:26–27)

4.6. Connected and Blessed

We also gain access to the Beatitudes from the heavenly kingdom and from Jesus' relationship with God. They offer joyful encouragement, thus *more* than mere ethical admonishment (Luz 2007, 188–90). They tell us that we are blessed because/when we are connected with the primal ground/God/the Whole. In light of my present approach, the "heavenly kingdom" *will* occur in this world whenever we experience connectedness. We will have an inner richness, even if we were poor before. We will be satiated, even if we were hungry before. And we will find consolation, even if we were weeping before.

Psychologically, it is no coincidence that we experience abject poverty (*ptwco,j / ptochos*), hunger, and grief. These states all express how we find our way into connectedness: by experiencing our naked essence and existential dependence, without any avarice and compensation. We therefore find connectedness by entrusting ourselves to the moment, as beggars do, who live from hand to mouth. Yet we also find our way inside indirectly, as hungry ones, in a state in which yearning still exists, as feeling and weeping creatures. How come? Grieving requires us to leave behind all our ego's glittering attributes: beauty, material wealth, power, and honor. On various occasions, Jesus said that the heavenly kingdom is almost impossible to reach if we are thinking in terms of property, achievement, and prestige. After his moving, loving encounter with the rich young man, Jesus says, "It is easier for a camel to go through the eye of a needle than for someone who is rich to enter the kingdom of God" (Mark 10:25). Yet, as Jesus adds (Mark 10:27), nothing proves impossible for God—in spite of all difficulties, the kingdom of God/heaven is *given* to us. It is/would be part of our primal ground.

The Beatitudes are primarily promises. In the end, we are all part of the Whole and *a priori* blessed. In our "unwrought" existence. In our essence. In that place where we rest on God, on the primal ground of our existence. In the Beatitudes, as when he speaks about the kingdom of heaven, Jesus refers to the *mode of being* (Fromm [1976] 2014). We cannot understand this in terms of having or craving power. We are openhearted because we are deeply satisfied, rooted, and connected. In this mode, we will (ab)use neither property nor power for our own purposes. Material wealth and power are not the problem. They are neither inherently good nor bad but belong to God. The problem is the fact that we have lost our connectedness and thus a natural way of dealing with worldly assets (chapter 6). We must overcome the need to compensate for the gap within us (chapter 2) by accumulating property and by identifying with ego-maniacal power. As Jesus says, "But it is not so among you; but whoever wishes to be first among you must be slave of all" (Mark 10:43).

"Blessedness" and the "kingdom of God/heaven" are gift and grace. We are given these experiences, which occur only ephemerally during our time on earth. Yet they are so fulfilling that they liberate us and make us capable of loving. We just are/would be loving creatures from within. We find this empowerment to goodness already in the Old Testament's commandments: God does not command us ten times that we "*must*" but that we "*will*." Notably, this happens after

Moses's encounter with God, which transcends every other experience (Exodus 19–20).

4.7. Spiritual Practice: Profound Acceptance and Relationship

What are the consequences for everyday spiritual practice, meditation, contemplation, and spiritual care? What does spirituality mean in terms of Jesus if we consider the relationship with the Father as the primal ground and bear in mind the kingdom of God/heaven and blessedness?

The relationship with the Father holds out a promise even today: we too are related and accepted without reservation.

- We are part of the "Father," his existence and power. We are grounded in *God* and can experience this inner primal ground. Seen thus, our identity has its deepest roots in the Whole, in what Richard Rohr (2009, 35) calls presence or nondual reality. The concept of God as the loving Father, along with his inherent order, truth, and fullness, means that we do not need to prove that we *are* in order. We are instead part of the divine order, from the primal ground up, and thus essentially we are "within" that heavenly and earthly order, and therefore "in order."

We are accepted, even if we are not consciously capable of such certainty, but have become overwhelmed, blocked, or even divided and guilty. Nevertheless, we do not fall out of the Whole but are always part of it.

- Where God is, there, too, is the "*heavenly kingdom.*" Insofar as we live from the primal ground (father, mother), we experience part of that fullness and "sufficiency" already in the here and now. I need not crave that fullness, nor worry about being loved and nurtured. Instead, I am loved ("from the primal ground up") and nurtured by the fullness of God as the Whole. Whenever greed rears its head within me, whenever I compare and grow envious, I am "beside" this divine reality, "out of order." Yet the door to return to God as the primal ground is open. I can begin afresh and define myself anew from there.

- Jesus appeals for a "*spirituality of abiding*" ("Abide in me as I abide in the Father"). Thus, poverty, asceticism, constant prayer, and persistent work are not absolutely necessary. Rather, I *am* blessed whenever I am in the midst of what I am doing, whenever I "*abide/stay*" in this connectedness (John 1:38–39; John 15:4). I even *become* blessed whenever I miss this connectedness. And when I can subsequently orient myself toward it.

- I can accept myself on my spiritual path. This happens when I am loved. Gregory of Nazianus (329–390) is known to have said what is not accepted cannot be healed. (See also C. G. Jung [1958, 339]: "We cannot change anything unless we accept it.") Conversely, what is accepted can also be healed. Salvation—that is, being healed—means something else than being medically healthy, capable of functioning, beautiful, and strong. It means being whole and being as we are as seen from God (*o[loj / holos*, "whole").

- I can accept God (as the Whole, as Father and Mother, as the kingdom of God/heaven) as the basis of responsible action, and even of spiritual existence. My first and most important spiritual challenge is *to care about my connectedness* as I do about my daily bread. I need to do this when I am well and when I am sick. We all can "cultivate contact"—through prayer, meditation, remembrance, and celebration.

Therefore I tell you, do not worry about your life, what you will eat or what you will drink, or about your body, what you will wear. Is not life more than food, and the body more than clothing? Look at the birds of the air; they neither sow nor reap nor gather into barns, and yet your heavenly Father feeds them. Are you not of more value than they? And can any of you by worrying add a single hour to your span of life? And why do you worry about clothing? Consider the lilies of the field, how they grow; they neither toil nor spin, yet I tell you, even Solomon in all his glory was not clothed like one of these. But if God so clothes the grass of the field, which is alive today and tomorrow is thrown into the oven, will he not much more clothe you—you of little faith? Therefore do not worry, saying, "What will we eat?" or "What will we drink?" or "What will we wear?"... your heavenly Father knows that you need all these things. But strive first for the kingdom of God and his righteousness, and all these things will be given to you as well." (Matthew 6:25–34)

We can understand these words as "You will" rather than as an enslaving "You must" or even as a cry to arms. The kingdom of God/heaven happens from within. Jesus tells us that in essence we are satiated and satisfied. This makes us thankful. We become grateful for the kindness of the creator and the creation, for everything that we are given. David Steindl-Rast makes the case for a life based on trust. He notes that we reap peace, "a sense of belonging and a firm anchorage in the eternal Now of the present moment" (Steindl-Rast 2010, 15). We might also call this "mindfulness." It is a state in which we are spiritually already in the kingdom of God/heaven.

But why are we so unaware of this happiness in our daily lives? Why are we unable to leap into the mode of being? I feel that a discrepancy exists between experiencing the heavenly kingdom and the "world."

CHAPTER 5

Jesus' Concept of the Human Being

5.1. The Human Being as a Subject

Jesus' concept of the human being was shaped by his concept of "God as Father and Mother" (see chapter 4), and by his own connectedness. How did Jesus speak about human beings? How did he behave toward them? I remember discussing Jesus with the members of a local parish. They described him as benevolent and esteeming as follows:

> Jesus is generous of heart and endearing. And yet these epithets are too harmless.

> Jesus is empathic and understands me without prior explanation. Nothing leaves him cold.

> Jesus is wise.

What do we know about Jesus' concept of humankind? His many healings suggest that Jesus knew exactly what the human being needed. His encounters with various people (disciples, teachers of the law, the sick, customs officials, women, etc.) and his speeches suggest that he accepted everyone, irrespective of status, background, and occupation. He rejected all contempt. He restored the dignity of the debased. And he saw the individual, the whole person. Those he met were *meant* as individuals: as subjects and friends, not as servants or slaves.

5.2. The Unrooted Person without an Inner "Lord"

For Jesus, our core is indestructible and that, in their essence, our actions and existence are fruitful (e.g., the seed that fell onto the good soil in the parable of the sower, Mark 4:8). He knew intuitively that we are ultimately part "of the Father" but have become disconnected from him. Thus Jesus must have realized that our good primal ground has largely been overshadowed, leaving our basic constitution no longer intact. The gospels reveal that Jesus was acutely aware not only of human want and fear but also of compensation patterns such as avarice, obstinacy, a thirst for power and glory, entitlement, and above all our remoteness from God. He admonished—indeed, warned—that humankind needs salvation:

"Repent, for the kingdom of heaven has come near" (Matthew 4:17).

"Stay awake and pray that you may not come into the time of trial; the spirit indeed is willing, but the flesh is weak" (Matthew 24:40–41; see also Matthew 12:43–45).

"They were like sheep without a shepherd"; he "had compassion for them" (Mark 6:34).

"But Jesus on his part would not entrust himself to them, because he knew all people ... knew what was in everyone" (John 2:24–25).

The exclamation "Oh, you of little faith" (*ovligo,pistoi*, Matthew 6:30; 8:26; 18:6) indicates that people's lack of trust and understanding made Jesus suffer. Time and again they failed to understand him—in particular, what the "Father" meant to him (primal ground, fullness, the kingdom of God/heaven). When Jesus told the disciples that he was going to the Father, Philip replied, "Lord, show us to the Father" (John 14:8). Jesus' reaction reveals his dismay:

> Have I been with you all this time, Philip, and you still do not know me? Whoever has seen me has seen the

Father. How can you say, "Show us the Father"? Do you not believe that I am the Father and that Father is in me? ... Believe me that I am in the Father and the Father is in me; but if you do not, then believe me because of the works themselves." (John 14:9–11)

Visibly moved, Jesus spoke in ever-new ways about the Father and the kingdom of God/Heaven. He also spoke about reversal and the evil powers in the world. He thus addressed a basic question of the Old Testament in his very own way: Who is the Lord (for instance, in Elijah: Yahweh versus Baal)? This question concerns the alternative "God or idol." For Jesus, this had a spiritual focus, not an academic one. The question, then, is not who or what God is. God is not endangered, but humankind is: Do we stand on firm ground (God/ Wholeness) or not? Do we revolve around an inner center (God as the Whole/a corresponding vision of development)? Are we centered on our own deeper, essential core or instead on our ego? Are we connected with what our life is worth entrusting to? In 1529, Martin Luther ([1529] 1908, 44) wrote, "Now, I say, whatever your heart clings to and confides in, that is really your God." Yet when we lose something greater as our "center," we are indeed disconnected. We become our own Master/"Lord"—along with our idols and false gods.

If we do not recognize God/the Whole as our inner core, as our center, the alternative is neither agnosticism nor atheism. The question is not whether I believe or doubt in God. We can still be oriented toward a final question and truth, toward ultimate meaning and purpose—even in doubt. The alternative is a closed heart. It is egotism, narcissism, and self-righteousness. A blindness toward the concerns of our fellows, as many Pharisees, scribes, and powerful people were at the time of Jesus. As C. G. Jung (1989, 325) wrote, "The decisive question for man is: is he related to something infinite or not? That is the telling question of his life. Only if we know that the thing which truly matters is the infinite can we avoid fixing our interest upon futilities, and upon all kinds of goals which are not of real importance." Thus the alternative: to be connected or to be disconnected.

Quite probably, Jesus saw his fellows not only as free and mature but also as lost, needy, and vulnerable. For him, we were "without a Lord/center" and removed not only from outer servitudes but also from inner connectedness. For Jesus, we are disoriented, wanting, greedy, captive, driven by external forces, and alienated from ourselves. Humankind is uprooted (and hence separated) from the Father. We lack the *foundation* to be genuinely free, trusting, and mature.

5.3. Jesus Becomes an Answer to Fear and the "World"

When he bade his disciples farewell in the Gospel of John (16:33), Jesus encouraged them (who would remain behind): "In the world you face persecution (i.e., you are afraid; *qli/yin / thlipsin*, "distress, suffering"). But take courage; I have conquered the world (*neni,khka / nenikäka*, "overcome")."

What do these peculiar words mean? Here, fear does not mean phobia (*fo,boj / phobos*, "inner anxiety"). Rather, it represents the pressure, plight, and suffering that overcome us from outside. Fear, moreover, corresponds to the "world" (*ko,smoj / kosmos*). In the beginning, meanwhile, the term *world* carries no negative connotations in John (e.g., in the Prologue; see chapter 10). Rather it represents the earthly, which is now negatively connoted. John speaks of the ruler of the world (12:31; 14:30). He is referring to Satan, who usurps humankind and abuses it for his own purposes. But we might also interpret this differently: in John 16:33, cited above, the "world" is what Jesus has overcome. Thus it represents what is surmountable. What holds true for us as individuals—that we are caught between what we *would* be (connected, fruitful) and what we *are* (uprooted, disconnected, empty or deficient in our hearts)—applies even more to the "world." It would be the garden of God but has become a place of fear, distress, and greed. It is the site of power struggles.

We can better understand the concept of the "world" in the Gospel of John if we ask *what* Jesus overcame. I suggest that he became an *answer to fear*. Jesus' closeness to God ensured that he was not separated from the Whole. His perception of reality was not egotistically focused. He—the mystic—saw beyond the normal human perspective. Emotionally, he also had different roots and possessed natural self-esteem; he experienced himself as borne by God. Based on his experience of the Father, Jesus lived and spoke out of a sensitivity beyond all fear, beyond time and space, beyond worldly categories. He must have known, intuitively, that primordial trust lies deeper than fear; than "the world" and its power structures, which the Pharisees, among others, justified, paradoxically, through recourse to "God." Jesus brings into play a different concept of God and another idea of power and truth. He also introduces a primordial trust that is justified *a priori* (i.e., biblically speaking, the world has been overcome). His message is that we are defined neither by primordial fear nor by its consequences. Even deeper, we are/ would also be carried by the Father. Or put in plain religious language, "God is stronger."

Arguably, Jesus knew fear. Yet his fears never resulted from primordial fear but corresponded to a specific situation (e.g., in Gethsemane, Mark 14:32–42; Hebrews 5:7). He "conquered" both those fears and those coping mechanisms that exist only because the ego has lost its primordial ground. The "world" stands for what has emerged *after* the overshadowing of the primal ground. It also represents what has therefore succumbed to ego-dominance (in mythological language, this means "beyond Eden"): a particular intrapsychic and cultural imprinting and dynamic (which I refer to later as "sin," see chapters 6 and 7).

The Gospel of John says that we, too, can surmount the "world" and "fear." I have observed this in some dying persons. Once they have left behind their ego-bound existence and its worries, needs, instincts, and patterns ("the world"), they are reconnected emotionally and visionarily (on near-death experiences, see chapter 2.4).

Jesus' mysticism went even further. His relationship with God overcame the all-too-human. The Father was alive in all of Jesus' actions and in his mere existence. Jesus was wholly united with the Father. Therefore, those who trust Jesus have already established a relationship with the Father. In Jesus, those who believe also encounter the Father and his benevolence. Many of us are helped by the fact that Jesus, who was mystically united with the Father, was also a human being. He actually lived on earth. Unlike God, who remains intangible, Jesus was/is closer to us, not only during his lifetime but also today. Because he was human, Jesus was/is a bearable counterpart—despite his oneness with the Father. He could/

can be approached. His contemporaries (the disciples, the sick) could trust him. And so can we.

We might also imagine this concretely. Like the patient who confided in me that when she fell asleep she imagined Jesus wandering from one village to another, emanating empathy and holiness. Let us not forget that whatever Jesus did or said, he also affected his surroundings as a human being. He *was* and *represented* the lived unity with the Father. As such, he was the answer both to our remoteness from God and to fear. In modern terms, Jesus *personifies* "primordial trust" as it were. He was a mediator, a spiritual shepherd, and a bridge for people to God—a personified answer amid their fear.

Many faithful Christians believe that the Mother of God acts as a similar bridge between abstract divinity and humankind. Worshipping Mary often means more than simply honoring the Mother of Jesus. Mary stands for an all-embracing mother, in whom we find refuge amid fear and need. Sustained and supported by her, we cannot fall out of all-encompassing divine benevolence.

> *During an operation, a comatose Italian patient, who only spoke broken German, saw "hats, many hats." She then dreamed about hats and felt chased. I was called to her bed and held her hand. She talked. Already our human contact*

*did her good. She was genuinely amazed when we began
interpreting the hats. I asked her what the hats had looked
like. "Colorful, red, blue—one was particularly important—
and huge." It had towered above her. At first, I was astonished
by the associations that this image triggered in me: wearing
hats, being sheltered, cared for. No sooner had I uttered this
thought, she cried out and breathed deeply. She wept for hours,
gripped by the image, and murmured from time to time:
"Mary . . . Madonna Maria, sheltered under a hat."*

*Another patient, a young dying mother, managed to let go
of her fear for herself and her child, which she would be
leaving behind. She found peace in the comforting thought
of God's mercifulness and womb. We can associate the
Hebrew word rehem (womb) with the verb rachem (to have
compassion) and with the noun rahamim, (womb compassion/mercy). This patient had an aha experience: neither she
nor her little daughter would ever fall out of this all-encompassing, womb-like, merciful God. This filled her with
joy. The following night she had an impressive dream about
a transformation. "There was a threshold in the air. Before
it, people spoke German; behind it, English. Before the
threshold stood real people, behind it 'ethereal creatures.' This
is what dying must be like." She wept when I mentioned
that English might also stand for the language of angels and*

praised God. Although she was terminally ill, the next day this woman referred to herself as "whole, saved,"—healed.

5.4. A Primordial Healing behind Jesus' Healings

Jesus not only proclaimed and taught. Beyond any doubt, he also healed. Who? And how? Superficially, we might say that the sick recovered, the lame were able to walk again, and the blind regained their eyesight. Each of these events would be inconceivable in the context of a modern hospital. Thus the incredible nature of Jesus' work (by today's standards) also distances him from us and makes him strange. No one understands.

But if we contemplate the stories of Jesus' healing, we will discover deeper, utterly comprehensible assertions. We can draw conclusions about *what* Jesus was meant to heal from understanding *how* his healing took place—beyond historical-critical interpretations. These claim, for instance, that several testimonies from the Early Church's oral tradition ("logia"; Gnilka 2010, 225) bear witness to the actual nature of Jesus' work. Or that the first evangelist (Mark) already had an older scripture before him (Gnilka 2010, 209).

Psychologically, Jesus' healing may mean being lifted up and delivered from external forces. Or rising from deep, deathlike regression or inner paralysis. For instance, Jesus took the hand of Peter's fever-stricken mother-in-law and lifted her up (Mark 1:31). He told the dead girl (whatever this means): "Little girl, get up!" (Mark 5:41). He also issued orders to give her food. He told a paralytic, "Stand up, take your mat and go to your home" (Mark 2:11).

Jesus' healing also involved regaining one's vitality and a foothold in life. Like the man with the withered hand, whom Jesus told, "Come forward . . . stretch out your hand" (Mark 3:1–5). For Drewermann (1987, 282), this man is "the symptom-bearer and victim of a self-affected, pathological religiousness," in which someone forbids themselves "to act by their own hand." Thus witheredness may stand for inferiority or inhibition. Healing, in this case, required the man to come forward and to stand in the center—before others, but also before himself.

Behind these healings stands *primordial healing* (Renz 2017): if we are healed in this way, we find our way back to ourselves and to the Father as the center of human existence. Primordial healing means reconnection. God, as the primal ground, already exists. And yet our remoteness from him requires us to find him again. We must *experience* not only him but also our primordial trust. The fact *that* Jesus healed is one of the most important answers to our fear and remoteness from God, to our uprooting and alienation.

But we should not read the often-cited assertion "Your faith has made you well" (Mark 5:34, 36, etc.) as an obligation to "believe in Jesus." Importantly, "Jesus never said egotistically, '*I* have healed you'" (Siebenrock, personal communication). Instead, he referred to the mature person's act of faith and trust. Thus Jesus relied on experience and on an authority within us. Biblically speaking, he relied on God, who is already *there*. We are healed when we engage with God and the primordial ground, and thereby risk being affected very personally.

5.5. Healing through Relationship

We can be healed. In the sense that we can be taken home (to the Father). How? Many biblical texts have suggested "Simply believe." Yet this eradicates neither diseases, nor fear, nor formative influences. "Coming home" is a *process*, also in the context of Jesus. Behind numerous biblical healings lies more than a straightforward narrative, as we see in the gospels. These concise stories, as told by the evangelists, detract nothing from their processual nature. When Jesus discharges the healed with momentous words (e.g., "Your faith has healed you"), he is recapitulating an entire process. These stories make sense if we assume that *Jesus united important salutary capacities in himself*. Immeasurable suffering, and the hope that arose from the healer's calling, drove those in search of healing to Jesus.

Yet how did the healing "work"? Much happened through "experiencing" Jesus and through his message of the benevolent Father. Relationship and relatedness are decisive in this respect. Encountering the man from Nazareth was a concrete experience. Jesus was a "person," a sympathizing individual who could be touched. He was human in everything he said and did. He touched, spoke to, and looked at those in search of healing as a Thou. He was saddened by transgressions. He insisted, he wept, and let himself be moved.

In several cases, Jesus healed through touch and relationship. He laid his hands on the sick (Mark 6:5). He took pity (Mark 1:41; 6:34; 8:2). He did not shy away from the leprous, but touched them (Mark 1:40–42). In turn, Jesus, too, was touched (Mark 3:10), if need be only by his cloak (Mark 5:27; 6:56). Even if this resonates with his inexplicable nature and authority (Jesus was aware that a power went forth from him, Mark 5:30), we should not neglect the concrete relational aspect. Nor his own relatedness to the Father. Jesus stood out because he was deeply connected and completely open to an essential encounter with the sick. His power sprung from his connectedness.

What did Jesus' healing change? The blind could see again, the deaf regained their hearing, the dumb their tongue. We may also read these events figuratively: they have to do with an inner opening. Our ego-boundedness, wherein we are isolated from God as the Whole; our closed heart, previously blind, deaf, and dumb to any connectedness with God, "opens up." We now are ready to be touched and reconnected. But how does this process work?

> They brought to him a deaf man who had an impediment in his speech; and they begged him to lay his hand on him. He took him aside in private, away from the crowd, and put his fingers into his ears, and he spat and touched his tongue. Then looking up to heaven, he sighed and said to him, "*Ephatha*," that is, "Be opened." And immediately his ears were opened, his tongue was released, and he spoke plainly." (Mark 7:32–35)

Here, healing essentially occurs through the material properties of human saliva. Rabbinic Judaism hailed saliva as a remedy, especially against eye diseases (Gnilka 2010, 297, 314). Yet instead of reciting the magical formula customary at the time, Jesus looked up to heaven—that is, consciously connected with the Father. His relationship with the Father was all-important. Gnilka (2010, 298) has highlighted that Jesus did not address the diseased organ, as Hellenistic analogies might lead us to expect, but the human being. This indicates the importance of personality and of relationship. He healed by entering into the primordial relationship with God, into the foundation of being. Moreover, the fact that the *ear* (the sick part of the body) is touched, directly and intensely, is a relational act. When we touch another person, this brings us very close to them. We either accept or confront them.

I therefore conclude that Jesus' main concern was openness—to be "open," as deeply as possible, through the "ear." The sick person does not need to actively hear but to become open, to be opened toward a deeper being, toward God, above all through the ear. The ear remembers our primal (e.g., embryonic) and final connectedness. The dying have taught me that listening and being "reconnected by the ear" are different. The dying rarely actively hear anymore. And yet they are connected, auditively and vibrationally, with their surroundings (ultimately, with the Whole/God) more than we are. They pick up much more than their disfigured appearance leads us to assume. Yet how does a healthy person enter this hearing state, this sensitivity, this receptiveness or mysticism? In particular, as it contrasts so starkly with the stupified state of our everyday consciousness ... with our apathetic, encapsulated existence? This is the question raised by the story of healing in Mark. His encounter with Jesus made the deaf man connected and whole (through his ear). It made his deafness and muteness irrelevant. Here, something was healed so deeply that even the man's tongue was released (Mark 7:35), allowing the (healed) man to talk about his experience. The story of the blind man of Betsaida is similar yet different (Mark 8:22–26). Jesus took the man's hand (he was born blind) and led him out of the village (note the parallel to "away from the crowd," Mark 7:33; see chapter 7). Then he put saliva on the man's eyes and placed his hands on him, in an intense statement of relationship. What strikes me about this story is Jesus' directive guidance, which is itself a relational event.

5.6. Healing Aims at the Newly Rooted, Essential, and Original Personality

What is healing directed toward? In an automotive metaphor, we are healed when we "go into reverse," even if we wish to move into a healthier "forward gear." Healing occurs at the root, in the energetic sphere (see the discussion of demons in chapter 7), and in our mind. It does so in the hope that a newly rooted person with a strong personality will emerge. Even if healing is directed to my inner child, this does not mean that I become a child or childish. It wants us to become whole and so natural as a child. The child theme may "empty ourselves" to the point of our "primordial essence," our inner child. "Let the little children (*paidi,on / paidion*, "child, infant, alumnus"; see also pedagogics) come to me, and do not stop them . . . for it is to such as these that the kingdom of God belongs. . . . Whoever does not accept the kingdom of God as a little child will never enter it" (Luke 18:16–17). Why, or indeed when, does healing occur through our inner child? Our nature and essence, as well as our woundedness, are more plainly evident in the child than in the adult. Under the sign of the (inner) child, those who are alienated from themselves will find their way back to their roots and deepest longings, to a place where our soul is naturally hopeful and still flourishing, blessed, free, and related. The inner child (the childlike) is not childish. No, it is original, uncorrupted, and capable of feeling. The (inner) child insouciantly accepts help and allows itself to be dependent. Similarly, Matthew said, "Unless you change and become like children, you will never enter the kingdom of heaven" (Matthew 18:1–5). Formulated as a promise, this passage also tells us, "whenever you become like children, you will be connected with the kingdom of God/heaven." Interestingly, Matthew associates this childlike state with reversal, with a spiritual process: we move backward (and forward) into connectedness, into mysticism.

Many adults find going back difficult because it means summoning the courage to be humble. We must leave behind the honors, the lavishness, and the comforts of this world. In contrast, the childlike state presents us with an opportunity that we should not underestimate. Here, in our spiritual-psychological nakedness, we can be touched as we were long ago. From here our creativity unfolds. From here we can experience what happiness, love, and sensory impressions are. From here we can also experience our astonishment and awe at the divine. Under the sign of the child we come to life, once again, far removed from disappointment and cynicism. This explains why as adults we seek relationships with children and blossom in this form of contact (which we cherished as children). This explains why the elderly return, increasingly, to the world of their childhood. Within our inner child, something is saved and becomes whole that otherwise suffers deprivation. Here, joy, sadness, undistorted fear, as well as fulfillment and being loved are all genuine experiences.

5.7. Spiritual Practice: Trust, Prayer, and the Motherly Therapeutic Jesus

What are the consequences for everyday spiritual practice, meditation, contemplation, and spiritual care?

Spirituality, in terms of Jesus' concept of humankind, means "Dare to believe, to trust, perhaps to pray, and to engage in an inner relationship with Jesus. Jesus is your therapist, too."

Believing can be an act of *trust*. Rutishauser (2011, 64) stresses that not merely religious or mystical experience may serve as the basis of a spiritual path, which may involve a "subtle narcissistic temptation." Just as memorable for the soul is the "basic category of trust," the courage to trust. Often we can only take a leap of faith into trust. Or we can let ourselves be carried, trustingly. This would be the aspect of the inner child.

Believing is *praying*, praying is believing. Praying, as a personal commitment, presents itself as a possibility for the upright person in his or her search for God. The many questions for the unfathomable, and wrestling with him, as Jacob does at the Jabbok River (Genesis 32:23–33), or the lament of the tormented—like mature gratitude, this is part of such a prayer. In prayer I can "show" myself to God. In the presence of the severely ill I always begin a prayer in a similar way: "God, whoever or whatever you are, here lies Mr. B . . ." I place this person's essential concerns before God. Then I invoke God. The German theologian Fridolin Stier (1984, 11), who wrestled with God all his life, wrote, "Most of what happens in my mind all day long belongs to the category of prayer." Concretely, prayer may involve various activities: to go on a pilgrimage, to work, to exercise, to go for mindful walks, to do yoga, to wait, to listen, and the like.

Spirituality, then, means *presence* and *perseverance*. Whether we do or do not, we can be present in the moment.

We are centered, neither distracted nor repressed. Some dying persons I have met would also liked to have been "present when death occurs." In itself, presence is a form of prayer and often a great art. In prayer—and knowing that, in essence, we are loved (chapter 4)—we manage to endure and to persevere. In this light, spiritual care often means affirming, supporting the sick in their hard-won patience, in their waiting and perseverance, and showing them our greatest appreciation and gratitude.

Christian prayer may be addressed directly to God, the Father, the Mother, and the Creator. Yet Christians may also accept Jesus' offer and address their prayers to him as the mediator. He then becomes our interlocutor, doctor, and therapist. Even Mary and the saints may—to some extent—become mediators, as long as we remain conscious of the fact that we should only give God our utmost adoration. In practice, accepting *Jesus as an inner therapist* means entrusting my essence, my worries, and my questions to him.

To our surprise, Jesus was often unafraid. He experienced no fear in the tempest out at sea (Mark 4:35–41), nor when confronted by demons and the obsessed (such as the man from Gerasa; Mark 5:1–20). Not even when the crowd wanted to hurl him over the cliff (Luke 4:29). Somehow, his primordial trust remained unbroken. Dogmatically speaking, he was "without sin." But what does that mean?

CHAPTER 6
Jesus' Response to Sin
MYSTICISM

6.1. The Dream of Becoming Ourselves without Separation?

What distinguished Jesus from us? What does being "without sin"—without separation—mean? What does sin mean?

In chapter 4.2, I mentioned two basic states of early human development: being connected with the Whole versus being disconnected from it. Here, I link the latter state—disconnection—to the difficult word *sin*. German *sünde*, "sin," derives from Middle High German *sonderung*, *sönderung*, "sunderance," "severance," "separation." The German *sonder(n)* is related to English *sunder*, which means "to separate, split, or break by force" (Hoad 1986, 472). The Old English *syn(n)* meant "wrongdoing," "offense," "enmity" (Hoad 1986, 439). Thus the word *sin* denotes separation, and as such a specific dynamic. The dynamic takes its name from its effect: the (nascent) ego detaches itself increasingly from reference and belonging. As a result, a break occurs between the ego and its origin. This raises two basic questions: What would we be if we were *not* separated? And how might we imagine development?

Theologically speaking, becoming an ego and the process of individuation are profoundly willed by God (see also von Rad 1975). It is as if the beginning of human life holds out a promise: that of becoming a strong personality while possessing a strong connection with the primordial ground, with a natural joy of life and curiosity. In this case, we can speak of an intact and strong ego-Self axis.[1] If we were like this, we would not be determined by greed, avarice, envy, or any other form of compensation. We would not be compelled to compare ourselves with what stands to our left or our right. Nor would we need to prevail over others or to keep up with the zeitgeist at any price. We would enjoy getting up in the mornings and working in God's "vineyard" during the day. We would look forward to "returning to God" in the evenings, uninterrupted by obstructive affects or drives. We would love God and the earth, ourselves, and our friends. We would appreciate our earthly lives but would feel that our ultimate home is in God. We would probably be quiet mystics, though also capable of social interaction and relationships and oriented toward worldly tasks. We would even approach human encounters and conflicts without any unnecessary fear and would be at peace with ourselves. Yet do we find such a person?

6.2. Jesus: A Life without Separation

We ought to imagine Jesus as such an ideal type. Church doctrine says that he was without sin. This makes sense if sin (in the singular) is understood as a dynamic of separation from our primordial ground (God/the Whole). Jesus had not lost his connection with God. Although various details about Jesus' life are unknown, we may nevertheless subsume it under the motto "A life without separation": Jesus' connection with the primordial ground and the Father was unbroken—that is, it was free of disruptive emotions, greed, or projections. He was strongly rooted (see the "mysticism of abiding"; chapter 4). In Jesus divine energy could flow freely. Even when afraid, shaken, or angry, he never lost his primordial trust for long. The hurt he suffered did not begin to fester. In modern terms, we might say that he was connected with the "web" of life and guided from within.

Despite his intense connection with God, Jesus was not naive, let alone childlike. On the contrary. The gospels and letters reveal a strong and wise personality. He endured his forty days in the (spiritual) wilderness despite temptations and hunger. After his baptism, he did not become a disciple of John the Baptist, but rather he had the courage to embrace a message of his own! Yet without losing any sense of reality. In the transfiguration, he did not want to build huts (Mark 9:2–13). Instead, he returned to the lowlands. Strengthened by his magnificent experience, he took upon himself the difficult passage to Jerusalem. Jesus was also strong enough to ward off the demons. Matthew (12:43–45) tells us that no evil force and spirits could enter Jesus' soul because this was filled by the Father. As such it was occupied and never "empty" (12:44). Today, we would say that Jesus was neither trendy nor his Father's puppet. On the contrary. He was mature and full of inner strength, wisdom, and empathy. He coped with emotional upsets and injuries on his own, impressively, yet not stoically. He lived in an inner presence, alertness, and commitment to the world.

What made Jesus so resourceful? Where did he draw his primordial trust from? Was his childhood sheltered, despite the severe difficulties of his times? Maybe. Nevertheless, the historical perspective leaves the question about Jesus' exceptional nature unanswered. According to John, Jesus "was" at the Father's side, near "the Father's heart" (1:18). From the beginning, and at all times. He was literally "in the womb and bosom of the Father" (*o`w'n eivj to.n ko,lpon tou/ patro.j*). According to Matthew and Luke, the stories about Jesus' childhood assume new meanings when we read them symbolically: on a deeper level, virginity means to be unmarried to the values of this world and therefore to be creative out of a great inner autonomy. Matthew and Luke also tell us that Mary was capable of such autonomy, which would only have been possible if she too was profoundly connected with God. Joseph dreamed about God and trusted these dreams, which also signifies a connection with God. The Gospel of Mark leaves this question aside.

According to Mark, Luke, and Matthew, Jesus' relationship with God intensified during his life. For these evangelists, it is conceivable that Jesus experienced individuation and a spiritual path. He too was maturing and learning (literally, he "gained in wisdom," Luke 2:40; Bruners 2015). I think that Jesus grew increasingly into his primordial trust and his determination, just as Dietrich Bonhoeffer, Edith Stein, and other heroes or mystics of our time have done. Jesus, however, surpasses even them. Karl Rahner (1966, 117) captured this development in the following formula: as our independence grows, so does our closeness to the Father.

Taken together, "an unbroken relationship with God" and "a strong personality" constitute a broad-based and highly developed pyramid (see figure 1, chapter 4.2). Jesus was God's dialogical counterpart, his covenant partner, and his Son—and to this extent he was unique.

6.3. Separation, Imprinting, and the Emergence of Subjecthood

Jesus' special case aside, what characterizes the processes of becoming human and becoming a subject? I felt truly enlightened when I realized that we need to understand *the phenomenon of sin psychologically*: as a process of "separation" that takes place in our early development. The word tells us a lot about human behavior in general and our own reactions in particular—beyond moralizing. Unfortunately, the phenomenon is "true," psychologically and mythologically.

Ego development as separation:

Separation already constitutes a *reaction* to something. According to my depth-psychological approach, it is triggered by the irritation and fear experienced in earliest human development. Essentially, separation means the detachment from the Whole—*more* than what would befit the natural process. The emerging ego separates itself and develops toward ego-centeredness. Separation is ego-development under slightly mistaken premises. Instead of emerging from interaction with the Whole, amid an atmosphere of trust, joy, and permitted being, the ego comes into being under the sign of fear and compensation such as having, coercion, greed, and ego-maniacal power. It must protect itself and revolves increasingly around itself. Already the minimal shift in emphasis—from the Whole to separation—resembles a category shift; the ego has fallen out of the original atmosphere of trust and joy. Primordial fear now overshadows or obscures primordial trust (see the shaded areas in figure 1, chapter 4). Our reflexes serve to ward off increasing fear. In this process, our energies are misguided already *during* ego *development*. Instead of being directed toward the entirety of creation and life, they are absorbed by the ego and by fear. Human motivation grows more and more ego-centered.

Even if we assume that human development and evolution are profoundly willed by God, this is not true of separation. Separation is a tragedy. Whereas it might be "accepted" or "taken on" by God—as were the dynamics ultimately leading to Jesus' death on the cross—separation is not "willed." It is not compatible with Jesus' concept of God (see chapters 4 and 9).

Although separation begins harmlessly and naturally, it degenerates into all sorts of excesses. It is impossible to precisely determine when the difficult inherent dynamic breaks open. Only retrospectively are we able to say, "Oh, that was when something bad began." False developments, however, began much earlier. Mythologically, they began with Adam and Eve. Ontogenetically, separation began in the mother's womb and during infancy, phylogenetically at the evolutionary stage of animals. In any event, the response to primordial fear (chapter 4) was aggression, either heightened or blocked ("to take the bull by the horns" and attacking or withdrawal, isolation, escape through the backdoor and lethargy). Separation has long ago become part of the human condition. It is characteristic of evolution, at least in our culture. Charles Darwin, the leading early proponent of evolutionary thought, spoke of *adjusting to the habitat* through variation and selection.

Separation, or increasing self-protection, arose whenever a certain level of irritation, stress, and earliest fear was exceeded among animals, primitive humans, embryos, and infants. This initiated behavioral patterns oriented toward egocentricity: alienation, defense mechanisms, and ego-competencies. The natural development—"from a state of being and participating in the Whole toward becoming a subject"—either occurred too abruptly or was not sufficiently dared. This misguided start negatively impacted human affects and further development: either affects became "a densely concentrated charge" or the human being remained inert and indifferent. Both our culture and most of its members have been shaped by such reactions.

Based on separation, our further development was determined by stress, self-protection, and coping with fear—in several respects:

1. *Objects*: safeguarding and must-have patterns developed into envy and greed. Group dynamics centered

on mimesis (see Girard [1972] 2005; Schwager 1999). *Having* prevailed over *being* (Fromm [1976] 2014) and led us to exploit the world's resources.

2. *Relationship*: compensatory strengthening of the ego, inflation to the point of narcissism, self-posturing, and displays of power. Group dynamics now concentrated on constant power struggles. Power was used and abused to strengthen the ego. Self-attributed power prevailed over love, self-reliance over relatedness. We reject our human condition of dependence.

3. *Energy*: splitting emerged, individually and collectively. I speak of an overshadowing amid the collective atmosphere (chapter 7; Renz 2018). The human being now became driven. No longer free, we became determined by anger instead of potential, and by depression instead of peace. Energies became misguided.

At some point, separation became a one-way route, leading to an impasse from which the ego could no longer retreat. It moved further and further away from the original atmosphere of permitted being, until the connection with the primordial ground—biblically speaking, the Father—was lost. Metaphorically speaking, the thread was severed, the umbilical cord cut. According to the biblical myth of creation, Adam and Eve were forced to leave Paradise. Yet this misguided development was based on tremendous distress and primordial fear.

Popular lore speaks of "formative influences" or "imprinting" rather than of separation. What is the difference? We may see formative influences also in positive terms. While separation means the *process* (i.e., the mechanism of self-extrication) and thus never carries positive connotations, imprinting means the *result* (i.e., a condition or humanity's starting point), which may also include resources.

Imprinting:

Imprinting and formative influences include motherly and fatherly love, corrective experiences, and maturation. They may hold a potential or remain an imposition. Separation is a dynamic term, imprinting a static one; the latter describes the state of "carrying baggage." This denotes what we take along in life, and whose specifications we can partly outgrow, partly not. We are all shaped. Imprinting comprises individual and cultural factors: every child grows into its personal, family, social, and cultural specifications and into the "human" condition. It does so in its own way, one that is possible at a specific point in time. The basic principle is: imprinting—not only genetic predisposition—forms the background of human action (see Renz 2017, 2018).

Together, genetic predispositions, environmental influences, good or ill fortune, and separation (which is more or less culturally shaped) constitute a common response pattern. All of these factors interact with one another.

Let me briefly explain the difference between imprinting and separation on the neurophysiological level. We are programmed in one way or another and exist within a web of traces and influences. Within this web, we are "moved into lane" in a particular way. Staying with this automotive metaphor, we are set on a particular track. Imprinting, though, represents a more or less salubrious, psychic-archetypal structure. In contrast, separation refers to a false dynamic and forms the backdrop to a less salubrious imprinting. As a result, difficult formative influences and separation mutually reinforce each other and have fatal consequences.

6.4. Fatal Consequences

Why is it so fatal if we are "moved into lane" on false premises? Well, because, biblically speaking, it is no longer God who "rules" our soul but our increasing ego. We are then *without* a Lord (chapter 5). And we easily misconnote our power. Our life is guided by self-determination. Yet today we consider this *normal*. As Max Weber ([1921] 1978, 53) observed, "Power [*Macht*] is the probability that one actor within a social relationship will be in a position to carry out his own will despite resistance, regardless of the basis on which this probability rests." What we call normal, however, is in fact determined by compensation. Fundamental human values have increasingly become misprogrammed. The consequences are manifold regarding the aforementioned three respects:

1. *Objects*: We now no longer simply exist. Rather, mimesis and greed gain the upper hand.

2. *Relationship*: We have lost the ability to be deeply receptive, reliant, and dependent. The passive, accepting side of a human relationship, symbolically the feminine (anima) within the man and the woman, is no longer accessible. Separation means that development occurs more or more in terms of the powerful, masculine way of coping with life. Collectively, patriarchy emerged. Group dynamically, competition, exclusion, and exploitation triumphed.

3. *Energy*: Future humans may be increasingly determined by external forces: their/our energies must fight against

inner "shadow forces." They/we are channelled into two kinds of patterns: either excessive aggression, performance orientation, and rationalism or regression, lethargy, and paralysis.

Even if misdevelopments can be corrected at a later stage, this is possible only as far as permitted by the ego, which has meanwhile emerged. Correction happens as far as the ego is still receptive.

6.5. Becoming Guilty

Where does guilt begin? We should not confuse separation (etymologically "sin") with becoming guilty. Separation begins before the emergence of the ego and "befalls" the human being. At some stage, however, it also becomes enforced by the ego, and we subsequently become guilty.

Separation (sin) and guilt spur each other on: their woundedness made humans extricate themselves from their original dependence. This process is ongoing. We became and are still untouchable. Interestingly, Augustine of Hippo and Martin Luther defined sin as encapsulation (*incurvatus in se*, "curved inward on oneself"). The phenomenon of encapsulation describes more than sheer imprinting because at some stage of development the ego *identifies* with isolation (i.e., self-absorption). In this state, we progressively set ourselves apart. At this point, sin (separation) becomes guilt: we are removed from the Whole, from everything closely related to God, even from our primordial ground. We define ourselves, as this process is called. The "Other"—which includes other human beings, God's numinosity, the world's suffering and that of Creation, and the like—is excluded. Beyond our perception. But precisely this coincides with what Western culture defines as normal and well-functioning. Separation (sin), our ego-based perception, has become the "normal state." Importantly, this shift began without any moral undertone.

The step to actual guilt, moreover to entanglement in sin, is small. Because once we have become separate, we are no longer capable of a higher or an external perspective. Separation (sin) clouds our view of the Whole and of the truth behind everyday phenomena. We keep our original fear at bay and choose not to probe more deeply into things or ourselves. Instead of seeing through what motivates our actions (fear, greed, power claims), we mask our motivations. This causes even greater suffering for those close to us: "I can hardly ever really get through to him"; "What she says is always half true but otherwise she's deluding herself." In regard to sin, we do not deal with what is totally wrong, or else it would be generally intelligible. This dynamic (sin) manifests itself, notoriously, in *half*-truths, cloudiness, and distortions. The transitions from separation (sin) to guilt are fluid.

> *I am thinking of the workaholic lawyer, for instance, who never managed to embrace his wife and daughter and to be a husband and father for them. But he didn't understand the implications of his behavior. Instead, he believed he was right and clung to his Protestant faith. Yet his original imprinting emerged as he lay on his deathbed: his extreme fear (Was it an inexplicable fear of closeness?) prevented him from allowing anyone near him. Looking back at his life, he must have covered this fear with his zeal for work. Now, on his deathbed, he was overwhelmed by fear. Yet, most impressively, this dying man, who had practiced law all his life, became aware of his guilt and managed to apologize to his family. He had a vision: he saw a court, though not like those he knew from his professional life. This inner court consisted of "a throne." After apologizing, and after an impressive display of mutual affection, which his wife magnanimously allowed to happen, the man was deeply touched and had a vision: "The gate is now open. Green." Was that the reopened gate of Paradise?*

Other severely ill persons dream when they become conscious of sin. They dream, for instance, of a frosted mirror or of one that once again shines resplendently. Or they look into the eyes of a loved one for the first time and are shaken; they feel looked at and allow others to look at them. A deeper truth may manifest itself symbolically on the deathbed. This is because, on this level, we can keep matters "closer to our chest" than in everyday consciousness. The lawyer mentioned above was an exception in this respect. His ability to feel and bear his guilt was an expression of a great personality. It distinguished him from others and set him free.

The path from separation (sin) to guilt is fluid also in life. We are often confronted with half-truths also in daily life. I am thinking of many people's experiences at work: innumerable meetings fail because things are obfuscated, hidden, "swept under the carpet." Conversations are no longer constructive or unifying but hurtful, pretentious, and ambiguous (double binds). They ought to deal with a particular issue, but they are actually about power, about being right, and about compensating fear. Obfuscation and half-truths usually create new injustice. Hurt and guilt continue. Our ego, burdened with diffuse guilt, reacts even more strategically and with more separation. It moves ever further apart and devises its own morality. Consequently, we neither search for the truth nor become conscious. Thus sin and guilt inherently prevent conscious realization. Obfuscation serves neither the truth nor the Whole but (the ego's) particular interests. And the ego refuses to feel ashamed or unmasked. Only afterward, facing a shambles, do we ask serious questions about where exactly guilt arose.

6.6. The Myth of Paradise and the Fall

Mythologically speaking, the dynamics of sin began with Adam and Eve. This means that primordial fear, separation, and imprinting coincide with the emergence of subjecthood, generation after generation. They are part of the atmosphere into which the coming generations grow. The German word *erbsünde* (ancestral sin) implies our ancestral inheritance. In contrast, Latin *peccatum originale* (original sin), preserved in many other languages, emphasizes the separation from the origin. It is one of my basic claims that primordial fear, separation, and imprinting all manifest themselves in the human unconscious. They do so because they are part of an early inner process. Elsewhere I have spoken of a transformation of perception (in Renz 2015; Renz 2016).

Creation myths describe exactly this transformation, which becomes a formative shift—for instance, from *inside* Paradise to the *outside*, where toil ("By the sweat of your face," Genesis 3:19) and an indefinable sense of guilt prevail (Genesis 2:4b–3:24). Yet what lies between these two states: guilt, a fall or a physical reality? I believe it is simply a shift in perception, from being inside and whole to recognizing our subjecthood and its ego-centered perspective—"Then the eyes of both [i.e., Adam and Eve] were opened and they knew [i.e., recognized] that they were naked" (Genesis 3:7).

Nakedness expresses our essence—as one aspect of interpretation. In our primal and final state of being, we no longer wear clothes and attributes to adorn and disguise ourselves—also psychologically. Several dying patients have taught me that, at some point, nakedness is no longer a problem, just as it is not for small children. However, nakedness also stands for our creatureliness and dependence—as another aspect of interpretation. When we feel ashamed of our nakedness, we all of sudden become aware of ourselves: we are no longer unified/whole and unquestioned. Instead, we are separated, lost, lonely, and "naked" (this is *the first aspect of primordial fear*; chapter 4.2). In this respect, naked means feeling unprotected and lacking deeper value. Yet feeling ashamed also describes *the second aspect of primordial fear*: our deepest reaction after being frightened, after suddenly experiencing "oppositeness." We find this experience described in Genesis when Adam and Eve "hear" God approaching (against the wind) and hide. They can only experience this fear because they perceive God as opposite. Before and beyond separation, the numinous was/is no problem. Perception was nondual. As the myth of Adam and Eva tells us, this primal experience of God as an opposite is *acoustic*. As a music therapist, I have come to understand that *a totality of sound* may make the ego feel defenseless and exposed. Sometimes, a shiver may run down our spine, whether we are children or adults. Inside us, something freezes when we feel overwhelmed. This may, for instance, be the loud sound of a gong, at that very moment when we would be receptive. According to this (biblical) creation myth, separation—indeed, even projection—began at a very early stage of human development, with Adam and Eve. All of a sudden, God, as the Whole, is described (and perceived) as terrifying, as the force that ejects human beings from Paradise. This resembles a very old projection (see Renz 2017; Renz 2018). In its wake, we feel lost more than ever. Catapulted out of the nurturing Whole, we become disconnected. And, as the myth suggests, we now even feel "guilty." But why guilty? Because we had no other explanation for the misery that catapulted us out of Eden. Our culture's spiritual imprint seems to be that we feel guilt although there is in fact none. Less radical creation myths of other cultures suggest a smoother separation, a gradual slipping free from God or the Whole. One Indian creation myth describes this process as purely accidental (see Renz 2018, 33).

Nevertheless, even if I am focusing on the tragedy—that is, the separation—of early human and cultural development, this does not change the fact that, deeper down, God/

the Whole "affirms" (von Rad 1975) and "wills" human life and evolution. I even speak of *an urge within God* (chapter 10), of his ever-new empathic collaboration with the human being: God institutes himself time and again in our life. He uplifts, corrects, and moves us. This corrective dynamic already began with Adam and Eve, when God made them garments of skin for their harsh and shame-ridden life outside Eden.

6.7. Exodus under the Sign of Blessing

Biblically, a next stage of experience is *exodus* under the sign of blessing. This is an important *corrective experience*. In the Old Testament, the separation and exile described by the creation myth were soon followed by a positively connoted exodus: Abraham, our forefather, stands for God-willed isolation and the coming of the Self:

> Go from your country and your kindred and your father's house to the land that I will show you. I will make of you a great nation, and I will bless you, and make your name great, so that you will be a blessing. (Genesis 12:1–2)

The flight of those gathered around Moses from Egypt might bear a similar title. Exodus stands for human development, individuation, and calling under the sign of blessing. Characteristically, the Bible (both the Old and the New Testaments) never mentions a return to Paradise—unlike the Qur'an. The Catholic theologian Roman Siebenrock (personal communication) states, "One can only live life forward."

6.8. How Did Jesus Respond to Separation?

Jesus' entire message and love, his life and death, constitute an "interruption in separation/sin." In Jesus, God attempts "correction" and reorientation: Jesus' person and behavior brought a new dynamic. Behind many of his healings stands a primordial healing of finding our way home to the Father/Whole (chapter 5). Jesus' empathy, healing, and love stood opposed to separation. We may understand his talk of the Father, of the heavenly kingdom, and of the blissful state in a new light against the background of the separated human being and humanity. For it was precisely here that the mystic of Nazareth made us the following offer: mysticism, returning to our roots in the Father, and thus gaining a new connectedness and a new(?) capacity for love.

Yet Jesus did not demand that we simply return. At the same time, he encouraged exodus: he demanded that the disciples leave behind their families, abodes, and customs in order to follow him and be guided by him on their path. Most importantly, Jesus announced *metanoia*. This meant reversal, conversion, "turning inward"; an inner return and thus homecoming. Metanoia was *the* Jesuanic reply to separation. Because we have fallen out of the Whole and are alienated from the primal ground, we need reversal, homecoming. This is how we might best understand Jesus' call: return is not a moral imperative but a promise, a gift, and mysticism. Yet metanoia is oriented both backward to the Father and forward with him. Jesus wanted to tell us: you have the chance to interrupt separation and imprinting, to turn inward. His call for reversal tells us that when he began his proclamation he believed that he could reach people through reason. But reversal and healing still need to happen deeply: emotionally. Etymologically, reversal also meant an emotional path and inner return, a "change of heart" (see chapter 1).

6.9. Spiritual Practice: Departure, Reversal, Contemplation

What are the consequences for everyday spiritual practice, meditation, contemplation, and spiritual care?

Jesuanic spirituality provides those suffering from separation and alienation with answers. These include "dare to go forth, to return, to retreat, and to reflect." Mysticism/the

Father is open to all of us. Exodus, as the journey toward inner autonomy, may be necessary in terms of developmental psychology (Drewermann 1991, 484–501). C. G. Jung speaks of individuation and argues that the coming of the ego is followed by the coming of the Self. On this path, psychotherapy, pastoral care, and spiritual retreats can prove helpful (Grün 1980; Rutishauser 2011).

But what might the difficult concept of reversal mean *today*?

- It is about finding our way home, about returning to the primordial ground and our roots (figure 1, chapter 4.3). This happens as a movement backward but also forward—for instance, when we draw new hope from meaning and fulfillment, as we often do in illness and suffering.

- Metanoia involves feeling and mourning ("Blessed are those who mourn," Matthew 5:4; "Blessed are you who weep now," Luke 6:21). And opening: our encapsulation is broken open, thus enabling us to be touched in new ways. Reversal can become an initial experience, by making us realize that there is enough (food, nurture, connection with the kingdom of God, love) for everyone. This happens to us whenever we experience transcendence (Renz 2016).

- Metanoia occurs in gathering, concentration, and integration: what is divided comes together in a new way.

- Metanoia occurs through decision and affirmation. It raises basic questions: "What do I orient my life toward?" (Rahner 2005; Rahner 2006; Rutishauser 2011, 65). "Who is my Lord?" In our daily life, we are able take this decision. In the case of severely ill patients, decisions may *occur*. "*Yes—meaning*," as one dying patient stammered, summing up this phenomenon, after his daughter had thanked him for dying the way he did.

In all these respects, metanoia is also mysticism. We may allow ourselves to be given and need not always take action. Spiritual and therapeutic schools remind us to be simply present. What happens just now may guide us. Mindfulness and contemplation. In conclusion, then, I do not mean reversal that occurs under threat or under the burden of guilt. No, I see such an inner return as promise and loving devotion, even if it often involves discipline, distress, and shadow work. However, the goal of reversal is new (in)sight, new hearing, new fulfillment. Biblically speaking, we gain the kingdom of God/heaven.

CHAPTER 7
Jesus and Evil

7.1. Evil: The Sum of Split-Off Energies

Jesus confronted evil (e.g., demons, obsessions). But what exactly is evil? Does it belong to the Whole, to God, or to the world? Where and when did evil begin? Where does it end?

The Bible locates human depravity (and thus the influence of evil) already in very early human development (e.g., the human races before the Flood and Noah's ark, the Tower of Babel, Sodom and Gomorrha). We have wrestled with evil since time immemorial, seeking explanations for its sheer extent. One prevalent theological explanation is that the human being is endowed with freedom and should be blamed for everything. To reason and think in terms of guilt has become part of our cultural heritage. We automatically search for cause-effect relationships, and this ends in feeling guilty. We blame others and we are blamed ourselves. Another explanation was that the devil is evil personified. Not that this changes its nature: evil remains elusive, then and now. Simon Peng-Keller (2010, 37), a Swiss theologian and professor of spiritual care, has argued that evil is a "non-objectifiable reality, which has haunted and affected all of us, and which nobody is able to distance themselves from on their own." Thus if we mythologize, we obfuscate. Eugen Drewermann (1977) chose the title "Structures of Evil" for his three-volume work on the phenomenon.

Evil becomes palpable in fairy tales and dreams: as a creature living in a dark forest, as a bewitched figure, as Bluebeard, as Iron John at the bottom of the pond, as a witch (a figure sitting on a fence, a liminal figure), or as a nixie. Fairy tales and dreams suggest that evil is detached from the flow of life and ultimately seeks one thing alone: a connection with life. Severed from all development, evil strives to make contact with the nurturing and the creative, with everything that promises life and future. Both within us and, secretly, also through us. Like a parasite, evil seeks to set aside part of these resources for itself. This mechanism threatens us since evil confronts us with the boundless, faceless, and dissociated. This is illustrated by fairy tales, for instance, when a stranger promises to help a distressed father if he promises to hand over "the young thing that has just been born in your house." As a rule, this is the newborn, which epitomizes the future and the power of renewal. The child is meant to satisfy the connection that evil desires with life (e.g., "The Nix of the Mill-Pond"; see Grimm and Grimm 1992, 470–74).

On the other, dreams may, for instance, confront us with peripheral figures (addicts, oddballs, thieves, other suspicious types). In them, the overshadowed urges toward conscious realization but remains unintegrable.

Psychologically, we can understand evil as the energies that are split off from the Whole. In a certain sense, this view concurs with Thomas Aquinas' *privatio*, the process of "cutting oneself off." For Aquinas, evil arises from *privatio* and involves splitting, an unconscious dynamic, which also became a dynamism. I am speaking of evil deliberately in the singular, because we are dealing with an infinite *sum* of unconscious energies. These contrast with the bounded, with what has become conscious, with the individual. We can imagine evil as what is already shadowed or obscured in our cultural heritage, as what lies between and behind our thoughts. It is a vibrational, unconscious, energetic phenomenon (Renz 2018). It is intangible and yet present. It is a hodgepodge of energies that, as a result of millionfold separation processes, are split off, trapped, blocked, and so deeply taboo that they can only ever appear distorted. This mixture consists of "alienation phenomena that have grown collectively" (Heinz Angehrn, personal communication). It wreaks havoc, it blurs, it makes us driven—yet neither obviously nor consciously. It is instead hidden behind our projections, fantasies of omnipotence, and dissociations.

In this respect, I would like to introduce the term *split off*. As Mephisto exclaims in Goethe's *Faust*, "I am the spirit of perpetual negation!" (scene 6, line 1338). We do well not to brush evil aside. It is an energy that is detached from divine volition and that acts "autonomously."

Yet does evil, in spite of all these dangers, ultimately rest on God? Is it also part of the Whole? If we take seriously the statement about God as the all-encompassing Whole, we must answer yes. In the end, evil will be (re)solved. Thus we need to think in terms of a tremendous process of gaining consciousness. In considering evil, I attempt to clarify neither its ontological status, nor its right to exist. What is crucial, however, is not only *how* but also *the fact* that evil is *experienced*. Human experience is perhaps our best chance of capturing the reality of evil in words. Many of us experience evil as a troubled state of arousal, as raging anger, as being seized by some violent force. We experience this power, which is itself impersonal, almost as a person. It dominates us. For instance, my dying patient's desperate wife was beside herself. She was virtually incited by something strange, by "evil." However, not only she but also I or anybody can suddenly feel governed by despair, by greed, by envy, by a need for revenge. In this state, we are perceived as "beside" or alienated from ourselves, as "out of our minds." If we look back at occasions when we were prompted by aggression (or were totally paralyzed), we are often unable to explain our behavior. We even struggle to become conscious of our motivation.

We need to distinguish evil from the vulnerable and emotionally unstable human being. Nobody is *a priori* evil, yet we all are sometimes driven or even obsessed. Evil acts autonomously. It tries to force its way into us ("I feel possessed," "It got the better of me," "It numbed me"). Whenever it finds a way of entering us, evil overcomes and takes hold of our soul. This is more likely to happen in a crisis, when deep wounds act as trigger points, when we are drifting through life spiritually impoverished, depressed, or unaware. Biblically speaking, evil seeks to enter us when we are in the wilderness (see the temptation of Jesus) or live in funerary caves (see the "possessed man" of Gerasa).

> *A pastoral carer had the following dream: "I am translating the Gospel of Matthew. Then the scene changes. I see my workplace: a beautiful, though empty room, with an opening as large as a trapdoor, which typically enough is called a 'leak' in the dream. New, faceless people keep entering the room through the opening. A man stands at the opening and says that it shouldn't be allowed to exist. I must first chase these people away before I can use the room for a meeting and repair the leak. But I will never be able to plug it completely. I must be on my guard."*

Is this dream a modern version of Matthew's account of the uninhabited house? Is it about "leaks" in our unconscious? Let us consider the corresponding biblical passage:

> When the unclean spirit has gone out of a person [Luther translates this as "ausgefahren," which means the spirit forcefully left him], it wanders through the wilderness looking for a resting place, but it finds none. Then it says: "I will return to my house from which I came." When it comes, and finds it empty, swept, and put in order [i.e., it looks like an invitation to come in, and is not already filled by the Lord], then it goes and brings along seven other spirits more evil than itself, and they enter and live there; and the last state of that person is worse than the first.... (Matthew 12:43–45)

7.2. Jesus Heals the Obsessed

Why should a book about Jesus also consider evil? Well, because *he* was able to confront evil. He knew intuitively about human vulnerability, about leaks and their causes, and about the difficulty of living in a spiritual home constantly threatened by intrusion. No one knew how to banish demons better than Jesus: he recognized, unmasked, and cast out demons and other evil spirits. He possessed more than the mere "skills" needed to handle these forces.

What does it mean that Jesus *healed* those who were possessed by demons? What does possession mean? The Catholic theologian Joachim Gnilka (2010, 226) has suggested that the idea of so many demonic possessions at the time of Jesus articulated "threats and fears in mythical language." Possession is indeed about mythical language, though not simply about fears but about *being driven* by outside forces. We certainly need to take the term *possessed*—and perhaps even the dimension of being cursed—seriously. According to Gnilka (2010, 223), *demons can cause illnesses* (e.g., the young boy who is seized by a spirit that leaves him speechless, Mark 9:14–27). Yet they may also literally *inhabit* a person (e.g., the possessed man of Gerasa, Luke 8:26–39; I have interpreted this story in Renz 2017). Jesus coped without much ado with both: the effects of demons and their existence.

In the Bible, *healing* often follows a similar course. First, the situation is described. Then, the evil spirit is cast out. In most cases, though, Jesus did not speak with the possessed but directly and authoritatively with the demon. He commanded the evil spirit that had seized a man in the synagogue of Capernaum to "be silent, and come out of him!" (Luke 4:31–37). In another case, he "threatened" the unclean spirit (Luke 9:37–43a). Or he cast out "the demon that was mute" (Luke 11:14). Jesus' words and actions are unequivocal and spoken out of a supreme authority. Nevertheless, the process does not end with exorcising evil. In a third step, the demon-possessed human soul must be turned toward God and toward a life that must be lived out of this (inner) center. In general, the healing procedure happens through relationship and on the level of relationship. When the healed are again deeply related, they are capable of facing reality. They can now be resocialized: the previously possessed half-dead boy is lifted up, taken by the hand, and returned to the Father. Some of the healed were advised not to return to their former surroundings, while others had to "confess" and go to the priest (chapter 5).

Throughout, Jesus' instructions attest to his profound knowledge of *dealing with taboos*. He distinguished taboo-breaking from the afflicted: he banished inscrutable powers and subsequently reintegrated the stigmatized into the community. Metaphorically speaking, Jesus illuminated the darkness that envelops a taboo and delivered the possessed individual from evil—which is indeed a redemptive act. Thus he represents light, the process of attaining consciousness (see below, chapter 10). Representing the light of rising consciousness, Jesus and his work were not only welcome but also feared. He became taboo himself, and in some cases was asked to leave a town or a region (Luke 8:26–39).

7.3. Conscious Realization: Jesus versus Demons

The concept of demons in the gospels is based on the later Old Testament and on early Jewish apocalypticism (Söding 2003, 519–49). Not only the development of Judaism but also Persian and Egyptian influences established distinct ideas about demons: evil spirits determined apocalypticism, demonized the world and history, and dualistically opposed God and his host of angels. Demons were said to come from fallen angels. Evil spirits were the absconded souls of the slain giants, themselves hybrid creatures, half divine (fallen angels), half human (Genesis 6:1–4; the Ethiopian Book of Enoch).[1]

Jesus was shaped by the early Jewish idea of demons, though not only. His worldview was neither purely dualistic, nor simply the result of his socialization. Instead, his whole *person* stands for the divine. He could deal with evil; he saw through the demons and cast them out. Therein lies the deeper meaning of Jesus' words: he is said to have broken Satan's rule (see chapter 3; Luke 10:18; Luke 11:20).

Archimedes, the Greek mathematician and physicist (287–212 BC) who discovered the lever principle, is supposed to have said, "Give me a lever and a place to stand and I will move the earth."[2] The Archimedean point is a theoretical "absolute vantage point," a fulcrum situated outside an experimental arrangement. It has long entered philosophy. Human beings sometimes search for an absolute point of reference. Jesus found such a point: *in the Father* and *in his connectedness with the Father*. He came to represent what can "unhinge" Satan, the "lord" of darkness and ruler of the world (John 12:31, 14:30). His ability was related to his mystical connectedness with the Father, from whom Jesus knew, based on his experience that a final victory over evil stems inherently from him. Jesus, moreover, participated in God's victory.

Interestingly, the unclean spirits and demons were the first to tell Jesus, "You are the Holy One of God" (Luke 4:34); "You are the Son of God!" (Luke 4:41). Thus, demons are somehow close to divine reality. Because they recognized Jesus, we need to place these forces on a similar spiritual level as Jesus. Unlike us mortals, evil spirits belong to a spiritual dimension, as we learn from the narrative framing the didactic tale in Job: "One day the sons of God came to present themselves before the Lord, and Satan also came among them" (Job 1:6). Yet demons do not represent substance but its opposite: the insubstantial, the ill-spirited, the nonperson, and the unperson. Demons are faceless bearers of energy. Simon Peng-Keller (2010, 37) quite rightly speaks of the "facelessness and anonymity of demons." Jesus, by contrast, was a "person." He had a profile, a human identity.

As I have mentioned, he lived very consciously. He represented and still represents the realization of consciousness (see the metaphor of light in the Prologue to the Gospel of John; chapter 10). This attribute—being conscious—explains both his superiority in his encounters with demons as well as their peculiar reaction to him (e.g., Luke 4:34; Luke 4:41). Like a quantum leap, *Jesus embodied and promoted the coming of consciousness in human development.* He left behind the old imprinting within humankind and himself became a new spiritual path. He also enabled us to become conscious. Yet *how* does this mystery of becoming conscious work? What exactly did Jesus do?

First of all, Jesus lived in a special relationship with God. He allowed himself to become aware—even of God as the ultimate taboo. Instead of trivializing, marginalizing, and reducing the numinous, he received God/the Whole. For Jesus, God, the highest power, was never "too much" or too close. I would like to illustrate this metaphorically: the sun was neither too hot for him nor to close to him. Thus God never represented the slightest taboo for Jesus, who was not subject to the patterns of separation. This enabled Jesus to bring light into darkness—for example, the human shadow.

A second aspect is Jesus' intuition. He intuitively exposed demons and their negative energies. He realized that evil transcends and undermines us, just as he knew intuitively that demons occupy and possess people. Evil encompasses more than individual human failure (although we should not downplay the human capacity for true guilt). Evil catches up with our weak points and literally "overpowers" us. Still, it is inherently tragic and remains locked outside. It has no chance of ever attaining a face, an identity, and thus a *raison d'*être. Yet Jesus knew. He saw through. He was thus not only able to heal the possessed (see chapters 5.4–5.6; 7.2) but also bring evil into light—to bring evil "home to the Father," where its energies can be neutralized and turned into positive energy.

We can understand evil as the opposite of becoming and being conscious. It has neither name nor identity. In early Jewish demonology, demons could not be named, for fear of invoking them. In the gospels, demons have no names, except Beelzebub, "the ruler of the demons" (Luke 11:14–23). Or, for instance, the possessed Gerasene (Luke 8:26–39) calls himself "Legion." This name does not express any particular identity but refers to the multitude that wishes to remain anonymous and thus unrecognized.[3] I interpret this as meaning that demons seem to resist recognition and naming (i.e., identification). They simply *refuse* to leave the secret zone. Rather, they hide behind anonymity, wreaking havoc in the dark taboo zone. They obstruct the attaining of consciousness in individual and collective maturation processes.

We struggle to perceive our own inscrutable motivations not only because we are indolent and weak but also because irrational forces prevent us from seeing things clearly. When we see this in others, we might say, "Oh, well, he keeps downplaying things" or "You know, she keeps creating new bearers of her projections."

Jesus attacked and unmasked evil. He spoke and acted in broad daylight, which may also represent the light of becoming conscious. And he demanded his disciples to follow his example:

> What I say to you in the dark, tell in the light; and what you hear whispered, proclaim from the housetops. Do not fear those who kill the body but cannot kill the soul; rather fear him who can destroy both soul and body in hell." (Matthew 10:27–28)

In this book, I discuss the claim that Jesus embodied, represented, and supported the coming of consciousness on several occasions (see chapters 1, 9, and 10). But why is conscious realization so important? Why is it even redemptive, indeed cathartic? What do we become conscious of? And in which context? In itself, the talk of "deliverance from sin or evil" is unintelligible. We must instead first gain a psychological understanding of the origin of evil and how energies work.

7.4. Splitting and Projection

Energies can, in general, serve two different goals: they can be part of the Whole, or stand apart; they can serve the Whole, or not. Thus they serve the ego and are split off from God as the Whole. Even if the evil was originally part of God, it was split off. This happened during human separation (see chapter 6). And vice versa: we became separated as a result of evil dynamism. Evil thus involves *splitting* and *projection* (due to disaffiliation, dissociation, splitting off). Like separation, evil results from prehistoric development.

The origin of evil:

The growing focus on the ego and its egocentric perspective in prehistoric human development meant that "something" was split off and "forgotten": the view of the Whole, indeed Wholeness itself, and our original experience of the Whole. The Whole was lost and went irrevocably missing. Mythologically speaking, the gates of Paradise were protected by a flaming sword. Every further dynamic and development were determined not only by what was desired but also by taboo, curse, and overshadowing—ultimately, then, by evil. Even if we interpret the flaming sword *positively* (von Rad 1975), that future humans should be protected against their experience of the numinous, something was nevertheless split off in our cultural prehistory at this point. Theologically, we began to come to terms with guilt (see Koelle 2015, 262–75).

Splitting and *splitting off* may help us understand evil. In its psychological meaning, the splitting mechanism is older and more encompassing than repression on its own. It arose *before the ego existed*, which would have been able to repress the negative forces. *Evil* and deeper down *God as the experience of the numinous Whole* could never become conscious. Our primordial fear stands in between and prevents us from experiencing the numinous. *Splitting* is a powerful word. It implies exclusion and taboo. What we feared primordially is excluded—that is, our earliest feelings of loss and our earliest impressions of facing an opposite (see chapter 4.2). In further human development, all those aspects that could have triggered primordial fear also remained locked outside: the excessive, the Dionysian, the sexual, the chaotic; the archaic, the distorted, the nauseating, and the corresponding bodily reactions (e.g., allergies, shivers, goose bumps) or intense emotions (e.g., envy, anger, hatred, and revenge). All of these aspects (and also others) have been taboo-laden since our earliest times.

In sum, what is split off is subsumed under the "undifferentiated mass." It continues to live—or rather to ghost—"menacingly in the underground." And it may develop into evil. Psychologically, splitting results in a severing of consciousness and the unconscious. We are unable to return to a state before the split.

The splitting mechanism is often intensified by *projection* (e.g., in the Fall, God becomes a supposedly violent and wrathful power). We are barely able to understand this mechanism. Yet it becomes acutely tangible, for instance, in the perpetrators and in the victims of wars and of sexual abuse: to continue living, those affected by such trauma must completely *shut out* their experiences, the evildoers, and often even the traumatic circumstances. Yet what was unbearable, still is. The result is a split (i.e., dissociated) personality. Germany's *vergangenheitsbewältigung* (coming to terms with the past) affects a first, a second, and a third post-Shoah generation (Koelle 2015). Another site of this split is the family drama: children only know the "good" attachment figure (children from broken homes sometimes also have an inflated, positive image of their parents). As a consequence of splitting, the terror of evil ravages uncontrollably in our unconscious. The dynamics continue: we even keep our shadow parts away from ourselves. In extreme cases of trauma, the split person has two sides. One side knows nothing about the other.

> *Splitting off is illustrated, for instance, by the dream-image of a fifty-five-year-old patient. She dreamed about her doctor, whom she had doubts about also in reality. In the dream, she saw him smoking shisha all the time, even when he was examining patients. Yet even more disturbingly, he was neither himself anymore nor alone: above his face and beside him stood two dragon heads. The animals smoked even more than the doctor and made sure he continued smoking without noticing what he was doing.*

Etymologically, the dragon stems from Greek δέρκομαι, "to see clearly, to glance dartingly." This recalls the earliest sense of confrontation and oppositeness. Dragons symbolize what triggers the second aspect of primordial fear (chapter 4.2). In the above dream, the first aspect of primordial fear is evident as addiction. What has been cut off is subsequently desired even more strongly. It is like a vicious circle: both aspects of primordial fear (forlornness and threat) are split off and constantly reproduced—intrapsychically and in group dynamics (see chapter 7.6). After her dream, this woman was prepared to encounter "two persons" in her doctor: one whom she knew and needed, one whom she had to reject.

7.5. Topography of the Unconscious II: The Split Human Being

In dissociated individuals, the nascent ego (the emerging pyramid) is split from its primal ground (see figures 2 and 3 in contrast to figure 1). Over the course of human history, this crack widened into a gap (chapter 2), an inner vacuum, which attracted outside influences.

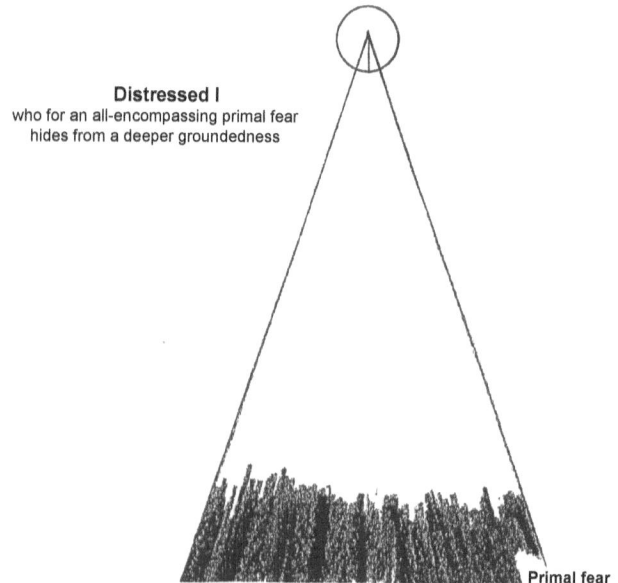

Distressed I
who for an all-encompassing primal fear
hides from a deeper groundedness

Primal fear

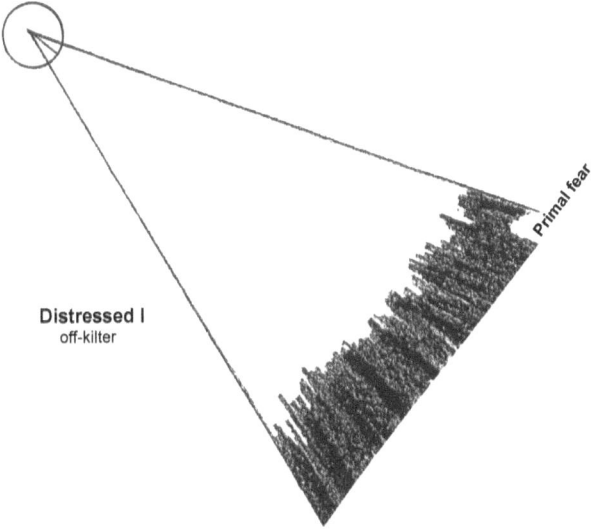

Splitting occurred very early, before the ego was consolidated. This meant that the ego now became determined by outside forces. It was forced to emerge under cursed conditions and became a "distress-ego." This term was coined by Erich Neumann, the German-Jewish psychologist and a student of C. G. Jung. Considering the structure of the human soul, Neumann spoke of a *more or less intact ego-Self axis* (see figure 1, chapter 4.3). For the unfortunate case, he coined the term "distress-ego" (Neumann 1988, 77). This ego stands on unstable ground, which provides too little support and nurturing (see figures 2 and 3). All of us have experienced both:

an ego *and* a distress-ego. Both are reflected in the psychic layers in our unconscious.

Whenever I need to better understand a person's biography and personality, whenever I seek to empathize with others, I think in terms of psychic layers: more recent impressions (e.g., school experiences) have laid themselves upon older ones (e.g., feelings during infancy). In chapter 4, I have tried to describe "a topography of the unconscious." Figure 1 (chapter 4.3) shows that while the ego is mostly separated from its primal ground and shaken by primordial fear, it still stands upon the Whole. Such an ego is *not entirely split off*. It is still capable of a loose connection, with the Whole and with its own hidden primordial trust.

Yet in the condition of dissociation and splitting off we are no longer able to restore any contact with what has become dissociated or alienated. What has been split off is no longer accessible to the ego. Like biblical demons, the dissociated must exist namelessly. Even our sense of a primal ground and safe origin can then be split off—that is, become taboo. This means that God/the Whole as the original *experience* moves into the distance, as suggested by Leibniz's deistic image of the watchmaker-God or that of the unearthly distant ruler. Or, vice versa, images of God reveal a trivialized, harmless, "affectionate God."

In my daily practice as an end-of-life carer, I sometimes face extreme cases of dissociation, patients who are affected by previously unconscious or tabooed guilt. They lack an inner responsible authority and the strength of personality to want goodness and reject evil. They move, anonymously, amid the crowd without ever becoming conscious. They do as others do. Near death, some nevertheless become capable of maturation:

> *In a very alert moment, one dying woman said that she didn't deserve to have children who had turned out so well. "Why don't you deserve your children," I asked. She replied that she had often been wicked and had made her children suffer. This evil streak overcame her, for instance, when she was taking a shower in the mornings, as if she were possessed. After a moment's silence, she added, "If Jesus were still alive, I would have asked him to (literally) deliver me from this state of possession." This was, she added, probably related to her sad and difficult childhood.*

7.6. Splitting and Mobbing

Splitting also occurs *in the collective*. Not only individuals but also collectives can be more or less conscious or unconscious. If enough individuals dare to strike out alone and take responsibility, this promotes consciousness in the collective. These individuals will also be able to influence how the collective approaches shadow themes. By contrast, a large number of unconscious hangers-on may turn the group into a crowd, which will (typically) easily allow itself to be carried away. This "crowd effect" provides repressed or taboo-laden energies with their main point of access. The crowd is susceptible to idols, trends, and atmospheres, and thus also to tantalizing, paralyzing, and disquieting forces.

Interestingly, the Greek New Testament distinguishes between the crowd or throng (*o`o;cloj* / *ho ochlos*, "the unconscious multitude"; e.g., Luke 4:28–30) and "the people" (*o` lao,j* / *ho laos*). The latter term also denotes those who gather and orient themselves toward their God and his guidance. At the time, it also meant the Jewish people and the eldest. This distinction makes psychological sense: the undifferentiated mass, with its unconscious thought patterns and behavior, can be manipulated by group dynamics (e.g., ganging up and rivalry, dissociated envy, stigmatization, and exclusion). Fanaticism, class and race struggles, witch hunts, and vendettas take effect in an unthinking mass of people and may also extend deep into public and ecclesiastical institutions. The masses are incapable of gaining consciousness on their own, or only to the extent that public knowledge progresses.

If we belong to the multitude, we constantly face two perennial questions:

1. Am I involved? Am I part of things? Am I liked or not? Am I "in" or out?

2. Do I appeal to others? Am I "hot"? Am I coveted in the group or despised? Am I someone or no one?

One of my patient's husbands recently asked me, "What is bad about such group behavior?" He wanted to understand the nature of demons and evil—also within himself and in his surroundings. I replied that continuing to live in the crowd stifles individuation, even if we are never able to know from the outside when exactly a congenial, creative dynamic changes into its ominous opposite. Just as we are unable to know when possessiveness or greed begins. We can, however, question ourselves. And we can observe and reflect on undesirable collective tendencies—for instance, toward eventism, constant availability and connectivity (via mobile telephones), extreme sports, or craving fun and entertainment. Nevertheless, we can still love life and its creativity.

The husband mentioned above then asked me, "Aren't these symptoms and tendencies caused by formative influences, stress, depression, or hormonal changes?" Once more,

I shirked a general(izing) answer. It is impossible to determine what can be attributed to individual instability or early imprinting and what, in contrast, arises from diffuse energies to the point of evil. Nevertheless, it makes sense if we consider evil to be real, at least in principle. We might define evil as a power that has become autonomous. Thus the *individual* is not simply a perpetrator but also a victim; nor is the *group* diabolical per se, but also vulnerable ("the spirit indeed is willing, but the flesh is weak," Matthew 26:41; see also Paul's Epistle to the Romans 7:18–25; Galatians 5:17). We need to be cautious instead of naive in dealing with the zeitgeist and collective dynamics. Group dynamics become problematic long before they degenerate into violence, which happens when certain behavioral patterns spread in a collective (e.g., an absolute craving for power, marginalization, derision, etc.). Today, such patterns begin in kindergarten. In human history, they began in primitive tribal feuds. That is, whenever our ego, our kin, or our clan needs to empower itself.

In terms of group dynamics, it is normal for an idol, a hero, or a king to become prominent, while the foreign, the weak, or the genius is ousted. Further, *separation follows the pattern of mimesis*: one becomes the coveted, the other the denigrated object. Collective processes work archaically—that is, in terms of association, representation, and surrogacy.

One becomes the hero and represents the ego or the group that needs strengthening (note the king's importance in ancient Israel, or the pharaoh's in ancient Egypt). The other becomes an outsider or is branded a failure. Either through his or her own fault or often accidentally, for instance, due to certain physical traits such as being particularly beautiful or ugly.

Which collective patterns were important at the time and in the society of Jesus? First, *revenge or blood feud*, as an archaic reaction to wrongdoing and injury; second, *scapegoating*—that is, casting out one's shadows and burdens. Over the course of human history, the first pattern (blood feud) had become more and more restricted long before Jesus, as in the Babylonian laws (ca. 2000 BCE) or later in Leviticus 24:20 ("an eye for an eye, a tooth for a tooth"). This meant that one could not avenge oneself *more* than the harm one had suffered. Jesus raised collective awareness of the absurdity of revenge and contrasted this archaic pattern with another: "If anyone strikes you on the right cheek, turn the other also" (Matthew 5:38–39; see also chapter 9).

The second pattern, the scapegoat mechanism, also follows the archaic principles of surrogacy ("one for all") and representation (the hero/king for the whole people). It turns an individual (the scapegoat) into a bearer of projections, upon whose back a whole group is "relieved" of its wrongdoing or guilt. Animal sacrifice (chapter 9) is one expression of such thinking. In the rite, it is an animal; in semiconscious group dynamics, it is a more or less random human victim, an outsider, a weak person, or an especially strong person, whose exceptional autonomy and mental power sets them apart from the rest. Such scapegoats made their opponents gang up on them (e.g., Pilate and Herod, Luke 23:12). They bring about catharsis in the whole group, which experiences a shift of energy that can barely be underestimated: the group's otherwise diffuse potential aggression is channelled and catalyzed (e.g., "I can be angry at him without exposing myself; I can explain my anger because everyone is angry at her").[4] Indirectly, this pattern also maintains community-establishing rules and taboos (e.g., the prohibition of certain images of God, concepts of purity at the time of Jesus). Moreover, it obfuscates: guilt does not become conscious and verbalized as it would through understanding, remorse, or conscious realization.

Yet Jesus behaved quite differently. He got along with those on the edge of society. He saw through collective mechanisms of ostracism, revenge, and annihilation. In the end, he even accepted being made a bearer of projections. But was he a scapegoat (chapter 9.2)?

It is always exceptional individuals and courageous and thoughtful persons, as well as solidarity movements, that challenge the absurdity of dissociation, revenge, or scapegoating, and thus the resulting dependence of individuals on group dynamics. Such autonomous individuals and communities give the collective dynamics of mimesis and stigmatization a new direction—namely, toward the attainment of consciousness. They initiate decades- or even centuries-long reconciliation processes and coming to terms with the past. These processes are aimed at revealing the long-term effects of discrimination, slavery, and other taboo-laden histories and guilt. They mark the beginning of a new spiritual path and other forms of togetherness. Such outsiders, however, have a difficult position—not only at the time of Jesus but also today.

To *overcome dissociation*, we need not only exodus and inner autonomy but also a long path of integration: we must accept and endure contrariness, unresolved issues, and polarities over a long period of time. In the Old Testament, our forefather Jacob already took this path. He had to learn to deal with his shadow in a new way and to face his hostile brother Esau.[5] By taking a circuitous route, one day he experienced *kairos*, a turning point: his time was mature enough for a new departure (see the modern phrases, "time is up," "the bad dream is over"). Esau rushed toward his brother, embraced him, and they both wept (Genesis 33:4). When whole groups take this path, they consist of several self-responsible individuals with strong personalities who unite and gather around a common cause.

7.7. Spiritual Practice: Vigilance, Shadow Work, Strength of Personality, Creativity, Gathering

What are the consequences for everyday spiritual practice, meditation, contemplation, and spiritual care? What does spirituality comprise in Jesus' sense if we consider the abysses of evil?

Various schools of psychotherapy and spiritual practices (e.g., Sigmund Freud, C. G. Jung, Stanislav Grof, Dalai Lama, Richard Rohr, Franz Jalics) have developed their own concepts of evil. Psychologically, confronting evil is about becoming conscious. It involves encountering the deeply shadowed contents of our soul (e.g., repressed envy). Formulated as a spiritual challenge, tackling evil means to consciously approach temptations. This involves spiritual discernment ("the distinction of spirits"; see Peng-Keller 2010, 35–36). When and to what extent do I say yes? When exactly do I say no? Spiritual teachers speak of enticement, catharsis, and passing the tests of life. Spiritually, dealing with evil is about recognizing spirits for what they are (e.g., greed, boredom, escapism) and letting them pass by (Grün 1980). Both (psychotherapeutic and spiritual) schools agree that we can never integrate evil on our own. Unlike personal shadow aspects, evil overwhelms us. We must take it seriously rather than make light of it or allow fear to paralyze us. If we are trapped in evil and dynamism, we need redemption (chapters 8, 9, and 10; see also Renz 2017). How then should we deal with evil? What did Jesus teach us in this respect? Below are five spiritual qualities that constitute *a spirituality based on Jesus*:

1. *Vigilance.* This is about discernment. Jesus' call for vigilance pervades the New Testament (Matthew 24:42, 25:13; Mark 13:35, 37; Acts 20:31; 1 Corinthians 16:13; Ephesians 6:18; Colossians 4:2; 1 Peter 5:8). Behind this call—and following Jesus' example—we must also recognize the need to become conscious. Translated into our present times, vigilance also includes rejecting destructiveness.

2. *Shadow work.* To become conscious, we must look into our own abyss as far as possible. Becoming conscious is opposed to repression and distraction. Even Jesus experienced spiritual darkness, for instance, in the story of temptation, at Gethsemane, and, as we may gather from the Lord's Prayer, also in general. He withstood by praying.

3. *Strength of personality*, as against remaining entangled in an unconscious, "mass" atmosphere. A strong personality enables us to remain fearless. This idea is far from naive, but necessary to avoid falling under the spell of evil or negativity. When he was confronted by demons, Jesus was not afraid because he knew that *God is stronger* than the dark forces. God, or in fact a corresponding concept of God, allows us to "believe and trust" (Rutishauser 2011, 65) despite omnipresent evil. Beyond that, we can also entrust ourselves to Jesus, as the one who defied evil. One of his exemplary reactions to the angry crowd occurred after he had read from the scripture in the synagogue:

> When they heard this, all in the synagogue were filled with rage. They got up, drove him out of the town, and led him to the brow of the hill on which the town was built, so that they might hurl him off the cliff. But he passed through the midst of them and went on his way. (Luke 4:28–30)

4. *Creativity*. Astonishingly perhaps, but creativity is the most important anthropological answer to tension, suffering, and evil. Music, art, literature, the expansion of knowledge and research have shaped history as much

as evil has. Every work of art transcends suffering, and only this makes it art. In creativity, some of the previously formless energy—including the inscrutable and the tabooed—takes shape and finds expression. What about Jesus, though? He was neither a musician nor a writer. And yet his message is original and ingenious. Jesus transcended the patterns and customs of his time. His source of trust and creativity was the Father. This is exactly what this book aims to show: *we must see Jesus as profoundly creative, as a mystic.* The emergence of his message was a highly creative process. His concept of self, of the world, and of God is a creative answer to evil.

5. *Identity and gathering (in consciousness).* Jesus distinguished evil (demons), which he rejected, from human beings, whom he cared about. In contrast to members of the crowd, those who gain a new identity become recentered and are hence able to gather among equals around Jesus as a spiritual path. Jesus said, "For when two or three are gathered in my name, I am there among them" (Matthew 18:20).

Taken together, these five qualities describe the *process of becoming conscious*. On our spiritual path, we are called to follow Jesus. At the same time, we can rely on him. He was a groundbreaker and paved our way. The *inner Jesus* is an even greater resource for many of us—like the severely ill—who are often no longer capable of an active presence of mind.

In the next chapter, I consider Jesus' most important answer to evil: love. For it is ultimately love that overcomes evil (and within love lies the mystery of God). But what kind of love?

CHAPTER 8

Jesus, the Father, and Love

8.1. Love That Liberates Us

Is there love that leaves us truly free? Love occurs between free agents, voluntarily, and involves great inner freedom. If it does not, it is not true love.

Is there any religion that leaves us truly free? Unless we seek and find religion out of our own free will, it will be neither liberating nor wholesome nor salvific. Because unless we are free, we will not become "centered"—or in Jesus' words, we will not become connected with the "Father." Despite centuries-long malpractice, religion is not about a struggle for power and authority. It is not about inhibition or prohibition, but about connection and reconnection.

Yet how can we be free if we are attached? We become free if what binds us, and what we are bound to, is so compelling, so magnificent or tender, that it attracts and touches us. Religion is/would be that kind of attachment that, if we live within and with it, breaks open the narrow categories of human thought and feeling. Just imagine God in this image: our connectedness with God, and thus God *himself*, surmounts our fears and narrow-mindedness. God *himself* opens us up and liberates us to ourselves, to our essence. Precisely this idea captures my working assumption in this book: the Father about whom Jesus speaks, but also Yahweh, who gave Moses the law, and further also the Whole/God, is the life-giving, nurturing, original, and ultimate power. In him and with him we can live truly free, unshackled. This is the major concern of Old Testament covenant theology. It is also Jesus' main concern, as becomes clear in the tale of the lost son, the "parable of the Father's love" (Ernst 1993, 340):

> Jesus tells the story of a father and his two sons (Luke 15:11–32). The younger son asked the father for his share of the property, traveled to a distant country, and squandered his share "in dissolute living." A famine occurred in the country, and the young man was hard up (Luther translated this as "he began to suffer want and starve" *auvto.j h*; *rxato u`sterei/sqai*; Luke 15:14). The lost son sought the help of one of the citizens of that country, who sent him to feed the pigs on his fields (*tou.j avgrou.j auvtou/ / tous agrous autou*). He would gladly have filled himself with the pods that the pigs were eating; but no one gave him any. Then he took stock of himself, packed

his things, and returned to his father. The father saw him approach from afar and had pity on him. He ran toward his son, embraced and kissed him. The son said, "Father, I have sinned against heaven and before you; I am no longer worthy to be called your son" (Luke 15:18–19). But the father had one of his slaves bring the best robe. He put a ring on his son's finger and gave him shoes for his feet. The fatted calf was slaughtered. And they began to celebrate.

This father's love is touching. It grants his son freedom, at first even to the point of extravagance and dire need. It also determines the atmosphere of the son's homecoming. The son receives pity, compassion, plenitude, celebration—and, which deserves special mention, *appreciation* (the best robe, the ring). Yet which love, which riches, which celebration, which level of experience or psychic layer does this story touch on? This question strikes me as crucial with regard to the elder son, who had stayed at home with his father and had worked hard in the fields. He grows angry and refuses to join the festivities, "to go in" (Greek: *eivselqei/n*). Because, as he exclaims, "For all these years I have been working like a slave for you, and I have never disobeyed your command; yet you have never given me a young goat so that I might celebrate with my friends" (Luke 15:29).

The story tells us that what matters is not achievement and property (having), nor measuring and being measured, nor earthly justice and morality. The theme of pig-tending points to a deeper psychic layer, one where the young man already "knows" about the existence, affiliation, and participation he is granted (in the Whole). The younger son's inner return (i.e., reversal; see chapter 6.8) already begins when he feels hungry while tending the pigs (i.e., when he becomes aware of his own need, of the gap within himself; when he is touched by his longing). He realizes that even the animals are better off. This realization expresses a profound crisis in his self-esteem. Symbolically, although shepherds are male, tending is a caring, motherly activity.

Symbolically, the *pig*[1] also suggests that the tale of the lost son is about earthy experience.[2] The pods (that the pigs were eating) also fit into this context: no one gives the young man any. Arguably, however, he does not take any himself, which would be an obvious thing for a starving person to do. Is he unable to grant himself this food amid his confidence crisis? His crisis is also a deep regression. Thus it is typical that when we are no longer capable of self-care (looking after ourselves), we return to infant-like, earthy experience. In this deep psychic layer, we can only be given. The alternative lies deeper down: we are either connected (i.e., fed) or disconnected (i.e., we starve).

"Returning home" to this inner, psychic layer, and experiencing overflowing (fatherly and motherly) love, heals and nurtures every starving, lost soul. The biblical story of the father and his sons seems to be about this spiritual reality, about returning to a fundamental participation in the Whole. The son (and also we) hear the message: "You are allowed to be and live. You belong and are welcome. There is 'plenty.'" Because he is reconnected with the Whole, the returning son can live as a free man, and not as a slave, in his father's house. Jürgen Habermas (2001, 6) states that God can determine the human being in the sense "in that He at once both releases and compels man to freedom." At the beginning of the parable, the younger son may have unconsciously been driven by such a "destiny." Out of his unconsciousness, he finds his way via a circuitous route—how else?—to conscious sonship, to a life of freedom.

What about the elder son? He remains outside. The father tries to gather him into the fold, too. He comes "out" to meet him (Greek: *evxelqw.n*) and makes a magnificent promise: "My child, you are always with me, and all that is mine is yours" (Luke 15:31). Uttered so directly, this promise is addressed only to the elder son. It is great even if it requires the son's loyalty. Yet the elder son does not understand his father's words. He is unable to relate the promise to himself. Has he not yet arrived inwardly at the place of celebration?

Or is he, in contrast to his brother, so disconnected when he returns home that he simply cannot understand such a promise? Did it express a state that he has never consciously made contact with? Has he remained too unconscious while remaining at home with his father? This would imply that he has never considered his family and its habits from an external perspective. He envies his younger brother. In terms of our world, this is quite natural. I also would feel jealous. But according to this particular father, there is no reason for the elder son to be jealous. Why not?

The father thinks in the category of being, his elder son in that of having. The father thinks in terms of self-evident participation and eschatological celebration, whereas his son argues in terms of right and wrong, performance and merit. These two levels are incomparable. Thus father and son talk at crossed purposes. The elder son seems to lack a crucial experience (individuation, finding his center, reconnection). He suffers from a hardened soul and unsettled scores. This state of mind separates him from his father's fullness. No earthly justice can heal the son's sense of shortcoming. What he needs, instead, is that great love that nurtures and helps him overcome his pain. And *this* is precisely how his father reacts to his son's need: lovingly, indeed endearingly. His words "My child" are crucial, because the parable otherwise consistently uses the word *son* (*ui`o,j / uios*). In ancient

Greek, "my child" (*te,knon* / *teknon*) is a term of love and endearment, which a parent used when they spoke to a child between the age of six and eight. We should imagine a gentle tone of voice, intent on conveying one feeling in particular to the child: "I love you." To this day, we can once feel again our inner child if we receive such love and gentleness. We find our way out of our hard shell and the armor we have surrounded ourselves with. We become open, receptive. The end of the elder son's story has probably not yet been written. Will he, too, find his way home?

Our experience of being loved, nurtured, and considered a free human being reaches deeper than any demanded virtuousness. Yet, in this light, how might we interpret the key commandment of Christianity?

8.2. The Commandment of Love: Can Love Be Commanded and Demanded?

Paul says: "For freedom Christ has set us free … do not submit again to the yoke of slavery" (Galatians 5:1). This contrasts freedom with circumcision—that is, adherence to the law: "… if you let yourselves be circumcised (translated loosely: as if you blindly obey the law), Christ will be of no benefit to you. …You have cut yourselves off from Christ; you have fallen away from grace" (5:2–4). Obeying the law, and lacking the necessary autonomy, the human being no longer lives in the freedom granted by God. "For you were called to freedom ... only do not use your freedom as an opportunity for self-indulgence [i.e., as a carte blanche for the needs of your flesh]; rather, serve one another humbly in love" (Galatians 5:13).

For Paul, love and freedom belong together. Freedom makes love possible. He considers love crucial: "You shall love your neighbour as yourself.... Live by the Spirit (Greek: *pneu,mati peripatei/te*, "walk by/be transformed by the Spirit"), and you will not gratify the desires of the flesh" (Galatians 5:14–16). Paul also identifies two different categories in this respect: the worldly (flesh, law, sin, and death) and the divine (spirit, the resurrected, grace; 1 Corinthians 15; Ephesians 2:1–10). Guided by the spirit, and connected with God, human beings experience themselves as capable of love and as free from all-too-human feelings ("desires of the flesh"). In modern terms, Paul conceives of human existence in terms of a theology of grace.

Yet are Paul's formulations enough to answer our doubts today and to refute the experiences of two thousand years of (violent) "Christian" history? Can love be lived as described by Paul—and as Jesus understood and bore witness to beforehand? How do we manage to reach beyond ourselves and thus become capable of loving our enemies and forgiving those who have wronged us? One of Jesus' authentic sayings on the ethos of love occurs in the Gospel of Mark:

> One of the scribes ... asked Jesus, "Which commandment is the first of all (*prw,th*, the highest)?" Jesus answered, "The first is, 'Hear, O Israel, the Lord our God, the Lord is one (*ku,rioj ei-j*, "*one* Lord"); you shall love the Lord your God with all your heart, and with all your soul, and with all your mind, and with all your strength. The second is this: You shall love your neighbour as yourself. There is no other commandment greater than these." (Mark 12:29–31)

According to Gnilka (2010, 163), this saying existed *before* Mark and was handed down by him with some minor additions. Jesus' words indicate that the commandment to love one's neighbor cannot be separated from the preceding commandment to love the Father. Yet this commandment represents no imperative, unlike the Ten Commandments in the Old Testament (Exodus 20:1–17; Deuteronomy 5:6–7). It does not tell us "You must" or "You should," but that we may expect certainty ("You will"). Based on a preceding, overwhelming experience with God (in the Old Testament: the departure from Egypt; for Jesus: his fundamental connectedness with the Father), human beings "will" love—that is, they will be able to love from within. Loving both one's neighbor (Leviticus 19:18; 19:34) and God (Deuteronomy 6:4–5) was already firmly anchored in the Old Testament. These two commandments were probably gathered into a dual commandment to love before the time of Jesus (see Theissen 2008, 11). This would explain why, according to Luke, the scribe (and not Jesus) cited both commandments (see the above-cited passage, Luke 10:26–27). Yet why do these two challenges concern the *same* theme?

The commandment to love describes an inner consequence and a spiritual reality: *if* we love God and the Lord with all our might, if we experience God as the Father, as Jesus did, if we are guided by the Spirit, and if we partake inwardly in the Whole/the divine, *then* some of its power of love will also emanate from us. Jesus does not describe a duty but an *inner wish or a longing* to love. This desire arises from rootedness. If we are connected with the Whole and are "blessed," we are able to love—not only ourselves but also others—and probably also creation. It is about moments of grace, in which we even love our enemies and forgive those who have wronged us. Such moments of grace express a *greater love*, indeed perhaps a trace of heaven on earth. Love thus becomes a joy, a voluntary intention among friends, rather than a prescribed mode of interaction between master and servant.

John's farewell discourses capture this atmosphere:

> As the Father has loved me, so I have loved you; abide in my love. If you keep my commandments, you will abide in my love, just as I have. . . . I have said these things to you so that my joy may be in you, and that your joy may be complete. This is my commandment, that you love one another as I have loved you. No one has greater love than this, to lay down one's life for one's friends. You are my friends if you do what I command you. I do not call you servants any longer, because the servant does not know what the master is doing. But I have called you friends. (John 15:9–15)

8.3. A Personal God: Love from an "I" to a "Thou"

According to Mark, Matthew, and Luke, Jesus seldom uttered the words "I love you." According to Mark, though unlike in the other two synoptic gospels, Jesus spoke these words to the rich young man, also because he *loved* him (Mark 10:20). Although Jesus barely mentions the term explicitly, he constantly bore testimony to love. His essence and behavior were shaped by love. He saw the human being—whether the outsider, the customs officer (Luke 19:1–10), the paralytic (Luke 5:17–26), or the ostracized woman who had sinned (Luke

7:36–50)—as a subject, as a Thou. He loved and respected the unloved. He did not abuse people as objects but met them eye to eye, from I to Thou (see chapter 6.1).

It is worth studying Jesus' capacity to love more closely. Christianity emphasizes ethical and charitable behavior, and as such the relation to the world. Compared to Buddhism, Christian love is world-affirming. Still, the term *world-affirming* falls too short of Jesus' intense love. Even if today the word *love* may sound worn out, no better word exists to describe how Jesus approached human beings, creatures, and things. He respected nature, the lilies in the fields; he appreciated and needed sanctuaries, which gave him a deeper sense of himself. He honored the Temple as a sacred place, as well as the rites and Passover. He loved his disciples, just as he loved serving them. He loved relationships. He loved being with his friends and enjoyed their companionship at table. He loved every individual, even his enemies, even if he did not condone their actions.

In this book, I do not mean love as opposed to hatred but to the need for power and to aloofness. Love is not about symbiosis but being connected in freedom, from one person's center to another's. A person who loves is emotionally connected. This requires a stronger personality than mere appreciation and mindfulness. It is *not about balancing* self-love and neighborly love, nor about engaging with others and then drawing boundaries. Jesus' love was "gift" and devotion. Yet this relational quality does not mean charitableness, nor disenfranchisement or emancipation, nor "merely" a humanitarian or philanthropic atmosphere. Love and devotion, as lived by Jesus, flow out of mysticism—that is, connectedness. They are motivated by the Father and by Jesus' deepest essence. He could only love by engaging radically with others ("entering into"). Yet he did not approach others indiscriminately. He was instead guided by inner coherence (harmony) and *kairos*.

Love raises a crucial question: Shall I risk a most intimate connection? Or shall I keep separating myself from the Whole? The difficulty is to remain receptive—that is, passive—and to admit my own sensitivity, vulnerability, creatureliness, and neediness. If we must keep resisting our dependence on others, we are unaware of dominating them and thus of suppressing ourselves. Our need for ultimate control already begins on the level of reflexes. Jesus' love of others and the world was not merely active, but it also involved suffering. His love was proactive and nurtured by his particular source: his connectedness with the Father. It also affirmed his personality, particular identity, determination, and patient endurance.

Yet what about us? Jesus loved and wanted us to have a distinct identity and dignity. In the healing narrative about the Gerasene demoniac, Jesus asked the man the all-important question, "What is your name?" (Luke 8:30; see also chapter 4). The man replied, "Legion." But this did not satisfy Jesus. He did not want us to be an anonymous entity but a Thou. Just as God meant us to be (for a more detailed interpretation, see Renz 2017, 214–17). We can see this, for instance, in his demand *not only for transpersonal but also for personal spirituality*. This kind of spirituality takes our personhood (the quality of being a person) and the lifelong coming of our Self seriously. The question is not how personal or how humanized we should imagine God—for instance, as a fatherly figure. In this respect, "personal" does not refer to God's essence, which we can never grasp, but instead to us as recipients. In becoming persons, we can neither avoid "God" as a counterpart nor our experience as his "opposite." This means that we can no longer just repress or split off our primordial fear. In my eyes, "related" captures matters even better than "personal": we experience ourselves as subjects, as individuals. This involves more than merely being part of an anonymous crowd; it means being "I" in the eyes of a Thou.

When Christianity embraces the desire for a "personal" experience of God, it thus follows the intuition that something inside us emerges in relation to our outermost counterpart, where it grows and from where we know who we ultimately are. God—the eternal one—resonates through us, as the Latin verb *personare* (to sound through) tells us. Here, too, we are, as with singing, an *instrument*. We are not identical with the divine, yet deeply connected with it. "Personal" means related and dignified. Hans Joas (2013, 52) speaks of the sacredness of the person, which accounts for the "irreducible dignity of every human being."

The famous German theologian Karl Rahner (1980, 450–66) struggled to capture this most extreme encounter with God in words. He speaks of the incomprehensibility of God and understands "God" as the final word before we fall silent (Rahner 2005, 85). Rahner sees us as figures persevering on the verge of God's unfathomableness. This, he suggests, makes us become aware that *something*—and not simply *nothing*—exists. Rahner speaks of "God," only to retract the word immediately (for his negative theology, see Rahner 2000). He realizes that any mention of God is merely approximation. According to Rahner, if we open up to this utmost relationship with God, we transcend or even overcome our self-entrapped ego. A modern expression for this process is "to let go."

Letting go brings us into *dialogue* with Eastern spirituality. Eastern cultures also impressively live love and serenity. Despite my utmost respect for those cultures, I must nevertheless question whether the same is meant in East and

West. Letting go and letting go are not identical. Nor are love and love. Jesus affirmed—indeed, even demanded—that we let go of everything in which the ego normally envelops and thus protects itself. Yet the dying Jesus let himself go toward the Father ("Father, into your hands I command my spirit," Luke 23:46). He also let go to find (see his parables about the kingdom of heaven) and to let himself be found. Letting go was an act of trust.

> *One of my patients once described the difference between West and East as follows: "The West can learn how to let go from the East, but not how to love. It's the other way around when it comes to love." The man was a former physicist and engineer and had lived in a Buddhist monastery for a long time to do maintenance work. He had loved the serene radiance of Buddhists, but had never quite managed to transfer their culture onto himself: "People there have no sense of identity. Identity is nothing bad. I love my wife more than anything else. I miss her, sometimes I make her happy, and I don't want to let go of that." The idea of engaging in a love relationship with God (and with his wife) appealed to the man. Later, now terminally ill, he didn't want to let his life simply fall into nothingness and utter futility, nor into the cycle of reincarnation. Rather, he sensed something else, something ultimate: "There*

is something," he stammered, seeming to want to teach physics to those gathered at his bedside. He drew formulas and graphic representations with sweeping gestures in the air. What was the purpose of this physics class? Amid his stammering, I recognized something "more." It was as if this dying man were encircling one last formula. Was he, too, an "Archimedes," one who ponders how to square the circle and who seeks that (Archimedean) point from which the world can be unhinged? What he saw inwardly remained a secret to us. Yet, for him, something became "apparent." He died peacefully. He had (in the truest sense of the word) left himself behind—and found.

8.4. Love according to the Gospel of John

The Gospel of John reveals more profoundly than the other three gospels the meaning and effects of love as lived and asked for by Jesus. The word *love* recurs throughout this gospel in various formulations and images:

"Do you love me (*avgapa/|j me / agapao*) more than these," the resurrected Jesus asked Peter at the end of the gospel (John 21:15–19). Peter replied, "Yes, Lord; you know that I love you" (*filw/ se / phileo*). Literally, this means "You know that I am fond of you, that I am your friend." Jesus repeated his question verbatim while Peter also repeated his answer verbatim. At first, Jesus' answer left Peter unmoved. Was this perhaps because of Jesus' choice of words?

Although they are often used almost synonymously, *agape* and *philia* (the corresponding verbs are *agapeo* and *phileo*) are nevertheless distinct. Etymologically, *agape*, *agapeo* (αvγα,ph, αvγαpα,w) means "to love, to content oneself with, to favor someone, to welcome someone, to long for someone." It is a generic word for "love." It can be applied to persons either superior, subordinate, or equal to oneself; individuals (Galatians 2:20) and gatherings (Ephesians 5:25). In the New Testament, *agape*, *agapeo* often denotes the Christian love of one's neighbor. This, at times, is an unconditional, also one-sided love centered on the other person. The noun *agape* often means divine love or the love brought about by God. This love is not exclusive or centered on one person (a partner) but inclusive and communal. Yet such a community of love does not necessarily mean an anonymous mass. In the Christian context, *agape* also refers to the celebration of the Eucharist in early Christianity. This love, if not meant simply as an ethically overelevated love, presupposes an inner connection with the Whole or—in Jesuanic terms—with the Father and his love (see also Kessler 2006, 35). When the gospels were written, *agape* was the common word for "love."

Philia, *phileo* has a more restricted meaning to *agape*, *agapeo*. It means personal affection and tenderness (*philos*, "to love," "to be dear"; *fili, a,* "love," "friendship"). *Phileo, file, w* means "to like" but also "to kiss, to look after, to host." It denotes a love based on feeling. We love what attracts us. The word is rarer in the New Testament: 'The Father loves [is fond of] the Son" (John 5:20); "The Father himself loves [is fond of] you" (John 16:27); "See how he [Jesus] loved him [Lazarus]" (John 11:36). The different meanings of *agapeo* and *phileo* help us to understand Peter: he loved Jesus impulsively, perhaps jealously, exclusively, and possessively and responded on this level (*phileo*). He did not understand *agape, agapeo*—that is, communal love. His next question makes this plainly evident: "What about him [the apostle John]?" (John 21:21). Nevertheless, Peter's love was genuine. He was sad when Jesus asked him a third time whether he loved him.

Jesus, the resurrected one, seemed to know that the human capacity for love was limited. He respected this limitation and yet asked or pleaded imploringly for more. In Peter's case, Jesus took up his disciple's word (*phileo*) at the third attempt, thus engaging emotionally with Peter. This saddened Peter, probably because he felt understood: "Lord, you know everything; you know that I love you." Next followed an actual calling: "Feed my sheep! ... when you were younger, you used to fasten your own belt and to go wherever you wished. But when you grow old, you will stretch out your hands, and someone else will fasten a belt around you and take you where you do not wish to go. . . . Follow me!" (John 21:17–19). Here, love, as Jesus saw it, becomes a true calling and a coming of the human Self (in C. G. Jung's sense; see introduction), in which the ego no longer "acts" but also lets itself be guided. For Jung, the second half of life is dominated by the deeper human Self. This is more encompassing than its associated conscious ego: the Self, increasingly gaining the upper hand, guides us—also to places where we would prefer not to go. If we allow ourselves to be led—as John says, immediately—we need not look to our right or to our left. Moreover, if we allow ourselves to be led, we remain with ourselves and can trust wholly in God. He ensures that different people can pursue their mission ("If it is my will that he remain until I come, what is that to you? Follow me!"; John 21:22). Our calling is a wise answer to our jealousy and gives us the freedom to love.

The passage about the good shepherd (John 10:1–21) is another important Johannine passage about Jesus' love and his concept of love: Jesus, the good shepherd, loves humankind (sheep) so much that he "gives" his life for the sheep (in the standard German translation). Luther, however, translates this as "he lays down his life." The passage is about devotion. Not in terms of leaving alone but of doing, as the choice of words suggests: Greek *ti,qhmi* (John 10:11, 17) means "to put, to lay, to place" in the sense of taking action. The theologian Max Küchler interprets this as follows: "The good shepherd commits his life to the sheep" (personal communication); he "puts it somewhere" or "lays it down," just as he is able to "take it up again" shortly afterward (John 10:17). Here, love is a gift that is actively and consciously given to an equal (who is addressed personally). For us in the West, the most impressive notion in the above passage is that the shepherd calls *each* sheep by its name. Whether we are healthy or sick, many of us infer this as meaning "God loves me, and I am worth it." I have seen four patients die while I was reading this passage to them.

The image of the good shepherd concludes with a magnificent promise: "I am the good shepherd. I know my own and my own know me, just as the Father knows me and I know the Father" (John 10:14–15). For once, Jesus' secret is revealed: the Father—He/It—is the Alpha and the Omega of the power of love. The First Letter of John, which emerged from the same community, puts it this way: "God is love, and those who abide in love (abide: *me,nw / meno*; see chapter 4.1) abide in God, and God abides in them" (1 John 4:16). The crucial word in John is love. It captures the atmosphere surrounding Jesus. And yet we should not attribute words like *love*, *devotion*, or *pro-existence* (existing for) too rashly to masochistic victimization. Nor does John advise us to either. At issue here is not *kenosis* ("self-emptying," Philippians 2:6–11) but a "gift," a divine giving. This is also true of another passage in the Gospel of John that took on an explosive force in ecclesiastical history: "For God so loved the world that he gave his only Son (Greek: *e;dwken* / "gave" in terms of a gift, a present), so that everyone who believes in him may not perish but may have eternal life" (John 3:16). This gift of God once again refers neither to the Passion nor to God willing Jesus' death (Kirchschläger, personal communication), as exegetes have claimed, quite unfortunately, for centuries. It is about a life-giving, Christmassy gift. The above verses have nothing to do with judgment and atonement. Instead, as John immediately adds, they concern salvation: "Indeed, God did not send the Son into the world to condemn the world, but in order that the world might be saved through him" (John 3:17). What, however, does "salvation" ("to save") mean? In this regard, we must reconsider the common interpretation of Jesus' death as sin offering and atonement (see chapter 9). For according to the Gospel of John, salvation occurs repeatedly, then and now, *through mystical relationship with the Father* and *through love* (which is also nurtured by the Father). Here, in the Gospel of John, the mystical relationship with the Father is linked with abundance and with "eternal life":

The Father loves the Son ... Whoever believes in the Son has eternal life" (John 3:35–36). "The Father loves the Son and shows him all that he himself is doing; ... Anyone who does not honor the Son does not honor the Father who sent him. ... Anyone who hears my word and believes him who sent me has eternal life. (John 5:20–24)

Instead of the "kingdom of God/heaven," a figure of speech used only in the Gospel of John (John 3:3–5), that of "eternal life" occurs here even more strongly. Eternal life is promised also to us. Receiving eternal life means to be "delivered from disconnection," which is caused by separation.

From a mystical perspective, deliverance from sin/separation already began in and with Jesus *before* his Passion and death: (a) through his unbroken relationship with the Father; (b) through his extraordinary behavior (into which we must factor the Father); and (c) through our metanoia/reversal. Whereas redemption was evidently concentrated in Jesus' Passion and death, this happened because he behaved unsurpassably amid his suffering, derision, torture, and crucifixion (see chapter 9.1–3). The Gospel of John expresses this fundamentally redemptive character of the Mystic of Nazareth through numerous "I am" utterances. It regards Jesus as the metaphor of salvation, as the light of the world (John 8:12), as the way, the truth, and the life (John 14:6), as the gate (John 10:7–9), as the bread of life (John 6:48). It does so not only with a view to his death.

We find an atmospheric concentration on the theme of love in the second part of the Gospel of John, at that point when it talks about the path back to the Father, about Jesus' imminent death, and about leave-taking/departure. It mentions the supper merely in passing (John 13:2), focusing instead on the washing of the feet:

> Now before the festival of the Passover, Jesus knew that his hour had come to depart from this world and go to the Father. Having loved his own who were in the world, he loved them to the end (*eivj te,loj / telos*, "to the extreme" "until the goal was reached").... And during supper Jesus, knowing that the Father had given all things into his hands ... got up from the table, took off his outer robe, and tied a towel around himself. Then he poured water into a basin and began to wash the disciples' feet. (John 13:1–11)

Even if they found this symbolic action deeply impressive, the disciples barely understood it. Why are the supper and foot washing thematically related? Why did the "Lord and Teacher" have to wash his disciples' feet? Superficially, this community of love reveals a reversal of values. It invalidates social hierarchies (teacher/student). It also overcomes interpersonal rivalries (see Luke 22:26). But is this actually true? This is where the disciples' failure to understand begins.

According to Jesus, a new community does not emerge when new hierarchies are defined and when people act charitably in order to make themselves look good. Such overinflated ethics are not the basis of a community of love. On the contrary. We become newly capable of love from within once we partake in the Father—a partaking that has remained unrevoked by God. We will then also experience the community of love that grows from our partaking. We can experience this community today, albeit only rudimentarily. Yet it remains a vision: an eschatological table fellowship (Matthew 18:1; Mark 9:33–35, 10:35–45). The key to all of this lies in the Father. Jesus wanted to reveal his secret—his unity with the Father and its plenitude—to the disciples. And he wanted them to partake in that secret:

> He came to Simon Peter, who said to him, "Lord, are you going to wash my feet?" Jesus answered, "You do not know now what I am doing, but later you will understand." Peter said to him, "You will never wash my feet." Jesus answered, "Unless I wash you, you have no share with me [which means: you do not partake in me, you are not connected with me and the Father]." Simon

> Peter said to him, "Lord, not my feet but also my hands and my head!" Jesus said to him, "One who has bathed does not need to wash, except for the feet, but is entirely clean. And you are clean, though not all of you." (John 13:6–11)

Jesus could not have expressed himself more clearly: outer cleanliness is not the essence but having a "share" with him and the Father. The essence is connection.

> After he had washed their feet, had put on his robe, and had returned to the table, he said to them, "Do you know what I have done to you?" You call me Teacher and Lord—and you are right, for that is what I am. So if I, your Lord and Teacher, have washed your feet, you also ought to wash one another's feet. For I have set you an example, that you also should do as I have done to you. . . . If you know these things, you are blessed if you do them." (John 13:12–17)

Yet do the disciples—and do we—understand? Once again, I recognize an alternative: disconnection, detachment versus connection; a distressed ego versus a trusting ego. In one case, compensation dominates—for example, clinging to greed, power, and competitiveness. In the other, an atmosphere of true love and devotion (foot washing) "exists," purely and simply.

Jesus—and he is probably the exception—united power and love. He made it clear that he was a teacher, but this did not prevent him from serving (foot washing). For him, power was "authority" (i.e., the power of a greater authority). Insight arises from participation, even for Jesus: he knew from being with the Father and following the *kairos* that his hour had come ...

8.5. The Supper Immediately before Death

In the three synoptic gospels (Mark, Matthew, and Luke), the supper before Jesus' death is a particularly impressive sign of his love. It, too, is about participation. In the Last Supper, Jesus enacted a highly concentrated form of the covenant between God and humankind. The supper illustrates this bond.

In biblical theology, the Jesuanic supper takes up the Jewish rite of Passover (Hebrew: *pesachim*; in Greek and the New Testament: "Pascha meal"). Mark, the first evangelist, chose a rough structure, one that followed the Passover festival[3] celebrated in Jesus' time: the climax is reached during the meal. The various gospels and the corresponding Pauline texts (1 Corinthians 11:23–25) vary slightly, which suggests that different customs and liturgies were practiced in the various communities (Mark's, Matthew's, etc.).[4] Yet the various narratives have the *same core message*: Jesus adjusted, even reinterpreted, the Passover of his time, shifting the festival *away* from the slaughtered lamb, through which Israel commemorated its rescue (Exodus 12–13, 16; 13:17–15:21), *toward* himself and toward his willingness to leave or to give his own life. As a result, the regulations for Passover (food, drinks, sacrifice, congregation) moved into the background. For instance, no special reference is made to the unleavened bread, although it was probably still used. However, Jesus explicitly adopted the metaphor of blood in the form of the wine-filled chalice. At the time, consuming blood, metaphorically or literally, was taboo among the Greeks, Jews, and Romans. Thus the blood of the Last Supper has a highly personal—Jesuanically shaped—symbolic value. When Jesus said, "This is my blood, the blood of the covenant, which is poured out for many [i.e., all[5]]" (Mark 14:24), he is referring to Moses, who took the blood, sprinkled it on the people, and said, "See the blood of the covenant that the Lord has made with you" (Exodus 24:8). Covenant meant relationship: both the Old and the New Testaments mention a God who seeks relationship. Yet Jesus extended the covenant from the twelve (patriarchs) representing Israel to *all*. This goes along with the idea that *all* of us have a place in God as the

Whole. Jesus also changed the content of the meal: bread and wine, as the metaphors of his body, were about Jesus *himself*, about partaking in him and with him in the Father (see the repeated "I am" utterances in the Gospel of John). Jesus, the mystic, may have sensed his effect as an intermediary. His words at the Last Supper are considered authentic and are constitutive for Christianity. Given the changes that Jesus made to the covenant, we are dealing with two equivalent interpretations: one Jewish, the other Christian (see chapter 3.1, note 3).

Whether or not the Jesuanic meal was celebrated traditionally as *remembrance* (Protestant) or as the *secret of transformation* (Catholic): its reenactment means that something may come to pass deep inside the human soul. Irrespective of the controversial question about the transformation of the divine substance (from bread into the body of Christ): when we take the Eucharist/Last Supper, a transformation occurs *within us*: something long forgotten and shattered once again becomes connected, whole.

A young dying woman heard a Swiss children's song in a dream: "Heile, heile Segen," (Healing, blessful healing). At the same time, she saw a pile of fragments. This happened at night, after she—touched by a text about Jesus—had received communion. She had no idea about the deeper meaning of communion nor that etymologically "healed/ unhurt" means whole (i.e., the pile of fragments becomes whole).

How are the Last Supper and the Passion linked? Jesus had deeply longed to celebrate the Passover meal with his disciples before his suffering (Luke 22:15). He "knew" that one of his disciples would betray him.[6] He also knew that the Son of Man "must" go his way, as scripture put it (Matthew 26:21–24; Mark 14:18–21; Luke 22:21–22). Although the gospels were not written until *after* Jesus' death, we may assume that, *historically*, Jesus saw the inevitability of his suffering and imminent death at this point in time.

The coincidence of the Last Supper and the Passion is not accidental. In fact, it is psychologically logical: it was precisely in the knowledge of his final hours that Jesus wanted to give himself as he had explained in the parable of the good shepherd (see chapter 8.4). I am *also* familiar with this from my practice as an end-of-life carer, though much more modestly, of course. I have in mind the final conscious stirrings and actions of *the dying*: the most affectionate words, the most magnanimous forgiveness, the infinite understanding and togetherness occur precisely now (see also Borasio's discussion of altruism, 2011). Superficially, this ability the dying have to love is often accounted for by the fact that they have nothing to lose. And yet these acts of a final giving of oneself reveal a greater mystery. I have observed that the dying sometimes already seem to have reached the light of heavenly experience (in Jesuanic terms, the kingdom of heaven) and wish to give themselves—as if fortified by that experience—at *this* very moment. For now, they are capable of love. Is it not until death that we become fully capable of love in the Jesuanic sense? And will we then be able to love? Jesus gave himself at the Last Supper, as symbolized by bread, chalice, and blood. And his giving blended seamlessly into the Passion.

8.6. Spiritual Practice: Love, Covenant, Acceptance

What are the consequences for everyday spiritual practice, meditation, contemplation, and spiritual care? What does spirituality comprise in Jesus' sense if we consider the dimension of love?

Love is not simply love. Can we, if we understand what he means, follow Jesus' way of loving a little bit? Can we let ourselves be touched by his love?

- Love, according to Jesus, is *given*. It is a power that ultimately needs to be situated in God/the Whole. To this day, the basis of the human ability to love remains the deep underlying experience of fundamental love (the Father who loves us unconditionally and releases us). God has integrated himself into human destiny. This is the basic statement of covenant theology.

- In everything that Jesus did and taught, in his speeches, in his silence and engagement, he lived one thing above all: love. This may also, to a lesser degree, happen inside us—in our being, doing, and enduring.

- A personal God: something truly fundamental ("from the foundations") occurs through relationship and relatedness. It involves various essential qualities: connectedness, reliability, responsibility, personhood.

- Love is directed toward response, and is comparable to the development from a one-sided to a reciprocal covenant. We respond to love primarily by *accepting* it, not by reinterpreting or by letting it roll off us like water. If we are moved in this way, at some point we will respond with love of our own accord ("from within").

One patient told me: "If I know I am inside HIM, I am fine. Then I feel tenderness toward those around me."

Love is indebted to a dynamics, and becomes a dynamics itself.

- Love manifests itself in our faithfulness and in our capacity to be resolute, even when we can no longer "love." Love gives and partakes in joy and suffering, in the suffering of others and in that of creation. In "compassion" (Metz 2006, 105–6), those who love let themselves be infected by the suffering of others and then discover some of that suffering within themselves. This extends beyond pity and is central to the Passion.

Love *redeems* us—to this day. Jesus' short formula of redemption is love, covenant, and connection.

CHAPTER 9
Redemption — Newly Spelled Out

9.1. Passion and Crucifixion: Searching for Interpretations

How can we understand Jesus' death on the cross? This question became fateful for the future of Christianity. No one knows with any certainty how Jesus understood his own death. And yet we may safely assume that in accepting his Passion and crucifixion, Jesus remained faithful to his Father's will: he went to Jerusalem, for instance, although he knew that he would face intense suffering there. He was aware of the death of the prophets and of John the Baptist. He had two concepts of interpretation: the Passion of God's servant (Isaiah 52:13–53:12) and the covenant between God and his people. Nevertheless, the interpretation of Jesus' death remains open. Already the scriptures have gaps. They are always shaped by the times, by their authors and their limitations. Already the evangelist and Paul probably struggled to grasp this incomprehensible death. In this book, I follow a particular line of interpretation: Jesus did not "seek" his death but accepted it as an act of his utmost faithfulness, to his message and to the Father, and as a consequence of his love. This approach avoids any masochistic interpretation of the mystery of the cross. Instead, the cross and the resurrection are the central statement about what love ultimately is and effects.

Mark's and Matthew's Passion narratives emphasized the apocalyptic events, the escatological tribunal, and the decision about good and evil (darkness, the torn curtain in the Temple;[1] in Matthew, also the earthquake and the opening of the tombs). Both apostles (Mark 15:34; Matthew 27:46) place Jesus' death within the context of the opening verse of Psalm 22 ("My God, my God, why have you forsaken me?"). Did Jesus die praying this psalm? (I discuss Jesus' godforsakenness below and in chapter 1). Luke, partly similarly, partly differently, highlights the theme of the righteous one with the narrative of Jesus being crucified between two criminals. Jesus' answer to the criminal who begged his pardon and feared God reveals his capacity for love, even amid utmost suffering. It also shows us how close he was to Paradise. So does dying inherently lead us to Paradise? John maintains his mystical, teleological view. He claims that Jesus' last words were, "It is finished" (*tete,lestai / tetelestai*; see the teleology in John 19:30), although he was dying on the cross—and was regarded by Jews at the time as a curse

(Deuteronomy 21:22–23; see chapter 3.1). In other words, the goal has already been reached.

In the course of Church history, interpretations emphasizing the connection between suffering and guilt have prevailed (e.g., Anselm of Canterbury and Martin Luther; see chapter 9, note 3). They include the notion of purchasing freedom and ransom money.[2] Further, they involve the theme of proxy: the suffering righteous one takes upon himself ignominy, misfortune, or death for the sinners. This theme is taken up in particular by Paul (2 Corinthians 5:21; Philemon 2:6–11; Colossians 1:19–20; see also Romans 3:25, 4:25). Yet we also find it in the institution narratives of the gospels (e.g., Matthew 26:28). It goes back to the servant song in the Old Testament (Isaiah 53:4–6). According to theologian Adrian Schenker (2001, 27–28), the concept of proxy in the Old Testament appears in this song, but also elsewhere: for instance, when righteous men such as Abraham and Moses stood up for the unrighteous, or when Jacob's son Judah offered to serve the sentence imposed on his brother Benjamin, who was pronounced guilty (Genesis 44:33–34). We find an even more radical instance among the Maccabeans (2 Maccabeans 7), when the last son prefers to die for God in the row of the seven martyrs than to live against him. In Jesus' case—here I refer to Paul, to Old Testament rites, and even to older scapegoat patterns—cultic themes were constitutive. Thus, historically, his death on the cross was mostly interpreted and celebrated as sacrifice and atonement (see the sacrificing of Jesus to satisfy God, the doctrine of satisfaction, and the "great exchange"[3]). According to such interpretations, Jesus offered himself as sacrifice. While ecclesiastical history has many concepts of redemption, none ever became exclusive or dogmatic. Instead, the popular belief in sacrifice described above has prevailed. Yet neither Anselm of Canterbury nor Martin Luther upheld this belief or an almost magical exchange in *this* way. It is also doubted today. Thank goodness.

So what remains? The theme of proxy, in the sense of an act of utmost love and devotion, is undisputed in Jesus' case. Yet we must still ask ourselves: What exactly did Jesus do? For whom? For which God? And on which grounds?

9.2. Was Jesus a Scapegoat?

Let me raise another question before considering *another* interpretation of Jesus' death: Which Old Testament, extra-biblical, and primeval influences already existed in Jesus' lifetime? Which notions of sacrifice and scapegoats, which ritual precepts, were common and remembered?

In the ancient Orient, sacrifice was meant to preserve and enhance the life force of the gods (see the Epic of

Gilgamesh or the derision in Daniel 14:1–22). But such notions were already rejected in the Old Testament (Psalm 50:12–16; Hosea 6:6; Amos 5:21–24; Micah 6:6–8).

The idea of sacrifice is ancient, both in biblical and extra-biblical perspectives. Psychologically, it probably underwent several shifts—corresponding to increasing human consciousness—for instance, from child sacrifice through animal sacrifice to the sacrifice of natural produce. In ancient times, child sacrifice probably also existed in the region of the later Israel: Jephthah, who presided over Israel for six years, killed his daughter to fulfill his oath (Judges 11:30–40). Ahaz and Manasseh, two ancient kings of Israel, are said to have sacrificed a son (2 Kings 16:3, 21:6). The story of Abraham's sacrifice (Jewish: the binding of Isaac, Genesis 22:1–9) emerged over a longer period. According to Reiterer and Unfried (2009a, 423), it eludes unequivocal interpretation. The depicted shift—from child sacrifice to animal sacrifice—might correspond to cultural progress. Further, the biblical narrative of Abraham reveals that sacrifice may also be a metaphor of extreme devotion.

In general, sacrifice increasingly assumed the function of recognizing God's superiority (see also Reiterer and Unfried 2009b, 564): "The correct attitude toward sacrifice allowed one to 'reach' God." A number of events were associated with sacrifice. Last but not least, the sacrificed animal or person served an important social function: it corroborated social values and cohesion (e.g., the celebratory banquet of those making the offering or a group scapegoating an individual). As Reiterer and Unfried (2009b, 564) have observed, clean herd or domestic animals were sacrificed (Leviticus 4:23; Deuteronomy 12:17). This class included the Passover sacrifice. Other classes were food sacrifice (Leviticus 2:15; Numbers 28:4–5), the burnt sacrifices (Exodus 30:8–9), the sacrifice of thanksgiving (Leviticus 7:12), the sacrifice of jealousy (Numbers 5:15,18), the initiation sacrifices of priests (Exodus 29:27), festival offerings (Exodus 23:18), purification offerings (Leviticus 12:6–7), guilt offerings (Leviticus 7:1–10:37), expiation (Leviticus 16:5ff.), sin offerings (Leviticus 4:24; Numbers 28;15), and peace offerings (Leviticus 3:1–17).

Regarding interpretations of Jesus' death, I need to highlight the Jewish and Old Testament ritual of the Day of Atonement (Yom Kippur; Leviticus 16:1–34). This was a day of fasting already at the time: the high priest absolved himself, the priests, and the people from sin. On this day, and only then, was the high priest permitted to enter into the Holy of Holies, the sacred enclosure, in the Jerusalem Temple. The details of instruction, which were originally meant for Aaron, Moses's brother, are interesting: he was allowed to enter the inner sanctuary in the Tent of Meeting (Exodus

40:2) only with a young bull as a sin offering and with a ram as a burnt offering. The Israelites also gave him two goats for sin offering and a ram for burnt offering. If he offered the young bull to atone *for his own sin* and that of his house, he had to cast lots for the two goats for the Israelites, one for the Lord and one for Azazel (a desert demon). The goat upon which the lot had been cast was brought before the Lord as a sin offering; the other was placed alive before the Lord to serve atonement and to be sent forth to Azazel in the desert.

The highly symbolic scapegoat rite for Azazel probably goes back to an even older custom that the Yahweh cult was not quite able to oust. In Jesus' time, this rite meant that the sins of Israel were placed upon the goat, which was driven out into the desert from the midst of Israel. The word *scapegoat* originates in this rite.

All these historical guidelines, which probably influenced interpretations of Jesus' death, were accompanied by a behavioral mechanism that has remained explosive yet hidden to this day. As they became more conscious (mythologically speaking beyond Eden), human beings entered into the perceptual modes and patterns of time, space, and causality. Thus arose an increasingly dualistic perspective. Henceforth, they recognized good beside evil and began to think in terms of cause and effect, fateful reward and punishment, deeds and consequences.[4] Where misfortune and inexplicable distress came over people, explanations had to be found: something or someone had to be "responsible" (i.e., guilty) for one's ill luck. Thus attempts were made to "banish" incomprehensible misfortune because it seemed explainable. At least in Abrahamic religions, thinking in terms of cause and effect, including "guilt" as an outlet, long served as *the* prevailing coping mechanism, collectively and individually. To this day, we make out the guilty party and scapegoat others in unconsidered, sudden reactions, even before we know the facts. Thinking in terms of guilt can be a way of diminishing—i.e., coping with—the incomprehensible (see chapter 7.1; Renz 2017; Renz 2018). René Girard ([1972] 2005) formulated this idea similarly, and yet differently.

This coping pattern also made cultural history. It explains the overfraught status of guilt in our culture. My experience with cancer patients has taught me that even they, as enlightened modern people, use this strategy: the scapegoats for one's cancer are one's previous doctor, one's former wife, God, and so forth. Only few patients accept their own responsibility (e.g., smoking, sunburn). And even fewer—among them academics, but also down-to-earth peasants, midwives, and educators, or in general mature individuals with much life experience and who have experienced much suffering—see through this scapegoating mechanism and take life as it is: good fortune beside misfortune (see Renz et al. 2017 for study results).

This scapegoat mechanism and (unconsciously) ganging up on others were probably already part of the human psychic structure and thus of the behavior common at the time of Jesus. Today we would compare them to suppression and projection as typical reaction patterns. Yet given such commonplace guidelines (extrabiblical and Old Testament), it is barely surprising that Jesus' death was interpreted in a dubious, magical fashion, in part already by Paul and the apostles (see above).

Did Jesus become a scapegoat? And did he become one in the usual meaning of the word? Did he become a bearer of projections? Our answer depends on our perspective. For the Romans, Jesus was a troublemaker; for the Jews, a blasphemer. In terms of the Yom Kippur rite (Day of Atonement), Jesus, as the theologian and Jesuit Raymund Schwager (1999, 91) explains, was "not a scapegoat, since the high priest at the hearing did not want—in his conscious intentions—to place the sins of others upon him but to condemn him for his own offenses." Yet neither was Jesus an accidental scapegoat, upon whom one could cast one's sins, as on the Day of Atonement. Instead, Jesus, like many other outstanding individuals, brought the rulers' and the crowd's wrath and projections *upon himself* through his speeches and actions. Beyond any masochistic interpretations, this was barely his intention, however.

Nevertheless, and precisely thus, Jesus literally became a scapegoat. Schwager (1999, 92) outlines the respective, two-layered process: the Romans, the high priests, the eldest, and the incensed crowd believed "(more or less honestly) that they have to reproach someone for something." Unlike the victim and third parties: they were convinced that Jesus (the accused) was being wronged; they accused the accusers of shifting their own problems and mistakes onto the accused (Schwager 1999, 92). If we follow both positions, then one party's word stands against the other's, at least on this (obvious) level. However, in a deeper layer, we must explore the projections and shadow material placed upon the scapegoat.

Why Jesus? Well, he "attracted" scapegoating because he was awkward and consistent in his speech and actions. His concerns and appearance went to the heart of his enemies' shadow: his success stoked envy and his message of direct, personal, and *immediate* access to the Father disempowered the powerful. Moreover, his message and his way of life were original (they stood alone). Yet, as such, he was vulnerable. In modern terms, one did not need to fear any lobby in Jesus' case. In this sense, he shared the fate of many other prophetic individuals and irksome individuals.

9.3. Jesus' Behavior Exceeded Human Limits

What was special about Jesus and his behavior? Scapegoating victims tend to despair when contempt and injustice escalate. They cannot bear this situation anymore. Sylvia Brinton Perera (1986) has suggested that amid the collective shadow material placed upon them, victims ultimately reject *themselves*. They are no longer able to love themselves and may grow angry. Their anger may be directed against themselves or against others, against God or against the world. Their reaction shows that they adopt the coping pattern described above: they must find someone to blame—just as they need to direct their anger against someone. If no one can be found, their unconscious blames itself (Renz 2018).

In contrast, Jesus—facing his accusers—showed no aggression ("Put your sword back into its place," Matthew 26:52; see also John 18:11). He did not act or react *to the outside*. He did not misappropriate (in any inflationary way) God's power (Matthew 26:53), nor did he ally himself with the world's most powerful. And he remained silent on the level of power and projection. Yet did this deprive him of all power? Did he succumb to suffering too rashly? I do not think so.

We need to understand Jesus' outer behavior in terms of a specific *inner* scenario, one that attests to his different kind of power and his strong personality. He was able to endure suffering and remain inwardly upright even amid his struggle. Despite facing extreme violence, he stayed strongly self-confident and capable of love and devotion. Jesus remained true to the Father, his message, himself, and his concept of the loving, nonviolent Father. Throughout, he counted on the Father. Normally, only highly sensitive and highly conscious people are even remotely capable of such behavior. Is *consciousness* both characteristic of and intended by Jesus (see chapter 7.3)? Is it a sign of the Father's presence within Jesus (see the metaphor of the Logos in chapter 10)?

This interpretation would illuminate the inscrutable nature of Jesus' act of redemption. It implies that Jesus, by consciously not avoiding the collective dynamics directed against him, brought something unholy and deeply cursed to light: a sum of collective shadow energies. In his case, these energies became concrete in the escalation of anger and hatred, accusations and projections, betrayal and, in general, the cursed energy and dynamics of the incensed crowd. Thus questionable semiconscious behavioral mechanisms such as "all against one" (mimesis), feuding parties ganging up on a common enemy (Herod and Pilate), taking revenge, and the senseless scapegoating pattern came to light. Although we cannot determine how consciously Jesus perceived these patterns, we know that he distanced himself *inwardly* from all these hostile reactions. He remained silent and aware of "being a king." By staying mentally alert, he renounced the energies of evil. There was no door within Jesus through which split-off energies could enter (see chapter 7.1). He did not let himself be enticed to counter violence with violence. Nor did he act in the heat of the moment. On the contrary, he was so self-contained, so contained in and connected with the Father, that he even asked God to forgive his enemies (Luke 23:24). Thus, for me, he even set them free so that they could (in principle) go back to God. God remained Jesus' reference point and thus helped him avoid a chain reaction or any entanglement in sin. This behavior was redemptive (see chapter 9.10). Importantly, it was not neurotically motivated. No, it was spoken out of Jesus' authority. Jesus thus showed us that, because he was connected, he did not even need to separate his enemies from himself. He *lived* what he commanded: faithfulness to the Father, to himself (inwardly), and to his neighbors.

A moment of (temporary) uncertainty occurred at Gethsemane, when Jesus asked the Father to let "this cup pass from me" (Matthew 26:39). Yet Jesus overcame his concern in the next breath and expressed even greater connectedness with God: "Yet not what I want but what you want" (Matthew 26:39). This inner event indicates—like Jesus' abandonment by God on the cross (chapter 1 and below)—an utmost spiritual challenge, one that Jesus evidently had to undergo himself. The fact that he came through this experience so "unscathed" attests to his utmost mysticism. He was a true mystic. Spiritually experienced, Jesus knew very well that he could only be redeemed and dissolved from such an inner struggle by saying yes (i.e., by living in an affirmative state). He also knew this because he was borne by the Father. In the final perspective, God-forsakenness—as many other mystics have experienced—nevertheless remains undergirded by God.

9.4. Jesus Redeemed Us by "Blazing Open Old Paths"

So what did Jesus do for us? What does his act of redemption comprise—with a view to his Passion? His behavior, as we have seen, interrupted futile retribution, the scapegoating pattern, and a politics determined by projection. He overcame the all-too-human and abandoned common behavioral patterns such as revenge, arbitrariness, and false adjustment. He did not "have" to win. Nor did he need to demonstrate power, nor to exercise violence, nor to expel victims. Nor did he have to "knuckle under," look away, or declare his solidarity with the masses. Nor was his identity that of a victim. He was not dissociated, nor self-destructive, nor self-condemning. Fully self-conscious, Jesus instead entered a nondual reality—that is, an undivided, final unity with the Father.

This (re-)connection with the Father even amid suffering is redemptive. Why? From what? And how exactly?

According to the old dogmas and belief systems, we are redeemed "from sin and from death." Yet what did sin mean? My answer is redemption "from separation" (see chapter 6) to reconnection. Redemption through Jesus does not just entail the tip of the iceberg such as surmounted greed and violence. Instead, Jesus renewed human life and development *from the root upward* through his connection with God. His life, message, and person enabled him to overcome negative, neurotic developments and split personalities. He went *behind* such dynamics and splitting by overcoming the division between God and the human being. In this way, he initiated a new path and redeemed human beings from age-old false paths of greed and violence. We are redeemed if we take this path. Or as Jesus says, "Follow me." "It" occurs by following him and "it" happens while being borne in God.

As Jesus tells us, his main concern was redemption. In the Last Supper, he followed a rite common at the time—commemorating the deliverance from Egyptian servitude—that he interpreted in a new light (see chapter 8.5). But who understood, and who understands, what he was doing? If we continue to interpret Jesus' Passion and death solely on the level of a magical, transcendental dissolution of guilt (a strange, inscrutable combination of the scapegoat and sacrificial lamb), we will not understand what Jesus—and within him the Father—actually accomplished.

Why can (or should) we not interpret Jesus' death in the usual context of *substitution and atonement*? The idea of Jesus being sacrificed to satisfy God, to make God merciful, is irreconcilable with Jesus' essence, person, and his relation to himself. It is incompatible with his way of entering into the Father's power and above all with his conception of God! Jesus spoke differently of God, for instance, in dealing with the Sabbath commandment or the Levitical purity laws. At the time, these purity laws rested on the idea that the human being "must purge himself of anything that might hurt the divinity and provoke its wrath" (Gnilka 2010, 279). Yet Jesus proclaimed a benevolent, fatherly-motherly God (chapter 4), who even wishes human participation in himself. Such a God needs no persuading!

And *sacrifice*? It is crucial *how* (i.e., in which tone of voice) we utter and hear the word *sacrifice*. I can agree to using this term if it means sacrificing ourselves and our ego, giving ourselves up, *devoting* ourselves. Jesus was faithful to his mission and the Father. He was devoted, out of love not out of duty or self-righteousness (as he told the Pharisees, "I desire mercy, not sacrifice. For I have come to call not the righteous but sinners," Matthew 9:13). Jesus' devotion did not mean that kind of sacrifice that seeks to satisfy God or accomplish seemingly magical redemption. With all due respect to two thousand years of Christian history and its foundations (biblical and extrabiblical), this view of Jesus' death is incompatible with his behavior. The man from Nazareth was neither a masochist, nor was he steeped in magical thinking. I don't think that he understood his suffering and death as substitutionary atonement that was considered necessary by God. For Jesus, God was like a father or a mother.

9.5. Passion and Crucifixion as Consequences of the Dynamics against Jesus

In which *other* ways can we understand Jesus' Passion and crucifixion? First of all, they result from the collective dynamics that arose *against* the man from Nazareth. Behind Jesus' story I recognize a drama that unfolds from the alliance between his enemies and the manipulable crowd. Once more, we must imagine a two-layered dynamic: the upper layer involves searching for factual arguments, while the lower focuses on sheer greed, for power and its defense. Like mobbing scenarios these days, no particular individual (Pilate, Herod, Caiaphas, or Judas) but a total dynamic turned the crowd into a mob. Those responsible lost sight of the facts and relations. Even his friends failed Jesus, they could no longer respond to this *dynamic*.

The dynamic was determined by patterns of evil that rejected conscious realization and refuted any attempt to gain consciousness (chapters 7.3–7.6). This dynamic allowed the energies to split off from the Whole to run riot. People were blind to this, which helps us understand that they were not Jesus' adversary but the power of evil. Jesus said so himself, "The ruler of this world has been condemned" (John 16:11) or he "will be driven out" because of his (Jesus') behavior. The gospels provide us a sense of the atmosphere at the time and raise a basic question: *What else could Jesus do than eventually accept his death?* It is not enough if we regard Jesus' Passion and crucifixion as the consequences of the sum of the events directed against him (see Raymund Schwager 1999). Jesus's behavior amid suffering shows us that his Passion and crucifixion expressed his utmost love, devotion, and consciousness. He lived these qualities despite impending captivity, torture, sentencing, and crucifixion.

9.6. Passion and Crucifixion as Utmost Love

Did Jesus have a choice? Could he have responded *differently*? First, his heavenly power could have intervened in the mobbing dynamics leveled against him. Already Matthew entertained this idea when he has Jesus say, "Do you think that I cannot appeal to my Father, and he will at once send me more than twelve legions of angels?" (Matthew 26:53). This sense of power, however, would have refuted the Jesuanic message, which meant another kind of power. Further, it would contradict the idea of a merciful, motherly-fatherly God, whom we need not fear. In performing a powerful heavenly deed, Jesus would have relativized his truly human existence and thus also his answers to our human distress and suffering. Yet even if Jesus renounced power, he was not "without power." Instead, he was powerful insofar as he did not claim power for himself. If chosen consciously, powerlessness is a strength.

Second, instead of accepting his death, Jesus could have revoked his message, his healing potential, and his conception of God. In particular, he could have avoided Jerusalem and could have fled. He could have surrendered to those in power. Or he could have collaborated with one or the other person. Yet would this have corresponded to his person, to his way of thinking, living, and loving?

Jesus took a different decision. He did not extricate himself hastily from his human existence (his first alternative), nor did he abandon himself to becoming too human (his second alternative). Instead, he *remained suspended in tension*. He bore his fate and accepted his suffering to the ultimate consequence. Amid all of this, he relied totally on the Father. Seeing through the patterns of evil, he sensed that it would end at some point, indeed that evil is already overcome *in the Father* (*in the Whole*). Whether consciously or intuitively, Jesus' loyal, trusting, and conscious attitude and behavior have given us his final answer to the question about redemption (deliverance) from separation, encapsulation, and arbitrariness: a new beginning, a new imprinting, constellates itself exactly through powerlessness, death, and resurrection; this enables even hardened souls to soften and become constructive—if the time is ripe.

Jesus died on the cross. I believe that his death was consistent with his message, behavior, and person. Although he did not seek this particular death, just as many Christian martyrs did not aspire to a violent death (see Siebenrock 2009, 15), his *actions* were consistent with his message and mission. He remained faithful to his message, to the Father, and to those he loved (see below for the notion of the "slaughtered" versus the sacrificed lamb). His unity with the Father gave Jesus the power to bear testimony, even on the cross. Even when facing death, he was still at home in mystery. His Passion remained a relational event until his death. His heart remained open throughout. Outwardly defeated, he placed himself—and his spirit—into the Father's hands as a free spirit (Luke 23:46) and exhaled. In my eyes, Jesus' death represents unconditional devotion and an ultimate statement about love.

9.7. Dignity and Freedom in Suffering

Was Jesus free when he was crucified? Many years ago, I was asked this question at one of my examinations as a theology student. My answer at the time was that Jesus, despite his crucifixion and total unfreedom, nevertheless seemed to possess an astonishing inner freedom. He was free from drivenness and affect, from blind adherence to laws and worldly systems, and thus free to consciously devote himself. At no point could evil enter him. This freedom liberated him from that particular dynamic.

What about his dignity? If Jesus prayed while he was dying, "My God, my God, why have you forsaken me?" (Psalm 22:1), then he probably also knew those words that occur later in the same psalm, "But I am a worm, and not human; scorned by others, and despised by the people" (22:7). Being forsaken by God is one of the utmost spiritual challenges, even today. Saints, yet also severely ill patients, report this experience. Inner derangement, which might coincide with utterly overwhelming darkness (Mark 15:33–34), is the reverse side of closeness to God. Experience tells us that accepting suffering while remaining related to God (see Psalm 22:20–32) usually leads to great dignity (see Renz 2015, chapter 2).

Jesus' dignity was evident even in his suffering and derision. He did not identify with the scorn, ridicule, and projections of others. Instead, he knew: "Yes, you say truly that I am a king" (John 18:37). Precisely this—as we know from those who have suffered violence and torture—is constitutive of how they might "feel" and react: whether they feel victimized or free. Whenever their transgressors do not possess them *spiritually*, victims preserve some of their humanity: they remain themselves, truly dignified. Yet if the torturers disempower them not only physically but also *spiritually*, the victims experience almost total abandonment or self-annihilation. This also explains the strange sadomasochistic treatment to which perpetrators subject their victims *spiritually*—for instance, giving torture victims a Bible yet nothing else in their cells; or threatening them in God's name or the devil's. Throughout, a *spiritual struggle* unfolds that we should not underestimate. It takes place not simply between perpetrators and victims but also *within* the latter. Ultimately this is a struggle between demons and the Holy Spirit.

These connections are important if we are to understand Jesus: he remained with himself and with God as the Father. Even when tortured, Jesus did not seem to be determined by the adverse circumstances. On the contrary. He displayed an impressive presence of mind, maturity, and serenity—even on the cross. These qualities bear witness to his utmost consciousness. As he approached death, Jesus lived a freedom that, rather than endured blindly, looked suffering vigilantly (fully present) in the eye. Until the end, Jesus was able to put questions to God. He withstood defamation and resisted the inner temptation to lose self-control and self-confidence in God. Crucially, he never turned away from God. Even if Jesus possessed an active free will, he bowed to God's will ("Yet not what I want but what you want," Matthew 26:39). Even amid his abandonment, Jesus was always borne by his personality, by the highest form of self-consciousness, and by his "attitude" (uprightness)—and therein by God. Amid his worst suffering, he still managed to act despite his horrific experience. To this day, Jesus' behavior exemplifies how we or how some of us are sometimes able to accept and experience our suffering and dying with dignity (Renz 2015, 34–40).

9.8. The Lamb of God as a Symbol of Devotion

But what does the symbol of the lamb of God mean if we leave aside its improper use? This symbol is difficult to understand. Years ago, I had a dream. In that dream, I kept hearing a special melody of the lamb of God, which I had known ever since childhood. In this dream, however, the words that I heard were different: "Lamb of God, you take away the suffering, have mercy, and give us peace." So instead of the common word *sin*, the song was about the suffering caused by separation, which I was about to formulate as a hypothesis at the time (see Renz 2017).

I was touched by the dream, yet I didn't understand. How does the lamb of God "take away suffering"? I began studying symbols and queried my theology professors. In general, the lamb represents the defenseless and the innocent of this world, upon whom the suffering of others is placed and who must endure this predicament instead of the guilty. Already children may face this imposition.

Next, I began exploring the symbol of the lamb historically: Where and how, in which writings and contexts, does the Old Testament mention "lamb," sheep," or explicitly "the lamb of God"? (The list below may be perused or skipped.)

- The secret revelation of John the Seer (who is not identical with the apostle) mentions a lamb—*avrni,on*—with seven horns (Revelation 5:6) that is slaughtered (Revelation 5:6,9,12; 13:8). Its blood (due to its violent death) has a cleansing power (Revelation 7:4) and defeats the devil (Revelation 12:10–11). Here, the lamb symbolizes powerlessness, one, however, which is also assigned power and sovereignty (see Hasitschka 1989, 96–97).

- In the Gospel of Luke, Jesus says, "See, I am sending you out like lambs (*w`j a;rnaj*) into the midst of wolves"

(Luke 10:3). In a parallel passage, Matthew speaks of sheep (*w`j pro,bata*) (Matthew 10:16). Both passages are about serving God with a certain attitude: righteousness and humility.

- The good shepherd looks after every sheep (Luke 15:3–6, John 10:1–10); the sheep is an unaggressive animal, whose obedience is mentioned in John.

- The later First Letter to Peter (1 Peter 1:19) speaks of a ransom through the precious blood of Jesus, of the lamb "without defect or blemish."

- Following the fourth servant song (Isaiah 53:7), Acts states, "Like a sheep he was led to the slaughter, and like a lamb silent before its shearer, so he does not open his mouth" (8:32).

- The Gospel of John speaks of the "lamb of God," particularly in the beginning. John the Baptist saw Jesus coming toward him and said, "Here is the lamb of God (*i;de o` avmno.j tou/ qeou*) who takes away the sin of the world" (Luther translates this as "which bears the sin of the world; John 1:29). Shortly afterward, when the Baptist saw "the Spirit descending from heaven like a dove, and it remained on him" (i.e., Jesus; 1:32), he testified to Jesus as the "Son of God" (1:34). The next day, he said, "Look, here is the lamb of God" (1:36).

It is undisputed that the apostle was thinking of Jesus' Passion, death, and resurrection when he proclaimed "the lamb of God" in verses that were written in a glorifying mood after Easter. Yet *why* was the metaphor of the lamb of all metaphors used? At Jesus' time, both Old Testament and extrabiblical guidelines existed for this usage:

- God's servant, who takes upon himself (as a proxy) the sins of others yet refrains from violence and remains silent out of inner strength (Isaiah 53; see Schenker 2001, 75–85).

- Jeremiah 11:29 (the lamb that is brought to slaughter). In Jeremiah—as in Isaiah's servant song—the lamb stands for "the prophet ... who is persecuted because of his message and whose life one is after" (Hasitschka 1989, 87).

- Psalm 44:23. Here the sheep is brought to slaughter as an image for those who are persecuted for God's sake.

- The influence of the lamb on the Passover festival (see John 18:28; 19:14,31,42; citing the passage about fulfillment, i.e., 19:36; see also 1 Corinthians 5:7; 1 Peter 1:19). Presumably, Jesus died when the lambs were slaughtered on Passover (see chapter 3).

- The influence of the noncanonical symbolism of the animal apocalypse (Ethiopian Book of Enoch, the Testaments of the Twelve Patriarchs). Here animal images (the sheep, the lamb, and negatively also the wolf) were regarded as symbols, and God was the Lord over the sheep and lambs.

- Referring to the sacrifice of Isaac (Genesis 22:8), the Targum Neofiti[5] suggested that Isaac himself was the sacrificial lamb and chose to sacrifice himself (see Hasitschka 1989, 59–61). Even if such an interpretation of the sacrifice of Isaac is questioned nowadays, the Targum Neofiti highlights the fact that transferring the image of the lamb onto a human being was not unusual at the time.

- The biblical expression "tam": although it is mostly not mentioned in connection with the lamb of God, I nevertheless refer to this Hebrew word (*tam*), which was common at the time. This attribute was assigned to very few human beings (in the Old Testament, to Noah, Abraham, Jacob, and Job). It meant upright, undefiled, "whole," very much in the sense of a lamb, which is without defect and blemish (impeccable and entirely itself) during its slaughter.

These remarks prompt several conclusions. First, the metaphor of the lamb of God symbolized Jesus's exceptional behavior in the face of violence and suffering. The ideas of powerlessness and defenselessness (barely any other animal is as passive during its slaying as the lamb) are crucial, as are the precepts of the prophets Isaiah and Jeremiah. Second, the lamb represents Jesus' innocence: a lamb is slaughtered without defect and blemish (see 1 Peter 1:19). It is unbent, entirely itself ("tam"). Third, the lamb of God refers to an intense relationship with the Father, an unconditional surrender to his guidance, an absolute loyalty. The animal in need of protection is both dependent and trusting. We may transfer this aspect onto human beings, who are sent out like lambs into the midst of the wolves. This puts our trust to the test. Fourth, the theme of the lamb fits other images that are characteristic of the Gospel of John and that corresponded to daily life at the time: water, bread, light, the way, the door, the shepherd, the vine, the grain of wheat, the bridegroom (see Hasitschka 1989, 54).

The crucial and controversially discussed question among theologians concerns the cultic dimension: Does Jesus' death represent *sacrifice* (see above) *or slaughter*? The latter would mean that he was murdered because others ganged up on him (leading to defamation, accusation, and even torture). Both interpretations are likely to have influenced the biblical authors. Yet they are differently salubrious. The image of the *slaughtered* lamb of God shows us—no less gruesomely than sacrifice, yet probably free from projection and inflated sacralization—that Jesus fell victim to the incensed crowd and accepted torture and crucifixion out of loyalty and devotion. Like a lamb, he did not put up a fight ...

9.9. The Secret of Jesus' Awakening

What has Jesus' awakening (i.e., his resurrection) to do with love? What do the metaphorical phrases "the victory of life" and "love over death" mean? Where does victory occur in this respect?

We have no historical evidence for Jesus' awakening. It thus remains a matter of faith and raises another question: Does God exist? Does a life-giving, renewing Whole exist? Yet this does not concern *how* Jesus' awakening (which we are unable to verify) happened. The crucial point is *that* it happened. Not the awakening itself but the many testimonies of those to whom Jesus reportedly appeared may claim historical value. How might we interpret the experiences of so many witnesses?

Theologically, we can understand Jesus' awakening as a mystery that originates in and is encompassed by the Father as the source of all sources. Schwager (1999) argues that this was how the Father confirmed his Son and his message. We can see Jesus's life, his speeches, healing, suffering, and death as the unfolding of a certain dynamic, as an increasingly intense drama. Below, I outline how I understand Jesus' life, Passion, death, and awakening (see Renz 2017, 238–60). These "five acts" partly follow Raymund Schwager (1999):

The Five Acts of Jesus' Drama

Act 1: The dynamic of invitation: Jesus' message and healing are first and foremost an invitation. We are all invited to participate in Jesus' cause—that is, we can all participate in the kingdom of God/heaven, at least in principle. The gospels primarily provide good news.

Act 2: The dynamic of escalation: Jesus' rejection by the rulers, the many projections and the ganging-up mechanisms that probably played out therein, follow a dynamic of escalation, greed, jealousy, and exercising of power.

No one except his disciples wanted Jesus. Yet no one could bear the thought of this extermination impulse entering consciousness. Nor did anyone take responsibility. Instead, one acted as an anonymous collective (see chapter 7.6 for a discussion of crowd or mob behavior).

Act 3: Death as a consequence of mobbing and the dynamic of devotion amid the Passion: Jesus died because the collective turned its back on him. His faithfulness to his message and to God—that is, the fact that Jesus remained true to himself and connected with the Father, even if this meant dying—is an expression of the highest love. It is devotion.

Act 4: Awakening (i.e., resurrection) as the "dynamic of God," as the "dynamic of life" per se. The mystery per se.

Act 5: The dynamic of a spreading spirit, from which spring enthusiasm, inspiration, and a new spirituality. And which moved the Pentecostal disciples to new faith and action.

Act 4—awakening—is a sign *from God*. It means that new life and new creativity will arise, and that love outlasts human greed and power. Pursuant to the laws of nature, spring brings new green after autumnal death and winterly frost. Human *nature*, moreover, generates new life even amid the greatest misery and war. The very same force enables us to love. Here, I speak of a *dynamic of love*. Instead of leading to embitterment, this dynamic makes us dare to take steps toward compassion and peace, even if this involves coping with hurt. It also represents spiritual strength and is evident, for instance, when an authority within us dares to hope and remains constructive amid collective resignation. This strength eludes rational explanation. It is either given to us from without or exists deep inside us. We cannot "make" it. It is grace.

In Jesus, this divine working took shape. The Father was involved in him. After Jesus' death, the Father lived on and so also the dynamic of love and increasing consciousness. This helped Jesus' cause to spread ever further.

9.10. The Quintessence of Redemption

In the previous chapters, I have developed a dynamic perspective on Jesus' life. I believe this is crucial to understanding redemption. How did Jesus redeem others? And wherein? What happened to his fellow humans at the time? How does "it" happen today? Let me outline the quintessence of redemption:

1. Jesus as a role model and as a person: his relationship with the Father and his extraordinary personality allowed the historical Jesus *himself* to embody a new connectedness. He personifies primordial trust, an answer to evil and dissociation; he is love personified. Nevertheless, as a role model, many people could perceive Jesus as "merely historical."

2. Message: his connection with the Father meant that Jesus could intuitively answer questions about human imprinting (see Renz 2017). We are redeemed if we understand and contemplate Jesus' speeches, parables, and healing stories. All of these can become an answer to our own distress. As a message, however, Jesus' redemptive potential reaches our mind and reason but not always the emotional depths of our soul. As a message, it could be dismissed (repressed) by so many.

3. Inner center and primordial image: Jesus' behavior was not affected by human imprinting (greed, a thirst for power, and glory). Instead, it burst asunder ancient false beginnings and initiated new reaction patterns, in a way perhaps comparable to a new neurophysiological programming. He thus prepared a spiritual path in the human soul, for his friends and for those wishing to

follow him to this day. Believing in and being able to rely on Jesus' way is a gift bestowed on Christians in the shape of Easter (and Pentecost). What we are unable to achieve ourselves, we can allow ourselves to be given. We can trust and follow the new initiation (and path) in our soul. The example of his anxious disciples shows that Jesus *himself* can become the center of the human soul (see figure 1) as well as a "Lord" for those who accept him. The apostles and disciples first locked themselves in the upper room (Acts 1:13) because they, too, had lost all orientation and structure when Jesus died. Later, they went out into the world, after being filled with the Holy Spirit, and proclaimed Jesus' message. Thus redemption occurs deep inside, through discipleship. Yet as a primordial image and center, Jesus remains pure experience, one that is reserved for "mystics."

4. A starting point for peace, for a new creativity, and for a newly ordered collective with a new group dynamics: What happened to the crowd? What happened to Jesus' enemies? The events surrounding the Passion brought to light the collective imprintings and behavioral patterns based on separation (e.g., revenge, scapegoating) and freed them toward transformation. Metaphorically speaking, the collective atmosphere was pried open.

It was able to change. Why? One point is that Jesus did not reduce his enemies to their negative behavior. Jesus even asked God to forgive his enemies. He thus released them into God's hands and acted as their advocate toward God. Even more crucially, Jesus thereby opted out of any power struggle. He let his enemies prevail and abandoned the old structures with no ifs or buts. What followed was not a struggle but a change of scenario, a vacuum. This enables a new perspective and opens up an opportunity. Let me illustrate this with an image from the theater. An act has just finished, the curtain has fallen, a sense of emptiness arises briefly, before another scene, another world, appears. This is how I imagine that most of Jesus' contemporaries experienced his death and awakening. The struggle between the incensed crowd and Jesus, the stumbling block (Greek: *skandalon*), was over. The struggle for victory and righteousness had been enacted. The Messiah had fallen silent and a deathly silence ensued. Many who had played along resumed their daily business, with their view of God and the world reaffirmed. Others—a precious few—stood still, touched by the incomprehensible events. They asked questions and perhaps even questioned themselves. Like the centurion standing guard over the cross (Luke 23, 47; Matthew 27:54), many of them realized the likes of us do not depart this life like that: "Truly this man was God's Son" (Matthew 27:54). Gradually, awakening from absorption, they still stood between these two scenarios. Yet a strange, deathly silence, perhaps their apprehension of a more comprehensive being, now gripped them. They no longer needed to prevail or to be right. Yet the vestibule for peace is at first a vacuum, the newly constituted order is unstable, impermanent.

5. A reversal of energy, the overcoming of separation and splitting: we need to see Jesus' greatest achievement *spiritually*. His person and behavior had overcome separation and splitting and consistently refuted their excessiveness, and thus also evil. Jesus had not let himself be confused. He had always seen through and confronted evil (see the healing of those possessed by demons). He did not even become embroiled with evil amid his greatest test, his Passion and death. He maintained—whatever confronted him—his identity as the Father's Son. In every difficult situation, he went to God, the One, and thus—united with the Father—he overcame splitting. Jesus trusted the Father, again and again. Redemption means a new beginning within the soul, as well as the new organization of collective structures. The

fact that this occurs when *someone* reveals the ancient imprintings and brings these before the Father has to do with God himself. It is the question about God per se. We need to think of God as the source of a new dynamic. Moreover, redemption from separation and splitting is given in the Father as the Whole, since time immemorial and forever. All it requires is that we are reconnected with the Father time and again. For this to happen, we must learn to overcome and endure the tabooed closeness to God (Tree of Life in Paradise). We must also endure God's all-encompassing love (he also loves our brothers, sisters, neighbors, and enemies; see John 21:22). Thus redemption is a reversal of energy and occurs through consciousness and discipleship. It *will* happen one day, and time and again, when we overcome our primordial fear and separation and find our way home to God. Biblical images of such an energetic turn include the victory of the lamb and of the light (Logos, consciousness) over darkness. The symbolism of the Catholic liturgy celebrated on Easter night takes up this victory, for instance, in the great hymn on the resurrection (Exultet). In terms of this symbol, Jesus' awakening defeats the powers of darkness. Today, we sometimes experience this overcoming or that "the time of evil is over."

9.11. Spiritual Practice: Second Identity, Peace, and Present-Day Experiences of Redemption

What are the consequences for everyday spiritual practice, meditation, contemplation, and spiritual care? What does spirituality comprise in Jesus' sense if we consider the question of redemption? Scapegoating has remained widespread until today. We must become aware of this unconscious pattern of behavior before we can—gradually—interrupt it. Our spiritual practice can help us turn inward. It can prevent us from identifying with our attributed role and from debasing others. From a spiritual viewpoint, we are always more than what others make of us.

Yet, guided by Jesus, our ground is already prepared and our path paved. Even despite great chasms and failure. "It" happens—through the processes of becoming new. Many of us experience Christ as an inner reality amid life and maturation. We see Jesus or the resurrected one in a dream. Some of us describe how we "see, hear, and understand in a new way." Still others feel newly borne and guided. They feel good and experience fresh "impetus" and "new orientation," either in reality or in their dreams. Time and again, we overcome our traumatic paralysis. Traversing long crises and becoming new, we find our way to new affirmation, new identity, and peace. Here are some present-day examples of redeemed existence:

"I have become someone else through my illness and must now try to live a new life in my old surroundings, which haven't changed, and stay alive" (a computer specialist and family father after suffering acute leukemia).

A woman going through a major marriage crisis dreamed the following abstruse words: "Peace among those whom he favors" (Luke 2:14). She heard angels playing music, but it wasn't Christmas music. When she associated her dream with the mystery of Christmas, she suddenly knew: "I want to make a fresh start to my marriage, as at Christmas. And all of a sudden, I also have the strength to do this."

When a patient who was struggling to get out of a coma was played Christmas music, she later described her experience thus: "Suddenly it was as if Jesus was standing next to me in a white robe. He said, 'Don't be afraid, I'll guide you.'" She then managed to regain her ego-consciousness and to return to her everyday consciousness.

During a long conversation, a Jewish patient of mine had a dream: He saw Jesus before him, who proffered his hand. Although the man was standing opposite, he still managed to shake Jesus' hand, as if "I had wings to fly over to him." For the first time, this staunch Jew did not feel that his own religion was being attacked by Christianity. He felt "inspired" instead (German: beflügelt, *"given wings").*

"This crisis has taught me how to marvel. I'm less afraid, and more curious and happier. The suffering in the world, but even more so its beauty, leaves me speechless. This is what it must have been like when Jesus lived. He opened people's eyes." These words were spoken by a forty-five-year-old woman whose cancer had confronted her with traumatic childhood experiences and had freed her from those physical symptoms and fears.

One severely ill patient dreamed that she had seen Jesus. *"He closes the dead person's eyes and opens the newborn's."* She died the next day.

"Jesus was lying on the bed next to me, on which my husband used to lie. Jesus was simply there" (a widow's dream who felt comforted in her grief).

"He/It arose in me and sang from within me" (as a leukemia patient dreamed one night, during which she mobilized so much energy that she was allowed to go home).

A crisis-stricken middle-aged woman had this dream: *"I had died. The coffin stood there. The funeral took place. Then I am walking, my arms and legs outstretched, as if I could fly, on the final stretch home to my Father. My robe, at first black and white, now becomes shiningly white and I 'know': The resurrected one is inside me."*

A seriously ill patient, who could barely see, told me about a dream in which he had *"found a so-called Jesus key while something like an alphabet was pressed into his hands." In the dream, he was able to read again.*

Other dream images describe redemption explicitly as an initiation, a paving of a way, a system. Thus, for instance, a friend of mine dreamed about a "railway track of redemption that leads through a bleak valley, first down, and then up again" (see the image of the former apostolic confession of faith, the descent into the realm of the dead, only to arise again on the third day). Further images include "a high-tech train set in primeval times," "a street amid a moonscape," "a path across the desert," "a passage through the original flood," "a silver-colored track on which a silver train takes the forsaken back home." All these dreamers were carried by trains and along paths and initiations. A direction emerged within chaos. Energies found orientation.

Amid a marriage crisis, one woman dreamed about that subterranean canal system beneath her marriage was about to come apart. Canals now needed to be installed even deeper to ensure that water flowed along the right paths, in the right direction. This image was accompanied by the strange words: "With religion it's like with a canal system."

After their dreams, these dreamers and many other patients (at least fifty) were now related differently to themselves and their inwardness, to God and the divine. They now had different roots. Their dreams strengthened and guided them to cope with their crises, for weeks, days, or simply for a brief moment. Months later, they interpreted their crisis as a creative process on their journey from one place to another. None of these fifty patients suffered from religious neurosis, nor was their experience neurotically motivated. They had instead made profound experiences with God/the Whole during their crisis or illness. Such experiences led them to another understanding of Jesus. For these people, Jesus did not simply pass away. No, he was/is mystically present. And they had quietly become mystics themselves.

Paul seemed highly familiar with this experience when he proclaimed, "It is no longer I who live, but it is Christ who lives in me" (Galatians 2:20). Moreover, "But by the grace of God I am what I am" (1 Corinthians 15:10). Paul's autobiograpical testimonies are among his most impressive words (1 Corinthians 15:1–11, 2 Corinthians 12:9; see Renz 2017). Although Paul and the dreamers/patients mentioned above had each received a new identity, their *old* life had not ceased to exist. No, it was now related to their new life.

Conceptually, *spiritual care* is about circumspection and refers to the word *spirituality*. In this book, it acquires a new—or rather its very own—dimension, one steeped in experience (see Fitchett and Nolan 2015; Lazenby, McCorkle, and Sulmasy 2014; Renz 2016). It should attend not only to patients' needs and conscious distress[6] but also to their transcendental experience (see Renz 2016) and thus its aspect of grace. Patients undergo deep processes: not only their needs change during their illness but so does their experience of who or what God is (Does he really exist?). "Easter experiences" are the peak experiences among many other religious experiences (e.g., being nurtured, comforted, borne) that I have observed and encountered in practicing spiritual care for twenty years (see the above examples of redeemed existence). This vast experience, which I could take part in by accompanying patients, encourages me to share their hope, or sometimes to hope in their place. Sometimes, my experience even gives me the courage to continue my work with terminally ill patients. My particular understanding of spiritual care tells me that redemption is possible even in the midst of an incurable illness. Indeed, it is precisely here that "it" occurs. In our inner search and maturation, all of us make similar experiences, whenever we accept what seeks birth or growth within us. This is part of our everyday spirituality. Waiting, relying on this, and facing ourselves leads us to ineffable, sacred, or deep spiritual experience (see William James [1902] 2012).

What does the Bible promise us in this respect? Which post-Pentecostal qualities do we find in the Bible? First of all, the capacity for peace, atonement, and "the forgiving of sins"—that is, the fruits of new identity and love. The resurrected one's greeting of peace stands out in the gospels: "Peace be with you!" (Luke 24:36). And so do John's words: "My peace I give to you. I do not give to you as the world gives" (John 14:27).

But how can a fate-ridden person imagine taking supper with everyone else? The victim beside the perpetrator, the deceived beside the deceiver? How can and should we still love beyond naivety? How can we share food and look each other in the eye unreproachfully? Some very few, very exceptional figures have achieved this: saints, or individuals such as Mahatma Gandhi or Martin Luther King. Biblically, peace, in Jesus' sense, is rooted in the Father, in connectedness. Reconciliation, which strives to be more than a truce, can emerge only from a new identity and a new atmosphere (in the generation of the sons, as the German word *versöhnung*, "atonement," might suggest). It overcomes us when the time is ripe. We can then feel for each other, momentarily or repeatedly, or are able to forgive each other. We are able accept our fate or to move toward each other. Sometimes, those whom fate strikes hard no longer ask, "Why me?" but "Why not me?" "Why should others always be affected?" The scars of old injuries still exist. At such times, they no longer hurt but are "transfigured" (see Drewermann 1989, 200).

Like Peter at the end of the Gospel of John (John 21:20–23), the human being still needs God's help even *after* such deep experiences of redeemed existence. In response to his anxious, envious question, "Lord, what about him [i.e., John the disciple]?" he received an overwhelming answer: God's promise of *his* own vocation. To the (entirely sufficient) extent that *we* are meant (called), and no one else, we are *protected* from our permanent reflex to compare ourselves with others, to compete against them. Peter's question reveals that he had momentarily fallen back into an all-too-human reaction: envy and jealousy. Only connectedness eventually makes us capable of gathering and community, in which all of us, no matter how great or how small, may exist according to our particular gifts.

CHAPTER 10

He Comes toward Me

JESUS THE LOGOS AND CHRIST

10.1. Human Development and Salvation History

Religions transmit *histories of salvation* and provide answers to deep human desires. When I was a theology student, salvation history was widely discussed, but I either didn't understand these discussions or I reacted allergically to them. Yet *which* salvation was meant? And whose salvation? Is salvation history manipulative? At the time, I took extra lessons (figuratively speaking) and understood that salvation is about interpreting our own biography differently, in another—and perhaps even brighter and transfigured—light. This raises several key questions: Do major lines run through our life, behind which God/the Whole might stand? Is a higher authority interested in our personal development? Such questions might provide answers even to our question about the meaning of life. However, the history of salvation always involves a basic decision: Do we or don't we believe such deep intuitions (see chapter 2.5)?

> *Seventy-year-old Mr. Camenzind looked back at his life, which had been fraught with suffering. He had always been plagued by illnesses and had suffered from depression for years. His wife had exploited him time and again, so that he finally decided to leave her. Now, he oscillated between despair and resignation. "Is there any sense at all?!" We had long discussions. He couldn't understand. Yet he realized that I wasn't lying. Being in hospital was a good experience: he had never experienced so much affection. A few weeks later, Mr. Camenzind was dying. He was barely responsive. His son and I were at his bedside. His son, usually quite a tough fellow, wanted to thank his father one last time: "Dad, I'm really proud of you. You're the first person in our family in a long time who hasn't committed suicide or sought assisted suicide. You've paved a new way for us." "What? Ahhh." The dying man opened his eyes and was visibly moved. That night, I remembered the question of meaning. When I returned to Mr. Camenzind's bedside the next day with his son, I continued our earlier conversation and said, "Mr. Camenzind, what you've achieved here, in your suffering, is meaningful. You've opened up a new way of dying to your family, your son, your nephews." After a visit from his extended family, during which the same issue*

arose, he stayed calm. He barely needed any painkillers until he died quietly—alone. Was this a story of salvation?

We can approach the big questions of life—What does it mean to be human? How do we develop as human beings?—both ontogenetically and phylogenetically in terms of salvation history. The basic tenets of religions and belief systems were developed in this way. Christianity, for instance, sensed that *God himself* existed both behind the historical Jesus and behind a great many early Christian experiences of the resurrected. These experiences became the basis for "writing a history of salvation," thus the belief in Jesus' resurrection may have ingrained itself in people at the time. Or it became a basic Christian tenet that not only Jesus but also the Father must be deeply compassionate. Or to ask about redemption represents a particular way of thinking. Christmas, Easter, and Pentecost are salvific answers that become concrete in the liturgy. They blend with historical moments and testimonies. They are not historical accounts but concern an emotional, spiritual moment.

Easter celebrates the resurrection of Christ, the life of the crucified Jesus. *Historically*, we must deal with many transcendental experiences of the disciples and others: they bear witness to their experience of Jesus—after his death. In *this* perspective, we do not know more. In terms of salvation history, we may take the disciples' experiences *as a sign of God*: Christians believe in Christ's resurrection and that this man was God's Son. For them—and psychologically speaking—Easter overcomes the (supposedly) definitive nature of death (which is symbolized by the denied access to the Tree of Life in Paradise). We recognize the relativity of our existence and of our "ego-death" (our usual way of thinking, needing ...). And we intuit a time and place beyond it. Throughout Jesus' Passion und death, the dynamics of love was stronger than the dynamics of evil.

Pentecost celebrates the Holy Spirit and the moment in which we are touched by God. *Historical evidence* exists for the disciples' experiences—also after the initial period, when Jesus was still close to them. We also have proof of Paul's spiritual experiences (although he never knew the earthly Jesus). Yet we need to place any interpretation in the broader context of salvation history. Accordingly, Pentecost overcomes the deep splitting in the human soul and the scattering of humanity across the world (into various languages and culture) as the result of hubris (mythologically, the Tower of Babel). A dynamic force is released: pneuma, spirit, spirituality. For Christians, the spirit of the Father and Son is still at work within us today. It enables gathering and community. As the one living within us, Christ is closer to us than the physical Jesus was.

10.2. God Comes toward Us—the Christmas Credo

Let me illustrate salvation history with the mystery of Christmas. In commemorating the birth of Christ, about which we have barely any historical knowledge, we celebrate the coming of the Son of God/the Savior/the Messiah (I have discussed these honorific titles in chapter 3). This is how Christian religion responds to the human separation from God. Christians believe that, in Jesus, God comes toward us and precedes us. The "distant one" draws closer—that is, the heavenly breaks into the earthly. Thus God is no longer sublime or totally unknown, even if he remains incomprehensible (see Paul in Acts 17:22–27). Consequently, the human being expelled from Eden is no longer entirely lost.

According to the mystery of faith and Christmas, the tenet that God, who has always existed and still does, has become immanent and visible in Jesus, is willed by God. Christianity believes that the Christ of all times was born with the historical Jesus and that this fundamentally changed the human condition and that of the world. At Christmas, many Christians still feel that heaven is open. The German theologian Gotthard Fuchs (2004, 183) speaks of God's descending movement: "In the eyes of faith, however, the searching God is always on his way to us; vice versa we are on our way with the question of God." A God who descends and approaches humanity is another proposition for our spiritual path than the soul's "mere" ascent to ever greater wisdom.

Historically, we know that early Christianity debated the question of Jesus (Was he human or was he the Son of God?). The Council of Chalcedon (451 CE) ended this discussion within the Church by declaring that human and divine nature coexisted in Jesus (i.e., true man and true God, not a demigod as was assumed in antiquity). Thomas Aquinas spoke of the unity of God and humanity becoming a reality in Jesus (*unio hypostatica*). Karl Rahner (1961, 162) formulated this idea as "independence and radical proximity": Jesus is uniquely rooted in God while remaining wholly himself. In other words, his relationship with the Father enabled Jesus to be who he was: entirely free (of foreign "masters"), sovereign, and loving. Based on his relationship with the Father, he became *personified love*. The *historical* moment in all of this is the mystic of Nazareth and his mysticism!

The evangelists used mythological-biblical images to retrospectively describe what can never become visible from the outside. Three evangelists (Matthew, Luke, John) inquired into the origins of the exceptional Jesus. Their main question: Where does he come from? While Matthew's and Luke's *accounts* of Jesus' childhood cannot claim *historical* meaning, they possess legendary, and thus even deeper *symbolic* meaning (I have compared the three ways of interpreting the Bible in the introduction). Matthew and Luke attempted to express what happened in constellations (the star of Bethlehem) and energetically: the shepherds "went with haste" to the child in the manger while the three wise men traveled from afar. Mary "treasured" what she heard and "pondered" it in her heart" (Luke 2:15–19). Elizabeth's child leaped within her (etymologically, "to hope" derives from to leap, to hop, to scuttle). These stories represent Jesus as a divine child, as a child born of the spirit (as told by both, the evangelists and probably also by the preceding oral tradition). So regardless of the biological question (i.e., the divine child and the virgin birth of Jesus), which remains unverifiable and a secret, Jesus was described accurately as astoundingly autonomous and as founded in God. Symbolically, "to be born of a virgin" means being generated neither by the male principle nor by worldly values (see also Drewermann 1986; 1991, 483ff.).[1]

The Christian legend of Christmas corresponds to a pre-Christian desire. The German theologian Hildegunde Wöller (1989, 22) speaks of archetypal psychic structures that existed long before the birth of Jesus. According to C. G. Jung, archetypes are the basic patterns of experience and lie concealed behind myths. At the time of Jesus, mythological themes such as the birth of "God's child in the womb of the virgin" and the birth of light (see the Gospel of John) were well known. They are confirmed by rites and myths in almost all cultures. Thus, two thousand years ago, people were still closer to their dream consciousness than we are today. If, for instance, the birth of Christ was said to have occurred in deep winter, after the winter solstice according to earlier pagan rites, this was not considered problematic at the time. However, even if we are alienated nowadays, these metaphors and themes are still alive in our deeper psychic layers.

The rational human being of the third millennium asks, what actually happened at the time? Did Jesus' birth really bring about fundamental change? And if so, how and why? Do individuals and communities find a new and better life in the light of that child today—beyond the sweet romance of Christmas? It remains an open question how far Jesus might become our primordial ground, and thus whether his "formula of redemption" (see chapters 1 and 9) is timeless. Jesus himself asked for discipleship. I believe in an individual spiritual practice that is based on a new understanding of the Holy Scriptures, which takes mystical approaches and metaphorical knowledge into account. The decision of faith still works subtly. Every year, all of us, even believers, face an inevitable question: How come the divine child is also born within us? How come Jesus Christ becomes present in our soul? This is the basic question of mysticism. Let me cite Angelus Silesius' (1932) *The Cherubinic Wanderer:*

"God must be born in thee
Though Jesus Christ in Bethlehem
A thousand times his Mother bore,
Is he not born again in thee
Then art thou lost for evermore."

Here we find the answer that the great German mystic Meister Eckhart (ca. 1260–1328) gave to the question, "Why did God become human?": "So that God may be born in the soul and the soul again in God (1979, 215; see also Keller 2011, 77). Thus, the fact that God's ground became *his*, and his ground *God's*, was crucial for Meister Eckhart. This, in short, is mysticism.

Below I try to interpret the prologue to the Gospel of John. Our knowledge of near-death experiences and many experiences of the dying are my key to—perhaps—gaining insight into the Prologue.

10.3. In the Beginning Was Logos, Not Coincidence or Forsakenness

John 1:1–18

In the beginning was the "Logos,"[2]
and the Logos was with God, and the Logos was God [toward God].

He was in the beginning with God [toward God].
All things came into being through him [the Logos],
and without him not one thing [of what has become] came into being.
What has come into being in him was life,
and the life was the light of all people.
> The light shines in the darkness, and the darkness did not overcome it.
> There was a man sent from God, whose name was John.
> He came as a witness to testify to the light, so that all might believe through him.
> He himself was not the light, but he came to testify to the light.

The true light,
which enlightens everyone,
(was) coming into the world.
He was in the world,
> and the world came into being through him;

yet the world did not recognize him.
He came to what was his own,
but his people [his own ones] did not accept [receive] him.
> But to all who received him, who believed in his name,
> he gave power to become children of God,
> who were born, not of blood or of the will of the flesh or of the will of man, but of God.

And the Logos became flesh
and lived among us,
> and we have seen his glory,
> the glory as of a father's only son,
full of grace and truth.
> John [the Baptist] testified to him and cried out: "This was he of whom I said, "He who comes after me ranks ahead of me because he was before me."
From his fullness we have all received,
grace upon grace.
> The law indeed was given through Moses;
> grace and truth came through Jesus Christ.
> No one has ever seen God. It is God the only Son [the only begotten one], who is God, who is close to the Father's heart, [bosom], who has made him known.

The Prologue is a composition. An original Logos-hymn (without the indented verses) was incorporated into the gospel and combined with other material (for a historical-critical perspective, see Schenke 1998; Gnilka 1983). It asks, how might we imagine the beginning of the extraordinary man from Nazareth? The Gospel of John answers this question with an ingenious vision: in the beginning was the principle of "Logos" rather than coincidence or forsakenness. The theme implicit in this theme is *the coming of consciousness*.

John's vision describes Jesus' origins with astounding accuracy in terms of the psychological patterns of *becoming conscious*. The Prologue resembles a creation myth, like Genesis 1 ("In the beginning God created the heavens and the earth").

The Prologue tells us, in the beginning, in the archetypal sphere, was the Logos. Only Logos. The term is crucial: *Logos* stands for Jesus and, beyond that, for a certain principle (effective words, the coming into consciousness, and the opposite of coincidence). The Greek $o`lo,goj$ means "word, report, speech, language, logic." The Semitic languages used "word" to refer to a dynamic event. Terms were "effective words" and followed the same pattern: "God spoke, and it was done" (see Genesis 1). Curses and blessings were effective words. According to Semitic thinking, they remained effective for four generations. However, the Prologue is not about curses and blessings but about redemption. For the Gospel of John, Jesus' existence marks a positive interruption, a turn of overall fate. The evangelist (and the group who shaped this gospel) was so moved by Jesus' work on earth that they saw a timeless working behind him: a potential that, in the beginning, was with God, and that was God himself (John 1).[3] In the historical Jesus, who lived with utmost consciousness (see his dealing with demons, chapter 7), and who advanced the coming of consciousness (see chapter 7.3), the Gospel of John recognized the timeless

Logos. There, the Logos stands for Jesus and also for all those qualities that he brought into the world with particular intensity: love, light, primordial trust, being related, spirit, and becoming conscious as the overcoming of sin (chapter 5) and evil (chapters 7 and 9).

According to its literal meaning, the term *Logos* (logic) also means the *opposite of coincidence*. The Prologue tells us that in the beginning there was not coincidence but the Logos. Everything came into being *from* the Logos, from this quality of being, and *in* this principle. Without the Logos, nothing came into being. Life was and began in it. Seen thus, the Logos transcribes God himself and the order inherent in him. In this respect, the Prologue is a *confession of faith*: "I believe in an ultimate pattern behind all things, in a primordial order, in a divine principle that forces its way into the process of becoming conscious. I believe in God as the creative primal ground" (see Kessler 2010). Moreover, "I believe that this principle became particularly effective in Jesus." And, finally, "I believe in the redeeming effective word, which entered the world with Jesus."

The language of the Gospel of John is special. It eludes most people today, except for those who have had deep spiritual experiences or dreams, and who are therefore able to feel their way into the initial and the liminal stages of life. Our liminal experiences help us grasp what it means if consciousness changes profoundly, from *everyday consciousness* through *dream consciousness* to our immersion in transcendence.

> *Thus, a man who lived in a mountain village dreamed about life taking place near the sea and in water. He took this to be a closeness to water, the prime and original element (amniotic fluid). In a dream, another man saw humans and animals that all had a spherical shape. Everything was round, and his association was "whole and holy." A third man only saw a black, glistening globe, from which light emanated.*

Each of these dreamers understood that transcendence—that is, roundness—is the ultimate reality and that a transition, as well as a state of transition (e.g., water), exists. People with near-death experiences and the dying describe this condition similarly: as a somewhat extreme state of transcendence, in which nothing exists except light, love (relational word), oneness with an all-encompassing force, and a transition to an utmost state of being. Already speaking about this condition moves them; they are "gathered," differently motivated, and oriented toward something deeper and higher than their ego. The Prologue describes transition, though in the opposite direction: from transcendence to everyday consciousness. Life began in the One. Yet the One is at the same time relationship, which existed already in the beginning. The Logos, too, is related to God from the beginning (see the Greek apposition, *pro.j to.n qeo,n*, "to or with ... God"). Transposed onto Jesus, this means that he was "related to the Father" and connected with him from the beginning. Thus he was a mystic. To the extent that we follow these patterns and emulate Jesus, we are also related and connected.

According to the Gospel of John, *only this particular mode of being existed in the beginning: primordial order, light, love.* From there, Jesus was given to us and directs us toward this mode of being. At this most extreme point, the metaphor of light does not yet represent the opposite of darkness. No ambivalence existed in the beginning. People with near-death experiences or the dying describe a "strangely radiant light," or a "primordial light," sometimes even a "dark light." The *One* is also love. It is fullness, emptiness (spatial dimension), meaning (fulfillment of the temporal dimension), and energy. In the beginning, there was no ambivalence, as the frequent reference to its "roundness" expresses.

Soon afterward, however, came differentiation, ambivalence, and tension. The corresponding images occurring in myths and deep dreams include chaos, dampness, greyness, and forlornness.

10.4. Darkness and Light—a Tension Inherent in the Whole

At some point, the Prologue speaks of darkness: "The light shines in the darkness, and the darkness did not overcome it" (John 1:5). An opposition, a polarity now emerges from primordial unity. The metaphor of light no longer represents a primordial light but instead the emerging Logos, crystallizing consciousness. (In this respect, it is worth noting the phrase, "I began to see the light," which implies the distinction between light and darkness and a sense of enlightenment). The emergence of polarity is symbolically coherent: the dying and people who have near-death experiences or deep spiritual dreams mostly "understand" the distinction between our divided, worldly state (everyday consciousness) and the undivided, primordial, and mystical state (see Richard Rohr's discussion of nondual reality in Rohr 2009). In everyday consciousness, their experience is temporal, concrete, polar, and causal. In the other, "transcendental state, none of this exists and all human ambition to rival or excel others is meaningless," as one elderly patient told me.

To understand the Prologue of John, we need to take into account that a category shift, a threshold or a crossing, occurs between these states:

Thus, one dying man stammered, "Two, three ... and now across, across—diagonally." His wife wanted him to be turned over. I explained that his words might also correspond to her husband's inner experience; he might no longer be experiencing things causally, or seeing things concretely, but was instead returning to another world. "Another world," he confirmed, "across, across." She understood and encouraged him. He died fifteen minutes later.

The Prologue here expresses this category shift in terms of a basic tension (light versus darkness): from now on, light stands beside darkness. Light emerges and represents becoming conscious, while darkness represents what resides in the unconscious. Figuratively, the unconscious is like the sea, while consciousness is the tip of the iceberg jutting out of the water. Because it is miniscule, and hence easily overlooked, consciousness constantly risks being flooded by the sea. We also experience the tension between consciousness and the unconscious in the liminal sphere between life and death.

Some people occasionally tremble or grow rigid in the transition and yet barely find any words for their distress: "White-black," "lost in no-man's-land," "in-between," "Something takes hold of me although there is nothing there," "I am tied up," "hot-cold." Others choose energetic images: "Pull," "fight," "power line."

The key metaphors of the Prologue are light and darkness.

The tension between consciousness and the unconscious also captures the difficult relationship between the individual, who emerges from the unconscious, and the world or the crowd. This view enables a new understanding of the Prologue to the Gospel of John, where darkness corresponds to the "world" (*ko,smoj / kosmos*; see chapters 5 and 7): "The true light, which enlightens everyone, was coming into the world. He [male, i.e., the Logos] was in the world, and the world came into being through him [male, i.e., *div auvtou / / di autou*]; yet the world did not recognize him. He came to what was his own, and his people did not accept him" (John 1: 9–11; see also John 3:19).

Yet the Gospel of John not only addresses the tension between conscious (light) and unconscious (dark) but also *a particular suffering*. The Logos—and with it also Jesus—is evidently unrecognized, lonely, and excluded. Why? How does this suffering occur in life and evolution? The Gospel of John offers no explanation. Yet since the Prologue is a hymn, and thus emerged from oral tradition, it also brought into consciousness transgenerational patterns, including the reflex of expulsion. A collective reflex against becoming conscious and against people who live consciously (they could bring into light what one wants to keep hidden). In this context, the assertions that "the light shines in the darkness, and the darkness did not overcome it" (John 1:5) are consequential. They are part of individuation and isolation. As Jesus' example shows, neither the unconscious individual nor the crowd (see chapter 7) understood the luminous consciousness of the Logos that came into the world. Here, the Gospel of John says the Passion stood over Jesus' life from the beginning. The Passion seems to be founded on God, and thus is allowed to exist. Yet similar suffering is, in general, part of processes of growing consciousness. People who advance consciousness endure suffering because they are first silenced or "die" before their knowledge becomes accepted. They are misunderstood and lonely. In the beginning of the Prologue, the terms *world* and *his own* refer to the Jewish people (they did not accept [receive] Jesus). Yet these terms also address the universal human reflex of expulsion and casting out those who advance consciousness. The crowd/darkness can never really approve of the individual's increasing consciousness and emergence (because he or she leaves the crowd, dares to live on his or her own terms, and to become conscious). The crowd reacts to such newness (which comes into existence through increasing consciousness) with fear and repulsion. Consequently, Jesus, who represents growing consciousness must have time and again faced the world's overwhelming lack of understanding.

At this point, the Prologue introduces an interesting expression: "did not overcome." Reassuringly, the original Greek also means "did not take hold of, did not destroy": *katalamba,nw / katalambano* means "to take hold of," "to understand," but also "to seize" in the sense of "to assail" or "to overtake." This word occurs in another passage in the Gospel of John: "So that the darkness may not overtake you" (John 12: 35). If we translate both meanings of *katalamba,nw* within the Prologue, then darkness is *not* able to understand the light/the Logos. Nor is it able to overwhelm or destroy it. Regarding Jesus, this means that what he brought into the world could not be stamped out—despite his crucifixion. Thus every insight, every piece of knowledge that enters into consciousness, exists irrevocably. Even if those who generate this knowledge are killed, knowledge *itself*—becoming conscious, that is, the Logos—is indestructible. Yet why, in the face of so much suffering, is it still worth daring to become conscious? This, I suggest, has to do with the mystery of God, with God's ultimate, utmost urge. We can imagine this as if God/the Whole urges toward conscious realization. But isn't it presumptuous to assume that an urge exists within God? Is God unfinished? In risking such an attribution here,

I do not mean that we should assume that God's essence is somehow deficient. Rather, it is about "longing" (for a counterpart, for likeness, for humans, for life and love). It is about a force or spirit within God (Holy Spirit), to which Stanislav and Grof (1990, 133) have attributed "intentionalism."

Looking at Jesus, the Father motivated him time and again to perform whatever he said or did. Jesus' way of life attests indirectly to the fact that the Father possesses "intentional force," a deep concern for humans. Already the Old Testament provides a similar image of God. It contains numerous reports of God pursuing the human being. He is "interested" in us. Why? Ecclesiastical history claims that human beings need this "for their salvation." I have a more open-minded view: God may be a God whose deepest interest is evolution, relationship, and human development! If we picture God dynamically, then patterns of energy also reside within him, including a striving for life, love, and becoming conscious.

Dynamically speaking, the beginning of life is not identical with its end. Development occurs between these poles. If precisely this interests God, then we can discover meaning even amid our most extreme suffering: what we endure and contribute flows as precious parts of a whole into greater development. Development is meaningful and springs from a corresponding urge within God.

The Prologue of John is shaped by such an epistemological perspective. It seeks to make us deeply astonished at God's large dimensions. The Logos, then, is "most deeply desired." And its suffering is taken for granted. At first, this holds true for Jesus: his life and suffering "serve" development per se. The same applies to other highly conscious people. Their suffering abides by a law inhering in all higher human development. Through suffering and after "crucifixion," the Logos also rises again in these persons' life, because it is God's energy. Yet who understands such a vision? According to the Prologue, the Logos (and such a vision) is accepted by *some* individuals. The Logos gave them the "power to become children of God" (John 1:12). Psychologically speaking, they are reconnected with the divine.

Pierre Teilhard de Chardin (1881–1955), the French geologist, paleontologist, theologian, and above all mystic, spoke of a spanning of consciousness,[4] which is more than merely blind instinct. He saw evolution as the *rise of consciousness*, as a very painful process, as a veritable crossroads. He speaks of the "spiritual energy of suffering" (1976, 245–49). Behind the world's suffering, he saw a time- and world-encompassing movement of becoming conscious and of unification. The force driving this movement is love, that particular energy that helps to increasingly unite humanity (see Haas 1971). According to the Prologue of John, we can recognize the personified Logos in Jesus Christ as well as the Logos in general as the force behind evolution. They are synonymous with the movement toward universal love. Thus these verses about suffering provide some sense of the high price that God evidently seems to pay for the eventually successful development of love. And this is ultimately redemptive.

10.5. And the Word Became Flesh: Jesus as the Conscious Realization Initiated by God

"And the Word became flesh and lived among us … full of grace and truth" (John 1:14). This verse definitely avows God's incarnation in the world (see Kessler 2006, 37). Here, "flesh" stands for the earthly, yet not in the same moralizing tone as in Paul.[5] Interestingly, ancient Greek does not use the term *soma* (see somatic), but *sarx* (*sa,rx / sarx*), which emphasizes transience and fragility as opposed to the well-formed, organized body. The message envisaged thereby is "The absolute divine became absolute fragility" (Max Küchler, personal communication). *Sarx* is not entirely neutral and contains an element of decay and separation. This heightens the assertion about God's solidarity with the world and the broken. Jesus is represented as a bridge between God and humanity, while *God himself* is intuited behind the birth of the Logos.

Although we celebrate the birth of Jesus year after year at Christmas, we barely realize what we were promised with the coming of the Logos: *the coming of consciousness initiated by God and oriented toward the final objective of all-encompassing love*. Becoming conscious is about being saved, held, and set free (from separation and splitting). It leads to a new capacity to love. From this final viewpoint, life is even "permitted" to undergo suffering as it was in the case of Jesus.

What exactly does *becoming conscious* mean (see also chapters 7.3–7.6)? It is not the same as acquiring knowledge; rather, it refers to an ever deeper illumination of traces that already exist unconsciously.

The Meaning of Becoming Conscious

Becoming conscious is an epistemological process, another kind of gaining knowledge: correlations and interconnections are derived not just logically but also associatively, intuitively, through the inclusion of primary perception (i.e., things that we notice for the first time). Becoming conscious is also a linguistic process, in that newness finds verbal expression. Our categories of thought are thus extended to the previously unthinkable. Becoming conscious involves emotional work that we should not underestimate: feeling or newly knowing an inner truth about ourselves is strenuous. It demands total engagement with what we are doing, thinking, and concealing. Also with what others and the world confront us with. This path leads us closer to the truth and dignity of our essence. Becoming conscious involves painful self-knowledge (Ursula Renz 2017) and the integration of shadows (see chapter 7). It brings to light what has long been forgotten, our culture's repressed material, unquestioned reaction patterns, down to deviancies, but also—by way of consolation—the deepest mystical secrets. And yet, however strange it may sound, becoming conscious does often not occur in everyday consciousness but in deep dreams, at the edge of the unconscious. When waking up, we seek to understand or stand on new ground.

Becoming conscious occurs not merely actively, but also passively. It is less about tackling things (male quality in men and in women) than about allowing things to happen (female quality; the anima in terms of C. G. Jung). Yet this—in contrast to actively acquiring knowledge—is barely possible for the split person. More than others, split persons need an understanding, loving person by their side: for instance, a partner, therapist, or pastoral carer, whose empathic presence lends some of their own emotional center to the split person.

Jesus, the mystic, was completely unseparated and undivided (see chapters 6 and 7). He was therefore especially capable of becoming totally conscious and permeable. Can Jesus, as Christ, also function as an anima for us? He was certainly aware of his special role, even if we cannot establish how he actually saw himself (for honorific titles, see chapter 3). We may consider the mediator's concern and charisma to be distinctly Jesuanic. In my eyes, Jesus initiated a shift toward coming into consciousness and toward human self-becoming: he brought "light into the world."

10.6. Finality or the Question of Why

Every final vision is an answer to the question "Why?" or rather "What for?" This is true for the Gospel of John and for Pierre Teilhard de Chardin: "If you could see what I see." This visionary, who devoted his life to describing the mystery of evolution, died—walking down a street in New York—on Easter Sunday, April 10, 1955.

Teilhard de Chardin discovered meaning even amid the greatest crisis. In the suffering of human beings, he recognized the potential for change and, in the most extreme case, for a leap within evolution. He spoke of *cosmogenesis*, the evolutionary becoming of the cosmos, which "unfolds through the consecutive thresholds of materialization, vitalization, and reflection" (cited in Haas 1971, 2:79). He also mentions other terms for these thresholds: *geogenesis* (materialization), *biogenesis* (vitalization, organic movement), *noogenesis* or *anthropogenesis* (reflection), and the hitherto hypothetical and visionary *Christogenesis* (see Teilhard de Chardin [1955] 1975). He considered the rise of consciousness to be the actual axis of cosmogenesis.

Geogenesis refers to the development of all matter (including stones) from a "primordial atom" (Teilhard de Chardin [1955] 1975, 300). Biogenesis marks the beginning and the development of life through the emergence of cells. Anthropogenesis (i.e., noogenesis) begins with the appearance of the first humans. Christogenesis involves a further thrust in the development of human consciousness toward a greater capacity for love, responsibility, and consciousness. It moves toward a final goal.

Teilhard de Chardin maintained that in the course of human development, divergence (separation, inequality, antagonism) makes way for convergence (alignment, rapprochement). Everything strives toward the Omega point, toward "a distinct Center radiating at the core of a system of centers" ([1955] 1975, 262). He considers the end of the world to be the overthrow of equilibrium. This detaches the perfect mind at last from its material husk, in order to enable its full weight to rest on God, on the Omega point ([1955] 1975, 287–88). This, however, does not occur without great suffering. Somewhat apocalyptically, Teilhard de

Chardin considers humanity to be confronted with the following alternative: either a civilization of love prevails or human life in its current form will perish.

Despite some problematic formulations, the work of Teilhard de Chardin expresses an impressive *final* view. He maintained that "the world holds no interest for me unless I look forward ,yet when my eyes are on the future it is full of excitement" ([1956] 1962, 104). He saw the Omega point in Christ. Moreover, "the universe is physically impregnated to the very core of its matter" ([1921] 1965, 57) with Christ's superhuman nature. Christ has always "put himself in the position (maintained ever since) to subdue under himself, to purify, to direct and superanimate the general ascent of consciousness into which he inserted himself" (Teilhard de Chardin [1955] 1975, 294).

Is there a higher striving for love? Hans Kessler (2006, 36) speaks of a movement toward devotion; all things strive toward the primal ground, the Creator, and the Father, "as the final goal." I would hardly have the courage to engage with such visions if it were not for those dying persons whom I meet in my work and who voice similar assertions:

> *"Light—a web of light that outshines everything" (through the patient's room).*
>> *"A green meadow," "a flower garden like Eve's."*

> *"I'm allowed to make a new beginning here, aren't I?"*
>
> *"I see a magnificently looking dress" (one patient's last words).*
>
> *"A city with geometrical shapes and towers" (an escatological city?).*

Other dying patients see a mediator ("a yellow-white angel, Jesus"; "the red Jesus is coming to fetch me"; "that's strange, I see Abraham, he's standing like a forefather over my father and is consoling me.") Or they describe "a bridge across, a ladder," "a ladder of light leading up to heaven." Most dying are without words. They are perhaps silently astonished, as the look on their face suggests. Some open their eyes once more before death, yet without actually looking at us (their carers or relatives). They look upward, as if they were living in another world. They look across to transcendence, yet in any event through us. I am impressed every time: someone who has not previously seen things this way, now sees things behind things.

> *Relatives might be helped if I, as an end-of-life carer, try to interpret the signs emitted by the dying. Yet I must be very cautious when asking myself what a particular patient might mean. Even if they remain silent, I sometimes deliberately ask the dying a question in the presence*

*of their relatives. For instance, "Do you see something?
Is it beautiful, or is it difficult? Both is fine with me."
Or "Would you like to tell or show us something?" The
reactions are often nonverbal: an intense look, increased
breathing, or a sound. It is not unusual for such moments
to amount to a profound experience for relatives. I try to
signal freedom and interest to every patient. How do they
feel? Some have a vision (Lawrence and Repede 2013;
Fenwick, Lovelace, and Brayne 2010; Nosek et al. 2015).
Others do not.*

What might lie behind the dying's "looking beyond"? Are they attracted by a final order or peace? By an ultimate meaning or even by a "divine urging"? By a teleological concern? Their testimonies suggest that for the dying, words and metaphors such as *light*, *paradise*, *permission*, *dignity*, and the *eschatological city*—as a symbol of the highest form of culture—express such final goals.

10.7. Spiritual Practice: Opening Ourselves to the Dynamics and to the Approaching God

What are the consequences for everyday spiritual practice, meditation, contemplation, and spiritual care? The previous observations have already led us straight to the core of this practical perspective. Essentially, practice is about taking patients seriously (when they have visions and when they do not). And it is about allowing their visions to take hold of us. However, visions not only concern the dying. They occur in everyday life, in contemplation, or when we are touched by music, love, or nature.

In the midst of life, we might ask ourselves why we should risk "God"? Why should we succumb to "divine striving"? Why is it worth considering Jesus in terms of salvation history? Why should we embrace the concept of grace? Well, because we thus enter the sphere of hope. And because such a final perspective is profoundly beautiful. Or at least this is what those "making this experience" articulate time and again.

Yet can grace, can God, can a conciliatory and an escatological view enter our soul? We can readily answer the question of hope as long as it arises from within us and is charged with energy. Yet finding hope in our darkest hours proves to be one of the hardest challenges of all. In their utmost despair, all I ask of patients is that they perceive whatever goodness comes toward them: a loving human voice, a friend who endures their suffering with them, a shaft of sunlight, the delightfulness of water. Enjoying small pleasures. Yet if they also silently endure and wrestle with God, the door to the dynamics of hope stands ajar.

"Even if God no longer wants me (!), I still want him," said one partially paralyzed patient who was struggling to place his difficult fate in larger hands. This made him feel better.

In terms of the model below (figure. 4), finality means that dying not only involves returning to our primal origin in the Whole. This might sometimes seem to be the case. Yet in going backward we also go forward. Our path to maturity leads us forward, sometimes even visibly to death.

On this path, when we die—spiritually speaking—we are not forlorn or alone, not even in our existential loneliness. Whether we are religious or secularized, we do not simply follow our path according to our worldview and our image of God. Rather, we are also slightly touched. Thus, in our existential loneliness before dying, we might be "touched" by the absence or dark side of God. Several dying patients who accepted even this challenge "felt" this subtle "presence of the absent God" or "the dark secret of God." Religiously speaking, we do not simply go toward God and return to the original Whole. Instead, God also approaches us from different sides (from below, from above, from within). As the German theologian Roman Siebenrock (personal communication) has argued, "The *cosmic* dimension of redemption must become present today. This is not bound to a particular religion and culture."

He Comes toward Me

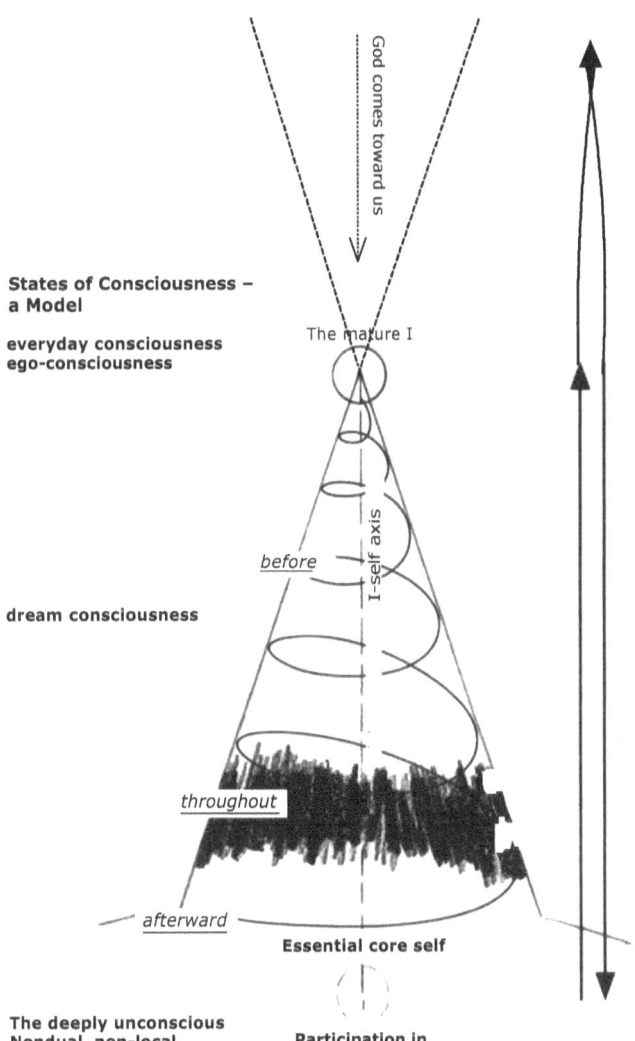

In terms of salvation history and finality, *Jesuanic spirituality* means that while Christianity should celebrate its festivals and hold on to the great power of the mystic of Nazareth, it should remain open to very different ways in which God comes toward us and in which the Logos seeks to assert itself.

Epilogue

Looking back at this book reminds me of its daring nature: I have presented Jesus as a mystic and have also tried to encourage readers to cherish their very personal experience with God, even in his absence. Consequently, the image of God presented here extends beyond traditional religion and opens up spaces for such inner experience. So, at the end of this book, we need to ask: How can we live as free and authentic human beings, as Christians, in a secular society? Working with patients from various religious backgrounds and with different worldviews in a medical setting (see Renz 2014; Renz 2015) for many years has strengthened my conviction that this vision of a religion that welcomes our freedom and personal relationship to God has a future.

Faith remains an option (Joas 2014). By definition, hope relies on finality. Yet we have no "guarantee" that risking such hope is worthwhile. Nevertheless, I still consider Jesus to be one of the most viable examples of a free and authentic religion in world history. Guides to spirituality exist neither in the therapist's mind nor in the public domain nor "on the open road." Instead, we find guidance in each and every one of us (see Jeremiah 31:31–34; Hebrews 8:8–12). Our experiences, dreams, and desires are what guide us.

Let me conclude with Dietrich Bonhoeffer's baptismal letter to Dietrich Bethge (cited in Bonhoeffer 2010, 389–90) and thank him for his testimony of faith and life:

> You are being baptized today as a Christian. All those great and ancient words of the Christian proclamation will be pronounced over you, and the command of Jesus Christ to baptize will be carried out, without your understanding any of it. But we too are being thrown back all the way to the beginnings of our understanding. What reconciliation and redemption mean, rebirth and Holy Spirit, love for one's enemies, cross and resurrection, what it means to live in Christ and follow Christ, all that is so difficult and remote that we hardly dare speak of it anymore. In these words and actions handed down to us, we sense something totally new and revolutionary, but we cannot yet grasp it and express it. This is our own fault. Our church has been fighting during these years only for its self-preservation, as if that were an end in itself. It has become incapable of bringing the word of reconciliation and redemption to humankind and to the world. So the words we used before must lose their power, be silenced, and we can be Christians today in only two ways, through

prayer and in doing justice among human beings. All Christian thinking, talking, and organizing must be born anew, out of that prayer and action. By the time you grow up, the form of the Church will have changed considerably. It is still being melted and remolded, and every attempt to help it develop prematurely into a powerful organization again will only delay its conversion [*umkehr*] and purification. It is not for us to predict the day—but the day will come—when people will once more be called to speak the word of God in such a way that the world is changed and renewed. It will be in a new language, perhaps quite nonreligious language, but liberating and redeeming like Jesus's language, so that people will be alarmed and yet overcome by its power—the language of a new righteousness and truth, a language proclaiming that God makes peace with humankind and that God's kingdom is drawing near. "They shall fear and tremble because of all the good and all the prosperity I provide for them" (Jeremiah 33:9). Until then the Christian cause will be a quiet and hidden one, but there will be people who pray and do justice and wait for God's own time. May you be one of them, and may it be said of you one day: "The path of the righteous is like the light of dawn, which shines brighter and brighter until full day" (Proverbs 4:18).

Notes

Introduction

1. This term refers to C. G. Jung's analytical psychology, but I understand it in an even deeper sense (see the model of the layers of the soul in chapter 4). Jung saw the ego as the perceiving function. Unlike the Self, the ego takes decisions and conscious action. These opposite poles—Self and ego—account for the interaction between the psychic forces (see Hark 1988, 71–72). "The Self is the center of personality. It is the arranging, steering, and symbol-creating function, the central archetype endowed with particular numinosity. Depth psychology's idea of the Self is a construct and points to the consciousness-transcending possibilities of relating to God and the cosmos, to crystals and animals, to being and everything that is. The beginnings of our psychic life seem to issue inextricably from this focal point, toward which all the highest and ultimate goals seem to move" (Hark 1988, 150–52).
2. Music-assisted relaxation involves guided body relaxation, often in combination with imagining inner images and a state of sensitivity. In the course of relaxation, patients are guided only by music. Suitable music includes repetitive monochromatic sound, simple melodies and sounds, or repeating the same rhythm.

3. "Jesus" here means the historical man from Nazareth, whereas "Christ" points to the human encounter with the timeless mystic. If we assume that Jesus was a mystic, and that his exceptional behavior extended beyond himself and his time, we will be able to establish a bridge from Jesus to Christ. My hope is that this approach will initiate a new culture of discussion beyond ecclesiastical and theological confines.

1   Jesus and God: A Mystical Connection

1. I have discussed the notion of primordial fear elsewhere (Renz 2015; Renz 2018).
2. I have interpreted the story of temptation elsewhere as an answer to the human structure of fear, desire, and power (Renz 2008a, 174–77).
3. Jewish tradition included early Jewish ideas of demons, the notion of Jewish instruction, the laws, and Jewish answers to the divine covenant.
4. Etymologically, German *leiden* (*lidan*) derives from traveling, journeying, experiencing, forever exposed to the prevailing conditions.
5. Often translated as "covenant," the Hebrew noun ברית *berīt* presumably derives from the Akkadian stem *bīritū*, "bond," "shackle." Other possible translations include "agreement," "obligation," "alliance." A *berit* (covenant) is concluded by an act of division, hence giving the Hebrew expression "to cut a covenant" (*karat berit*, Genesis 15:18). Presumably this goes back to the blood rites that affirmed legal agreements at the time of Abraham. Modern variants include ribbon-cutting ceremonies to formally declare a bridge open.

6. This resembles a mathematical formula, which is also the quintessential outcome of years of research. Provided the evidence and derivation are correct, a dissertation submitted in the field of mathematics may consist solely of a formula.
7. The inner dimension, the inner path to God, is also contained in the symbolism and history of the word *faith* (Hebrew: *amanah*, from which derives *amen*; Greek: *h` pi,stij / pistis*). Originally this meant to tie or bind oneself to the truth, which persists (Isaiah 7:9) and can be relied on. In the cult of ancient Babylonia, a path was paved in the desert to transport the giant statues of the gods. In their Babylonian exile, the Israelites took up this cultic image (see Deutero-Isaiah: to pave the way for the Lord). But they also used the word to mean an inner path to Yahweh. He was not meant to be worshipped with (movable) statues but as the utterly reliable, unalterable, invisible God, who could be trusted. God's magnificence (Hebrew: *dAbåK' kabod*; Greek: *do,xa*, *doxa*) also comprises his unalterability and reliability. *Kabood* means "weight" or "force" in a positive sense, "honor," "power," or, more loosely, "presence." One gave glory to the Lord, the God of Israel (Joshua 7:19; similarly Psalm 96:7). The corresponding verb means to "become heavy," "to honor."

2 Absent Mysticism and Awakening

1. The Greek word *gnosis* (*gnw / sij*) means "knowledge," "insight." It represents a worldview according to which the world is fundamentally depraved. It is the outcome of a failed creation, for which an equally inept God or creator (demiurge) is responsible. This creator wages a constant battle against the good God

(dualism). While humankind is part of the divine sphere, the demiurge's mishap has made it part of the earthly world. Living in an inimical world, human beings—and this idea is typically Gnostic—need to *free themselves* through knowledge and spiritual ascent. Gnosticism condemns the body as evil. In its eyes, self-redemption occurs through human beings remembering their actual divine origin—that is, through spiritual-psychic introspection. Gnosticism was widespread among intellectual and religious circles in the first and second centuries CE. In the history of the Church, it was combatted as heresy, leading to the exclusion of numerous writings with Gnostic resonances (e.g., the apocryphal Gospel of Thomas) from the later biblical canon (the collection of Holy Scriptures).

2. The root meaning (*evsw,teroj*) refers to what lies within or behind—that is, to secret knowledge.

3. Puchalski et al. (2009) reported the proceedings of a Consensus Conference on improving the quality of spiritual care as a dimension of palliative care. The conference involved forty American experts from various fields, including physicians, nursing staff, psychologists, social workers, spiritual caregivers, and hospital directors. They demanded that spiritual care should be integrated into good palliative care. The group defined spirituality as "the aspect of humanity that refers to the way individuals seek and express meaning and purpose and the way they experience their connectedness to the moment, to self, to others, to nature, and to the significant or sacred" (Puchalski et al. 2009, 887).

4. Nouwen never disclosed his friend's name.

3 Jesus the Mystic: A Historical View

1. The word *Palestinian/Palestine* (literally, the land of the Philistines) has existed since its first mention by Herodotus in 540 BCE. It was revived by the Romans, who divided Palestine into three parts (Prima, Secunda, Tertia) and thus supplanted the common word *Judea*. Until the foundation of Israel on May 14, 1948, one spoke of Palestine and Palestinian Jews.
2. Kefar Nachum or Kfar Nachum (*kfar*, village; the modern German word *kaff* can also be traced to this root).
3. Regarding the relationship between Judaism and Christianity: Christians consider (and need to consider) Jesus in terms of his childhood, his religious upbringing, covenant theology, and Old Testament promises. Nevertheless, Jews cannot follow such interpretations of the Torah and the Prophets. Jews and Christians have *a* common prehistory and history, from which arose two equivalent interpretations. This, I believe, is the basis for Jews and Christians to engage in dialogue.
4. According to Deuteronomy (21:22–23), when someone "is executed, and you hang him on a tree, his corpse must not remain all night upon the tree; you shall bury him that same day, for anyone hung on a tree is under God's curse." Paul took this up in Galatians (3:13) and in 1 Corinthians (1:23).
5. This would have been the fourteenth of Nisan in the year 30.
6. Among others, the Roman author Tacitus or the Jewish historian Flavius Josephus. See Tacitus, *Annals* 15.44; see also Flavius Josephus, *Antiquitates Judaicae* 18.63–64 (Theissen and Merz 1998, 64–71, 81–83).
7. See Theissen and Merz (1998, 93–124); Jeremias (1971, 38–45); Meier (1991, 167–95); Breech (1983).

8. See the following passages: "Is not he (God) your Father, who created you, who made you and established you" (Deuteronomy 32:6); "For you are our father, though Abraham does not know us and Israel does not acknowledge us; you, O Lord, are our father; our Redeemer from of old is your name (Isaiah 63:16); "As a father has compassion for his children, so the Lord has compassion for those who fear him" (Psalm 103:13). See also Isaiah 64:7; Tobit 13:4; Wisdom 14:3; Sirach 23:1,4; Sirach 51:10. The famous Jewish prayer *Avinu Malkeinu* (which Rabbi Akiva cites in the Talmud; its age is unknown) also begins with the words "Our Father, our King" and is prayed on Rosh Hashanah (New Year).
9. Mark 1:9–11; Matthew 3:17; Luke 3:22. For similar yet different instances, see John 1:33–34 and the so-called Gospel of the Nazarenes (NazEv sec. 2). See Webb (2000).
10. Translator's note: At the author's request, these are literal translations from the Greek. The present tense has been omitted, in contrast, for instance, to the KJV and the NSRV.
11. The Didache is an early Christian treatise written in the first century (Theissen and Merz 1998, 19; 30).
12. In Hebrew, the word *heaven* took the plural (*schamajim*); in Greek, the singular (*uranos*). It was originally (Genesis 1:1–2) thought to be a sphere that curves around the earth, which was conceived of as a disk. This sphere consists of several layers and includes stars, a firmament, and the like. The Book of Daniel speaks of the "King of heaven" (4:37). The heavenly kingdom is the translation of the Hebrew term for "kingdom of the heaven."
13. Asking for bread is intelligible also without the attribute *evpiou,sioj*. It is about food in both a material and a figurative sense

(see Matthew 4:4; Luke 14:15). Parallels to Old Testament prayer literature include several passages in the Psalms: Psalm 78:20, 24–25; 105:40 (God gives manna, bread from heaven); Psalm 104:14–15; Psalm 132:15 (God satiates the poor with bread). If we consider *evpiou,sioj* (being, belonging), then, as Hasitschka (personal communication) claims, this also concerns "the bread needed for the respective day" or "the bread needed to exist" (*evpi*, and *ouvsi,a*, "existence, subsistence, substance"). Hasitschka (1989, 42) also speaks of the bread that "I am" for today (*eivmi*, "I am," *w;n ou=sa o;n*, "for the respective day"). Overall, this is a petition against fear!

14. Translator's note: at the author's request, these are literal translations from the Greek.
15. For angels as the sons of God, see Job 1:6; for the one anointed by the Lord (David?) as the son of God, see Psalm 2:7; for the chosen people/Israel as the son of God, see Exodus 4:22 and Wisdom 18:13; for the people as the children of the Lord, see Deuteronomy 14:1; for the sons of Israel as the sons of the living God, see Hosea 2:1. In the New Testament, the list extends to the peacemakers as the sons of God (Matthew 5:9 and 5:45).
16. *Kyrios*: The Greek Septuagint (from the Latin *septuaginta*, "seventy"), a translation of the Hebrew Bible, translated YHWH, which was unpronounceable in Hebrew, as "Kyrios." When Christians took up this word, which reflected its Greek influence, this also involved the Septuagint tradition—that is, the veneration of Yahweh recorded there. Messiah: David, too, was anointed, literally making him a *maschiah*/messiah (*mischcha*, "to anoint").

17. Gospel of Thomas 82, taken from van Ruysbeek und Messing (1993, Logion 82). This word of Jesus occurs similarly also in Origen (see Limbeck 2009, 372; Ernst and Kogler 2009, 13; Reichardt 2009).
18. For instance, Xerxes, if he so desired, could stride across the sea (according to Chrysostom, the first-century Early Church Father) (Cotter 1999, 155–56); apparently, Buddha could miraculously cross from one side of the swelling Ganges to the other (see Klatt 1990); and according to the third-century philosopher Iamblichus, Pythagoras could calm the waves of rivers and oceans to enable effortless crossing (Cotter 1999, 144).

4 Jesus' Concept of God: An Answer to Fear

1. Grief: "... and began to be grieved and agitated ... I deeply grieved, even to death" (Matthew 26:37–38); "Jesus began to weep" when Lazarus died (John 11:33–35). Anger: "You brood of vipers" (Matthew 12:34; 23:33); "He looked around at them with anger; he was grieved at their hardness of heart" (Mark 3:5); his anger at the cleansing of the Temple (Mark 11:15–17; Luke 19:45–46; Matthew 21:12–13); "Zeal for your house will consume me" (John 2:14–17). The key phrases in this respect include the various lamentations and exclamations of woe.
2. Where exactly the Gospel of John originated is the subject of ongoing discussion: Kirchschläger (personal communication) suggests northeastern Palestinian, whereas Ernst (2009, 386) maintains it emerged in Syria and was redacted in Asia Minor. Its Semitic lexicon and syntax point to a Judeo-Christian contest. It includes three references to the fact that those who

testify for Jesus will be excluded from the synagogue (9:22; 12:42; 16:2). The distanced language of the later version indicates that a break with "the Jews" has already occurred. The fact that Jewish customs were explained at the time (2:6; 11:55) and that Hebrew and Aramaic terms were translated (1:38,41; 4:25) suggests that the gospel was intended for a pagan-Christian community.

3. Kirchschläger (personal communication) mentions that the gospel might have been a *consensio* in the apostolic tradition (see the Muratorian fragment, dated to the year 200 and found circa 1740). It is disputed how well the final redactor of the gospel knew the other gospels. There are points of contact and differences. In any event, the redactor saw no need to reproduce the existing gospels, either because he assumed they were known or because he barely knew them himself. According to Bultmann (1973), other sources also existed (the source of wonder, Gnostic revelations, the Passion narrative). Brown has divided the development of the community into four phases: the Prologue including Jesus' preexistence, which is unacceptable to Jews, was written *before* the exclusion of John's community from the synagogue (see Ernst 2009, 385).

4. Kirchschläger: "The Greek (present) tense emphasizes the permanent validity of the question 'Where are you staying?' and points to an *inner* abode" (personal communication).

5. The temporal reference (the tenth hour) makes the above passage particularly important. The Gospel of John contains only four references to time (Kirchschläger, personal communication). In the Greek, "they dwelt/stayed" is no longer in the present but in the aorist form, indicating that the disciples lived with Jesus in a *single, completed action*. Thus they

participated in his abode in the Father as best as they could as finite human beings.

6. Of Jewish faith, Herzka was professor of psychopathology at the University of Zurich. He supervised my first dissertation.
7. Intrauterine hearing: As its ears and brain develop, the fetus (also the embryo?) blocks out the rather noisy surroundings in the mother's womb. It filters its mother's voice and heartbeat and hears them more intensely for the purposes of orientation (Salk 1973; Tomatis 2005; Parncutt 2006).
8. Ontogenetically, this means the nascent ego (that of the fetus or the newborn).

6 Jesus' Response to Sin: Mysticism

1. On the concept of the Self, see endnote 1 in the introduction. The ego-Self axis describes the relationship between the ego and the Self (see figure 1, chapter 4.3). It was first introduced by Neumann 1989.

7 Jesus and Evil

1. The Ethiopian Book of Enoch 15 is based on an even older book of Noah's.
2. Translator's note: Archimedes's famous assertion was quoted by Pappus of Alexandria, *Synagoge*, book 8, c. 340 CE. It is also found in John Tzetzes' *Chiliades* 2.13.
3. For an interpretation of this tale, see Renz 2017, 214–17. Beside this interpretation in terms of individual psychology,

there are political interpretations, of course, according to which "legion" refers to the Roman occupying power.
4. This psychological mechanism occurs, for instance, when the member of a sect leaves the community and thereby creates even stronger ties among the remaining members. In slightly objectified terms, this mechanism is also evident in politics—namely, the pattern of creating new problems to divert attention from existing ones.
5. See Neumann 2015.

8 Jesus, the Father, and Love

1. On account of its rich progeny, for instance, among the Egyptians, Greek, and Celts, the pig is a common fertility symbol. It was sacred to the Celts at times. In Greco-Roman antiquity, it was among the sacrificed animals. At the latest since medieval contests, where piglets could be won as prizes, it stood for undeserved luck (note the German expression *schwein haben*, "to be a lucky pig"). Nevertheless, various cultures despised pigs as lowly creatures because of their gluttony and rummaging (see *Herder Lexikon* 1978). Its dirtiness—pigs love wallowing in mud—refers, for better or worse, to a profound connection with Mother Earth, whether dry or moist. Yet despite their bad reputation, pigs are actually quite clean. Voss (1988, 123) regards pigs as a symbol that should be associated with the "matriarchal level of energy."
2. Depth psychology links this experience to matriarchy. See, among others, Neumann (1955).
3. The festival of Passover commemorates the meal taken by the group gathered around Moses before the Exodus (see

Exodus 12 for its cult-establishing function). The Mishnah, which explains the religious laws pertaining to the *pesachim*, determines the proper celebration of the night of Passover. The destruction of Jerusalem and the Temple (70 CE) made it impossible to slaughter the Easter lamb in the Temple. The entire celebration, including the Easter slaughter, was now moved to the domestic (i.e., family) sphere. The Passover meal was taken late and quickly. The food and drink recalled the bitterness of the original night of Moses's group. Structuring moments were interspersed during the meal, for instance, the preparing of the cups (the mixing of liquids), which was accompanied by prayer and instructions. The second cup was central as drinking it recalled the night of the former Exodus and appealed to the meaning of that night in the expectation of the coming, restored kingdom. In the circle of those seated—who would lie down at important cultic moments—one chair was left empty for the prophet Elijah. At around midnight, the procedure had to be completed (Küchler, personal communication). It was characteristic of Passover that the poor could also take part.

4. Besides mentioning instructions for drinking, Mark's gospel, and only his, says that they all drank from the same cup ("and all of them drank from it," Mark 14:23). The interpreting words, "This is my blood, the blood of the covenant, which is poured out for many" (Mark 14:23–24), follow thereafter, in contrast to the Catholic Eucharist. Matthew emphasizes the forgiving of sins as the effect of the meal (and not of baptism). Matthew assumes that people already knew what the Paschal lamb was about. Paul and Luke both give voice to recollection: "Do this in remembrance of me"; Luke refers to bread/the

body (22:19), Paul to the cup/blood (1 Corinthians 11:25). Luke highlights the aspect of desire: "I have eagerly desire to eat this Passover with you before I suffer" (22:15).

5. Although German [and also English, for that matter—translator's note] says "many," other languages reveal that it is about "all."

6. And the traitor? We need not dwell on Judas, but it is worth noting that in the end, "sharing"—that is, partaking in God—does not occur without the traitor's involvement. It seems to me that in this respect the evangelists remained behind Jesus and his secret, and were unable to understand.

9 Redemption—Newly Spelled Out

1. The curtain in the Jerusalem Temple was meant to separate the Holy of Holies, where God was present and where the Ark of the Covenant once stood (see Exodus 40:3; Leviticus 16:2), from the rest of the Temple, where the Israelites gathered. Only the high priest was permitted to enter the innermost, most sacred area once a year (on the Day of Atonement; Leviticus 16:2; Numbers 29:7–11). The torn curtain enables everyone to enter into a relationship with God. This amounted to the Jerusalem cult being abolished as the exclusive place for an association with God and as the only place of atonement.

2. Just as slaves in antiquity were set free after payment of the ransom, according to this interpretation, Jesus' death set free humanity from sin and damnation (see Mark 10:45; 1 Corinthians 6:20; 1 Peter 1:18–19).

3. The doctrine of satisfaction goes back to Anselm of Canterbury (1033–1109). While the notion of the "great exchange,"

which was picked up, among others, by Martin Luther ([1520] 2013), does not occur directly in the New Testament, it does appear in this sense in Paul, in 2 Corinthians ("For our sake he made him to be sin who knew no sin, so that in him we might become the righteousness of God," 5:21), and in Philippians ("Though he was in the form of God, did not regard equality with God as something to be exploited, taking the form of a slave, being born in human likeness ... he humbled himself and became obedient to the point of death ... on the cross. Therefore God also highly exalted him," 2:6–11). The second-century Epistle to Diognetus (9:5) contains the following words: "O the sweet exchange (ὢ τῆς γλυκείας ἀνταλλαγῆς), ... that the iniquity of many be concealed in One Righteous Man, and the righteousness of One should justify many that are iniquitous!"

4. The deeds-consequences connection is a common concept in Bible studies that was introduced by Klaus Koch ([1955] 1991), a Protestant Old Testament scholar. It refers to Old Testament wisdom literature, according to which God ensures that those who do his will in this world fare well (i.e., enjoy a long life and have many children and herds), whereas those who disrespect his will, harm themselves. Since the category of eternal life did not exist at the time, reward and punishment were not shifted into the hereafter. Prayers, reversal (i.e., repentance), and sacrifice in the Temple could assuage the negative consequences of sinful behavior. Wisdom literature includes the books of Job, Ecclesiastes, Proverbs, the Song of Solomon, the Book of Wisdom, and some of the psalms. However, wisdom literature also existed in Nordic or Egyptian contexts (e.g., the Maxims of Ptahhotep, ca. 2450 BCE)

and in Syrian cultural centers. Thus, such thinking was widespread. The deeds-consequences connection was the subject of controversy already in the Old Testament, as the example of Job suggests. Jesus also resisted this thought pattern, for instance, in the Sermon on the Mount, where he said that God lets his sun rise on the evil and on the good (Matthew 5:45). Another example is the man who is blind from birth, in whose case Jesus refutes any connection between the man's (and his parents') sins and his blindness (John 9:1–41). Jesus *physically* opposed this thinking in the Passion. Jesus sees one solution to the problem of justice in justice being done *after* death, in the Last Judgment (e.g., the poor man named Lazarus, Luke 16:19–31). As a mystic, however, Jesus knew that a wholly different justice existed (see chapter 4). His image of God and of the human being was different.

5. Targum Neofiti (or Targum Neophyti) is the largest of the Western Targumin on the Torah. Its 450 folios cover all the books of the Torah.

6. According to Selman et al. (2014), spiritual care involves three main questions: First, how do we help nursing staff, physicians, and other carers address spiritual issues? Second, how can we capture the spiritual needs of patients and their relatives? Survey instruments have been developed accordingly. Third, which interventions help us to react to spiritual needs and distress?

10 He Comes toward Me: Jesus the Logos and Christ

1. The "divine child" is a mythological theme. A. L. Seifert (2001) suggests that it exists in "figures in which the divine principle manifests itself as a child or in its childhood state. In analytical

psychology, it is ... a term for certain qualities of the Self." Many cultures produced this symbol already thousands of years ago. "Whether these were children of the gods, like the Greek Apollo and the Indian Krishna, or whether they were important human beings, like Jesus ... or ... Gautama, who later became Buddha, these children were always given divine names, because they were associated with particular abilities" (A. L. Seifert 2001). The early childhood of divine children is often difficult (e.g., Moses), and yet life then prevails after all.

2. I have consciously used the original Greek term *Logos*, which I will interpret later in this chapter.

3. Note the similar beginning of 1 John, which emerged later from the same community: "We declare to you what was from the beginning, what we have heard, what we have seen with our eyes, what we have looked at and touched with our hands, concerning the word of life."

4. Regarded along its axis of complexity, the universe is, both on the whole and in at each of its points, in a continual tension ... and thus of interiorization. Which amounts to saying that, for science, life is always under pressure everywhere" (Teilhard de Chardin [1955] 1975, 302; 1966).

5. Paul placed blood, flesh, sin (singular), death, and the law on the *one* side, and the spirit, the divine, the resurrected one, and grace on the *other* (see 1 Corinthians 15; Galatians 5:16–22; Ephesians 2:1–10, etc.).

References

Angelus Silesius. 1932. *Selections from The Cherubinic Wanderer.* Translated by J. E. Crawford Flitch. London: Allen & Unwin. Original work published in 1675. Retrieved from http://www.sacred-texts.com/chr/sil/scw/scw05.htm.

Benedetti, G., and P. M. Furlan, ed. 1993. *Psychotherapy of Schizophrenia: Effective Clinical Approaches–Controversies, Critiques and Recommendations.* [Proceedings of the 9th International Symposium on the Psychotherapy of Schizophrenia, held in Torino, Italy]. Seattle: Hofgrefe & Huber.

Bonhoeffer, D. 2010. *Letters and Papers from Prison.* Edited by J. W. de Gruchy. Translated by I. Best, L. E. Dahill, R. Krauss, and N. Lukens. In *Dietrich Bonhoeffer Works*, vol. 8, edited by C. Gremmels, E. Bethge, and R. Bethge, with I. Tödt. Minneapolis: Fortress Press.

Borasio, G. D. 2011. *Über das Sterben: Was wir wissen, was wir tun können, wie wir uns darauf einstellen.* München: Beck.

Breech, J. 1983. *The Silence of Jesus: The Authentic Voice of the Historical Man.* Philadelphia: Fortress.

Bruners, W. 2015. *Wie Jesus glauben lernte.* 2. Aufl. Freiburg i.Br.: Herder.

Buber, M. 1991. *Tales of the Hasidim.* Translated by O. Marx. New York: Schocken Books. Original work published in 1947.

Bultmann, R. K. 1973. *The Johannine Epistles: A Commentary on the Johannine Epistles*. Philadelphia: Fortress Press.

Childs, B. S. 1993. *Biblical Theology of the Old and New Testaments: Theological Reflection on the Christian Bible*. Minneapolis: Fortress Press.

Cotter, W. 1999. *Miracles in Greco-Roman Antiquity: A Sourcebook*. London: Routledge.

Drewermann, E. 1977. *Strukturen des Bösen*. Bd. 1–3. In *Paderborner Theologische Studien*. Bd. 4–6. Paderborn: Ferdinand Schöningh.

———. 1986. *Dein Name ist wie der Geschmack des Lebens: Tiefenpsychologische Deutung der Kindheitsgeschichte nach dem Lukasevangelium*. Freiburg i.Br.: Herder.

———. 1987. *Das Markusevangelium: Bilder von Erlösung: I. Teil. Mk 1,1–9, 13*. Olten: Walter.

———. 1989. *Ich steige hinab in die Barke der Sonne: Alt-ägyptische Meditationen zu Tod und Auferstehung in Bezug auf Joh. 20/21*. Sonderausgabe. Olten: Walter.

———. 1991. *Tiefenpsychologie und Exegese. Bd. 1. Die Wahrheit der Formen: Traum, Mythos, Märchen, Sage und Legende*. Olten: Walter.

———. 1994. *Discovering the God Child Within: A Spiritual Psychology of the Infancy of Jesus*. New York: Crossroad.

Erikson, E. 1980. *Identity and the Life Cycle*. New York: Norton. Original work published in 1959.

Ernst, J. 1993. *Das Evangelium nach Lukas*. 6. überarb. Aufl. Regensburg: Pustet

Ernst, M. 2009. "Johannesevangelium." In *Herders Neues Bibellexikon*, edited by F. Kogler, 384–86. Freiburg i.Br.: Herder.

Ernst, M., and F. Kogler. 2009. "Agrapha." In *Herders Neues Bibellexikon*, edited by F. Kogler, 13. Freiburg i.Br.: Herder.

Fenwick P., H. Lovelace, and S. Brayne. 2010. "Comfort for the Dying: Five Year Retrospective and One Year Prospective Studies of End-of-Life Experiences." *Archives of Gerontology and Geriatrics* 51 (2): 173–79.

Fitchett, G., and S. Nolan. 2015. *Spiritual Care in Practice: Case Studies in Healthcare Chaplaincy*. London: Jessica Kingsley.

Fromm, E. 2014. *To Have or to Be?* London: Bloomsbury Academic. Original work published in 1976.

Fuchs, G. 2004. "Die Kirchenkritik der Mystiker." In *Die Kirchenkritik der Mystiker: Prophetie aus Gotteserfahrung*, edited by M. Delgado & G. Fuchs, 165–86. Fribourg: Academic Press Fribourg.

Girard, R. 2005. *Violence and the Sacred*. Translated by P. Gregory. London: Continuum. Original work published in 1972.

Gnilka, J. 1983. *Johannesevangelium*. In *Die Neue Echter-Bibel: Kommentar zum Neuen Testament mit der Einheitsübersetzung: Bd. 4*. Würzburg: Echter.

———. 2010. *Das Evangelium nach Markus* (Studienausgabe). In *EKK Evangelisch-Katholischer Kommentar zum Neuen Testament: Bd. 2*. Neukirchen-Vluyn: Neukirchener.

Grimm, J., and W. Grimm. 1992. *The Complete Fairy Tales of the Brothers Grimm*. Translated by J. Zipes. New York: Bantam Books.

Grof, S., and C. Grof. 1989. *Spiritual Emergency: When Personal Transformation Becomes a Crisis*. Los Angeles: Tarcher.

Grün, A. 1980. *Der Umgang mit dem Bösen: der Dämonenkampf im alten Mönchtum*. Münsterschwarzach: Vier-Türme-Verlag.

Haas, A. 1971. *Teilhard de Chardin-Lexikon: Grundbegriffe, Erläuterungen, Texte*. Bd. 1–2. Freiburg i.Br.: Herder.

Habermas, J. 2001. "Faith and Knowledge." Acceptance speech, Peace Prize of the German Book Trade 2001. http://www.friedenspreis-des-deutschen-buchhandels.de/sixcms/media.php/1290/2001%20Acceptance%20Speech%20Juergen%20Habermas.pdf.

Hark, H., ed. 1988. *Lexikon Jungscher Grundbegriffe*. Olten: Walter Verlag.

Hasitschka, M. 1989. *Befreiung von Sünde nach dem Johannesevangelium: Eine bibeltheologische Untersuchung*. In *Innsbrucker Theologische Studien: Bd 27*. Innsbruck: Tyrolia.

Herder Lexikon: Symbole. 1978. M. Oesterreicher-Mollwo (Bearb.). Freiburg i.Br.: Herder.

Huber, M. 2012. *Trauma und die Folgen*. 5. Aufl. Paderborn: Junfermann.

Jálics, F. 2011. *The Contemplative Way: Quietly Savoring God's Presence*. New York: Paulist Press.

James, W. 2012. *The Varieties of Religious Experience: A Study in Human Nature*. Edited by M. Bradley. Oxford: Oxford University Press. Original work published in 1902.

Jaschke, H. 2000. *Jesus, der Mystiker*. Mainz: Matthias-Grünewald-Verlag.

Jeremias, J. 1966. *Abba: Studien zur neutestamentlichen Theologie und Zeitgeschichte*. Göttingen: Vandenhoeck & Ruprecht.

———. 1971. *Neutestamentliche Theologie: 1. Teil. Die Verkündigung Jesu.* Gütersloh: Mohn.

———. 1976. *The Prayers of Jesus*. London: S. C. M. Press.

Joas, H. 2013. *The Sacredness of the Person: A New Genealogy of Human Rights*. Translated by A. Skinner. Washington, DC: Georgetown University Press.

———. 2014. *Faith as an Option: Possible Futures for Christianity*. Translated by A. Skinner. Palo Alto, CA: Stanford University Press.

Jung, C. G. 1958. *Psychology and Religion: West and East*. Translated by R. F. C. Hull. In *The Collected Works of C.G. Jung*, vol. 11, edited by H. Read, M. Fordham, and G. Adler. London: Routledge & Kegan Paul.

Jung, C. G. 1969. *Archetypes and the Collective Unconscious*. Translated by R. F. C. Hull. In *Collected Works of C. G. Jung*, vol. 9, pt. 1. Princeton, NJ: Princeton University Press.

Jung, C. G., and K. Kerényi. 1969. *Essays on a Science of Mythology: The Myth of the Divine Child and the Mysteries of Eleusis*. Rev. ed. Translated by R. F. C. Hull. Princeton, NJ: Princeton University Press.

Jung, C. G., and A. Jaffé. 1989. *Memories, Dreams, Reflections*. Rev. ed. Translated by R. Winston and C. Winston. London: Collins & Routledge.

Keller, H. E. 2011. "Damit wir Gott Gott in uns sein lassen." In *Mystik: Die Sehnsucht nach dem Absoluten*, edited by A. Lutz, 74–77. Zürich: Museum Rietberg; Scheidegger & Spiess.

Kessler, H. 2006. *Den verborgenen Gott suchen: Gottesglaube in einer von Naturwissenschaften und Religionskonflikten geprägten Welt*. Paderborn: Schöningh.

Kessler, H. 2010. *Evolution und Schöpfung in neuer Sicht*. 3. Aufl. Kevelaer: Butzon & Bercker.

Kirchschläger, W. 2011. "Tod, Auferstehung und Erlösung: Bibelorientierte Anmerkungen zur Soteriologie." In *Der Jesus des Papstes: Passion, Tod und Auferstehung im Disput*, edited by H. Häring, 57–82. Berlin: LIT.

Klatt, N. 1990. *Jesu und Buddhas Wasserwandel*. Göttingen: Klatt.

Klinger, E. 1994. *Das absolute Geheimnis im Alltag entdecken: Zur spirituellen Theologie Karl Rahners*. Würzburg: Echter.

Koch, K. 1991. "Gibt es ein Vergeltungsdogma im Alten Testament?" In *Gesammelte Aufsätze: Bd. 1. Spuren des hebräischen Denkens: Beiträge zur alttestamentlichen Theologie*, edited by B. Janowski and M. Krause, 65–103. Neukirchen-Vluyn: Neukirchener. Original work published in 1955.

Koelle, L. 2015. "Schuld als Aufgabe: Deutsche Theologie der dritten Nach-Shoah-Generation und ihre Vergebungsdiskurse." In *Schuld: Theologische Erkundungen eines unbequemen Phänomens*, edited by J. Enxing, 262–75. Ostfildern: Matthias Grünewald.

Kogler, F. ed. 2009. *Herders Neues Bibellexikon*. Freiburg i. Br.: Herder.

Küchler, M. 2014. *Jerusalem: Ein Handbuch und Studienreiseführer zur Heiligen Stadt.* 2., vollst. überarb. Aufl. In *Orte und Landschaften der Bibel: Bd. 4,2.* Göttingen: Vandenhoeck & Ruprecht.

Lawrence, M., and E. Repede 2013. "The Incidence of Deathbed Communications and Their Impact on the Dying Process." *American Journal of Hospice and Palliative Medicine* 30 (7): 632–39.

Lazenby, M., R. McCorkle, and D. P. Sulmasy. 2014. *Safe Passage: A Global Spiritual Sourcebook for Care at the End of Life.* Oxford: Oxford University Press.

Limbeck, M. 2009. "Jesus von Nazaret." In *Herders Neues Bibellexikon*, edited by F. Kogler, 370–73. Freiburg i.Br.: Herder.

Lommel, P. van. 2010. *Consciousness beyond Life: The Science of the Near-Death Experience.* New York: HarperOne.

Luther, M. 1908. *Luther's Large Catechism: God's Call to Repentance, Faith and Prayer; the Bible Plan of Salvation Explained.* Translated by J. N. Lenker. Original work published in 1529. https://openlibrary.org/books/OL7000889M/Luther's_large_catechism.

———. 2013. *On the Freedom of a Christian.* Translated by J. Frymire. Indianapolis: Hackett. Original work published 1520.

Luz, U. 2007. *Matthew 1–7: A Commentary.* Edited by H. Koester. Translated by J. E. Crouch. In *Hermeneia: A Critical and Historical Commentary on the Bible*, edited by H. Koester, H. W. Attridge, A. Y. Collins, E. J. Epp, H. J. Klauck, and J. M. Robinson. Minneapolis, MN: Fortress Press.

Matthews, B. 1993. *The Herder Dictionary of Symbols: Symbols from Art, Archaeology, Mythology, Literature, and Religion*. Wilmette, IL: Chiron Publications.

McGrath, P. 2002. "Creating a Language for 'Spiritual Pain' through Research: A Beginning." *Supportive Care in Cancer* 10 (8): 637–46. http://dx.doi.org/10.1007/s00520-002-0360-5.

McMahon, R. 2006. *Understanding the Medieval Meditative Ascent. Augustine, Anselm, Boethius and Dante*. Washington DC: Catholic University of America.

Meier, J. P. 1991. *A Marginal Jew: Rethinking the Historical Jesus*. Volume 1 of *The Roots of the Problem and the Person*. In *The Anchor Bible Reference Library*. New York: Doubleday.

Meister Eckhart. 1979. *German Sermons and Treatises*. Translated by M. O'Connell Walshe. London: Watkins.

Merton, T. 1981. *The Ascent to Truth*. New York: Harcourt Brace Jovanovich.

Metz, J. B. 1980. *Faith in History and Society: Toward a Practical Fundamental Theology*. Translated by D. Smith. London: Burns & Oates.

———. 1994. "Gotteskrise: Versuch zur 'geistigen Situation der Zeit.'" In *Diagnosen zur Zeit* by J. B. Metz, 76–92. Düsseldorf: Patmos.

———. 2006. *Memoria passionis: Ein provozierendes Gedächtnis in pluralistischer Gesellschaft*. Freiburg i.Br.: Herder.

Moser, T. 1976. *Gottesvergiftung*. 2. Aufl. Frankfurt a.M.: Suhrkamp.

Nahm M., B. Greyson, E. W. Kelly, and E. Haraldsson. 2012. "Terminal Lucidity: A Review and a Case Collection." *Archives of Gerontology and Geriatrics* 55 (1):138–42.

Neumann, E. 1955. *The Great Mother: An Analysis of the Archetype*. Translated by R. Manheim. Princeton, NJ: Princeton University Press.

Neumann, E. 2015. *Jacob and Esau: On the Collective Symbolism of the Brother Motif*. Edited by E. Shalit. Translated by M. Kyburz. Asheville, NC: Chiron Publications.

Neumann, E. 1988. *The Child: Structure and Dynamics of the Nascent Personality*. Translated by R. Manheim. London: Karnac.

Neumann, E. 1989. *The Place of Creation: Six Essays*. Translated by H. Nagel, E. Rolfe, J. van Heurck, and K. Winston. In *Essays of Erich Neumann*, vol. 3, Bollingen Series. Princeton, NJ: Princeton University Press.

Nosek C. L., C. W. Kerr, and J. Woodworth et al. 2015. "End-of-Life Dreams and Visions: A Qualitative Perspective from Hospice Patients." *American Journal of Hospice and Palliative Medicine* 32 (3): 269–74.

Nouwen, H. J. M. 2002. *Life of the Beloved: Spiritual Living in a Secular World*. New York: Crossroad.

Parncutt, R. 2006. "Prenatal Development." In *The Child as Musician: A Handbook of Musical Development*, edited by G. E. McPherson, 1–31. Oxford: Oxford University Press.

Peng-Keller, S. 2010. *Einführung in die Theologie der Spiritualität*. Darmstadt: Wissenschaftliche Buchgesellschaft.

Perera, S. Brinton. 1986. *The Scapegoat Complex: Toward a Mythology of Shadow and Guilt*. In volume 23 of *Studies of Jungian Psychology by Jungian Analysts*. Toronto: Inner City Books.

Perrin, N. 1976. *Jesus and the Language of the Kingdom: Symbol and Metaphor in New Testament Interpretation*. Philadelphia: Fortress Press.

Peter, T. R., and C. Urban, eds. 2004. *The End of Time? The Provocation of Talking about God: Proceedings of a Meeting of J. Cardinal Ratzinger, Johann Baptist Metz, Jürgen Moltmann and Eveline Goodman-Thau in Ahaus*. Translated by J. M. Ashley. New York: Paulist Press.

Puchalski, C., B. Ferrell, R. Virani, S. Otis-Green, P. Baird, J. Bull, ... and D. Sulmasy, 2009. "Improving the Quality of Spiritual Care as a Dimension of Palliative Care: The Report of the Consensus Conference." *Journal of Palliative Medicine* 12 (10): 885–904. http://dx.doi.org/10.1089/jpm.2009.0142.

Rad, G. von. 1975. *Old Testament Theology*. Study edition. Translated by D. M. G. Stalker. London: S. C. M. Press.

Rahner, K. 1961. "Current Problems in Christology." In volume 1 of *Theological Investigations: God, Christ, Mary, and Grace*, translated by C. Ernst, 149–200. Baltimore, MD: Helicon Press.

———. 1966. "On the Theology of the Incarnation." In volume 4 of *Theological Investigation*, translated by K. Smyth, 105–20. New York: Herder and Herder.

———. 1967. *The Christian of the Future*. Translated by W. J. O'Hara. London: Burns & Oates.

———. 1971. "Christian Living Formerly and Today." Translated by D. Bourke. In *Theological Investigations*. Vol. 7. In volume 1 of *Further Theology of the Spiritual Life*. New York: Herder and Herder.

———. 1980. "Warum lässt Gott uns leiden." In *Schriften zur Theologie* by K. Rahner, bd. 14, 450–66. Einsiedeln: Benziger.

———. 1997. *The Need and the Blessing of Prayer*. Translated by B. W. Gillette. Collegeville, MN: Liturgical Press.

———. 2000. "Experiences of a Catholic Theologian." Translated by D. Marmion and G. Thiessen. *Theological Studies* 61 (1): 1–15.

———. 2005. *Foundations of Christian Faith: An Introduction to the Idea of Christianity*. Translated by W. V. Dych. New York: Crossroad.

———. 2006. Alltagstugenden. In *Sämtliche Werke: Bd. 23. Glaube im Alltag: Schriften zur Spiritualität und zum christlichen Lebensvollzug*, A. Raffelt (Bearb.), 125–38. Freiburg i.Br.: Herder.

Ratzinger, J. (Benedict XVI.) 2007. *Jesus von Nazareth: Erster Teil. Von der Taufe im Jordan bis zur Verklärung*. Freiburg i.Br.: Herder.

Ratzinger, J. (Benedict XVI.) 2011. *Jesus von Nazareth: Zweiter Teil. Vom Einzug in Jerusalem bis zur Auferstehung*. Freiburg i.Br.: Herder.

Reichardt, M. 2009. Worte Jesu. In *Herders Neues Bibellexikon*, edited by F. Kogler, 806–7. Freiburg i.Br.: Herder.

Reiterer, F. V., and R. Unfried. 2009a. Kinderopfer. In *Herders Neues Bibellexikon*, edited by F. Kogler, 423. Freiburg i.Br.: Herder.

Reiterer, F. V., and R. Unfried. 2009b. Opfer. In *Herders Neues Bibellexikon*, edited by F. Kogler, 564–65. Freiburg i.Br.: Herder.

Renz, M. 2010. *Der Mensch—Wesen der Sehnsucht—connected or disconnected: Texte und Musik für unsere Sehnsucht und Spiritualität*. [Mit einer CD]. Paderborn: Junfermann.

Renz, M. (August 30, 2013). Religionen sind eine existenzielle Antwort—doch worauf? *Neue Zürcher Zeitung*, 23. Abgerufen von http://www.nzz.ch/meinung/debatte/von-derselbstbefragung-zumaustausch-1.18141197.

Renz, M. 2015. *Dying: A Transition*. In *End-of-Life Care: A Series*, edited by K. Anderson. New York: Columbia University Press.

Renz, M. 2016. *Hope and Grace: Spiritual Experiences in Severe Distress, Illness and Dying*. London: Jessica Kingsley.

Renz, M. 2017. *Erlösung aus Prägung: Botschaft und Leben Jesu als Überwindung der menschlichen Angst-, Begehrens- und Machtstruktur*. 2. überarb. Aufl. [Mit einer Klangreisen-CD]. Paderborn: Junfermann.

Renz, M. 2018. *Angst verstehen: Tiefer als Ur-angst liegt Ur-vertrauen*. München: Herder.

Renz, M., M. Schuett Mao, D. Bueche, T. Cerny, and F. Strasser. 2013. «Dying Is a Transition." *American Journal of Hospice and Palliative Medicine* 30 (3): 283–90. http://dx.doi.org/10.1177/1049909112451868.

Renz, M., M. Schuett Mao, A. Omlin, D. Bueche, T. Cerny, and F. Strasser. 2015. "Spiritual Experiences of Transcendence in Patients with Advanced Cancer." *American Journal of Hospital Palliative Care* 32 (2): 178–88. http://dx.doi.org/10.1177/1049909113512201.

Renz, M., O. Reichmuth, D. Bueche, B. Traichel, M. Schuett Mao, T. Cerny, and F. Strasser. 2018. "Fear, Pain, Denial and Spiritual Experiences in Dying Processes." *American Journal of Hospital Palliative Care* 35 (3): 478–91. http://dx.doi.org/10.1177/1049909117725271.

Renz, U., ed. 2017. *Self-Knowledge: A History*. Oxford: Oxford University Press.

Riedel, I. 1994. *Tabu im Märchen: Die Rache der eingesperrten Natur*. 4. Aufl. Solothurn: Walter.

Rohr, R. 2009. *The Naked Now: Learning to See as the Mystics See*. New York: Crossroad.

Rutishauser, C. 2011. *Vom Geist ergriffen, dem Zeitgeist antworten: christliche Spiritualität für heute*. Ostfildern: Grünewald.

Ruysbeek, E. van, and M. Messing. 1993. *Das Thomasevangelium: Seine östliche Spiritualität*. Translated by E. Thielen. Solothurn: Walter.

Salk, L. 1973. "The Role of the Heartbeat in the Relations between Mother and Infant." *Scientific American* 228 (5): 24–29.

Sand, L., P. Strang, and A. Milberg. 2008. "Dying Cancer Patients' Experiences of Powerlessness and Helplessness." *Supportive Care in Cancer* 16 (7): 853–62. http://dx.doi.org/10.1007/s00520-007-0359-z.

Schelbert, G. 2011. *Abba Vater: der literarische Befund vom Altaramäischen bis zu den späten Midrasch- und Haggada-Werken in Auseinandersetzung mit den Thesen von Joachim*

Jeremias. In *Novum Testamentum et orbis antiquus. Studien zur Umwelt des Neuen Testaments.* Bd. 81. Göttingen: Vandenhoeck & Ruprecht.

Schenke, L. 1998. *Johannes: Kommentar.* Düsseldorf: Patmos.

Schenker, A. 2001. *Knecht und Lamm Gottes (Jesaja 53): Übernahme von Schuld im Horizont der Gottesknechtslieder.* In *Stuttgarter Bibelstudien.* Bd. 190. Stuttgart: Kath. Bibelwerk.

Schromm, M. 2015. [Rezension des Buches *Die Verzauberung der Welt: eine Kulturgeschichte des Christentums*, von J. Lauster]. *Christ in der Gegenwart* 67 (13): http://www.christ-in-der-gegenwart .de/aktuell/extras/rezensionen_details?k_beitrag=4427693.

Schwager, R. 1999. *Jesus in the Drama of Salvation: Toward a Biblical Doctrine of Redemption.* Translated by J. G. Williams and P. Haddon. New York: Crossroad.

Schwienhorst-Schönberger, L. 2007. *Ein Weg durch das Leid: das Buch Ijob.* Freiburg i.Br.: Herder.

Seifert, A. L. 2001. Kind, göttliches. In *Symbol Online.* Abgerufen von http://www.symbolonline.de/index.php?title=Kind _göttliches.

Selman, L., T. Young, M. Vermandere, I. Stirling, C. Leget, and Research Subgroup of European Association for Palliative Care Spiritual Care. 2014. "Research Priorities in Spiritual Care: An International Survey of Palliative Care Researchers and Clinicians." *Journal of Pain Symptom Management* 48 (4): 518–31. doi:10.1016/j.jpainsymman.2013.10.020

Siebenrock, R. 2009. *Christliches Martyrium: Worum es geht.* In *Topos-Taschenbücher: Bd. 662.* Kevelaer: Butzon & Bercker.

Söding, T. 2003. Wenn ich mit dem Finger Gottes die Dämonen austreibe ... (LK 11,20): die Exorzismen im Rahmen der Basileia-Verkündigung Jesu. In *Die Dämonen - Demons: die Dämonologie der israelisch-jüdischen und frühchristlichen Literatur im Kontext ihrer Umwelt*, edited by A. Lange, H. Lichtenberger, and K. F. D., 519–49. Tübingen: Mohr Siebeck.

Söding, T. 2011. *Die Verkündigung Jesu—Ereignis und Erinnerung*. Freiburg i.Br.: Herder.

Steindl-Rast, D. 2010. *Deeper Than Words: Living the Apostles' Creed*. New York: Image Books/Doubleday.

Stier, F. 1984. *An der Wurzel der Berge: Aufzeichnungen II*. Freiburg i. Br.: Herder.

Teilhard de Chardin, P. 1962. *Letters from a Traveller*. Translated by R. Hague. London: Collins. Original work published in 1956.

———. 1965. *Science and Christ*. Translated by R. Hague. New York: Harper & Row. Original work published in 1921.

———. 1975. *The Phenomenon of Man*. Translated by B. Wall. New York: Harper Perennial. Original work published in 1955.

———. 1976. *Activation of Energy*. Translated by R. Hague. New York: Harcourt.

Theissen, G. 1983. *The Miracle Stories of the Early Christian Tradition*. Edited by F. Riches. Translated by F. McDonagh. Edinburgh: T & T Clark.

———. 2008. *Die Weisheit des Urchristentums aus Neuem Testament und ausserkanonischen Schriften*. München: Beck.

Theissen, G., and A. Merz. 1998. *The Historical Jesus: A Comprehensive Guide.* Translated by J. Bowden. Minneapolis, MN: Fortress Press.

Tomatis, A. 2005. *The Ear and the Voice.* Translated by R. Prada and P. Sollier. Lanham, MD: Scarecrow Press.

Tresidder, J. 2005. *The Complete Dictionary of Symbols.* San Francisco: Chronicle Books.

Voss, J. 1988. *Das Schwarzmond-Tabu: Die kulturelle Bedeutung des weiblichen Zyklus.* Stuttgart: Kreuz.

Webb, R. L. 2000. "Jesus' Baptism: Its Historicity and Implication." *Bulletin for Biblical Research* 10 (2): 261–309.

Weber, M. 1978. *Economy and Society: An Outline of Interpretive Sociology.* Translated by E. Fischoff et al. Berkeley: University of California Press. Original work published in 1921.

Wöller, H. 1989. *Ein Traum von Christus: In der Seele geboren, im Geist erkannt.* 2. Aufl. Stuttgart: Kreuz.

About the Author

Monika Renz is a practicing psychotherapist, music therapist, theologian, and spiritual caregiver and has been head of the psycho-oncology unit at St. Gallen Cantonal Hospital, Switzerland, since 1998. She holds a Ph.D. in psychopathology and in theology/spirituality. An international lecturer and the author of several books, her research focuses on dying, spirituality, and spiritual care and can be found at www.monikarenz.ch.

www.ingramcontent.com/pod-product-compliance
Lightning Source LLC
Chambersburg PA
CBHW030105010526
44116CB00005B/102